GOD as Trinity

GOD as Trinity

Relationality and Temporality in Divine Life

Ted Peters

Westminster/John Knox Press
Louisville, Kentucky

Book design by Laura Lee

First edition

Published by Westminster/John Knox Press
Louisville, Kentucky

This book is printed on recycled acid-free paper that meets the American National Standards Institute Z39.48 standard. ∞

PRINTED IN THE UNITED STATES OF AMERICA
9 8 7 6 5 4 3 2 1

Library of Congress Cataloging-in-Publication Data

Peters, Ted 1941-
  GOD as Trinity : relationality and temporality in the divine life
  Ted Peters.
      p.   cm.
  Includes bibliographical references and index.
  ISBN 0-664-25402-0 (pbk. : alk. paper)

  1. Trinity. I. Title. II. Title: Relationality and temporality in the divine life.
BT111.2.P48 1993
231'.044--dc20   92-1739

Contents

Preface

All too often, books on the Trinity begin with an apology, usually because this doctrine is thought to be out of date and boring. I offer no such apologies. Trinitarian thinking has proved to be one of the best-kept secrets in theology during the last half of the twentieth century. Perhaps more than any other locus of theological discussion, Trinity talk has provided the opportunity for serious consideration of the nature of God and for understanding the work of salvation.

In this book I will tackle two closely related tasks. First, I will chronicle the quiet conversation, the whispering about the Trinity that has been taking place in theological corners while other, more boisterous themes have been playing center stage. As this conversation proceeds, I will make note of the issues and points of conflict that energize Trinity talk in our era. I will examine closely the transcripts of the core conversation that begins with Karl Barth and Karl Rahner and continues today with Eberhard Jüngel, Jürgen Moltmann, Robert Jenson, Wolfhart Pannenberg, and Catherine Mowry LaCugna. What one hears here is that through the incarnation God has experienced otherness, and through the power of the spirit God is experiencing an integrating wholeness. The result is that relationality has become a key theme in today's Trinity talk. As we pay heed to this conversation, we will listen as well to what is being said by process theology about the becoming of God, by feminist theology about sexism in trinitarian language, and by liberation theology about divine and human community.

The second task will be to say something constructive, to advance the conversation to a new level. In particular, this volume seeks to address the relationship of God's eternity to the world's temporality. The central question will be this: How can an eternal God act in, and be affected by, a temporal world? This question is made difficult because traditionally Christian theologians have assumed that eternity should be defined in terms of timelessness. Eternity has been thought to be a form of absoluteness that is exempt from the passage of time and its accompanying deterioration and death. Inoculated with eternity, God appears immune to infection by the passage of time. It would seem that if eternity is assumed to mean timelessness, then God could not be related to our world of time.

I would like to work here with the notion that the question of the tie between eternity and time is a subquestion within the larger concern over the absoluteness and relatedness of God. I will formulate the larger concern in terms of the paradox between the beyondness, or transcendence, of God, on the one hand, and the intimacy, or presence, of God, on the other. The paradox is key, because it opens up the double truth that God is both beyond and intimate, both absolute and relative. God, the transcendent one, is also related to the most intimate depths of ordinary human existence. In the Father-Son relationship, the eternal and ineffable Father becomes intimately related to the incarnate Son who takes up residence in the ordinary world of time and space that we humans share. In the Son-Spirit relationship, the historical person of Jesus Christ is freed from his finitude to become spiritually present in the faith of believers in all lands and all epochs. In the Spirit-Father relationship, the whole of creation, redeemed in Christ, becomes eschatologically restored to an everlasting harmony within the divine life.

To think of God as Trinity helps to answer the question of this volume because it affirms that the word "God" applies to both sides of the ledger, to both eternity and temporality. As the incarnate one, as Emmanuel, as God with us, God is temporal. The eternal one enters time, and time thereby enters the divine life. And it stays there, even unto eternity.

One implication is that eternity cannot adequately be understood if conceived of as simple timelessness. Eternity and time cannot be mutually exclusive. Somehow, eternity must incorporate time. This leads to the thesis of this volume: the incorporation of time into eternity takes place through the eschatological incorporation of the temporal creation into the eternal perichoresis of the three persons that characterizes the trinitarian life. The eternity-time paradox is resolved eschatologically. This is what this volume attempts to underscore and develop in today's Trinity talk.

This is essentially a constructive argument. It is not a historical argument. I acknowledge that historically it was not simply the problem of the relation between eternity and time that drove the fourth century theologians in and around Nicea and Constantinople to produce the formula of one *ousia* in three *hypostases*. Yet the problem of the relation between eternity and time helped to frame the issues in both the fourth and the present centuries. Furthermore, as we will see in the exposition of today's Trinity talk, the Nicean settlement left an unsatisfactory resolution to this problem. It left us with an eternal immanent Trinity with only a dubious tie to the economic Trinity responsible for the saving work in history. It is this tie that this volume tries to tighten.

The constructive contribution to the conversation I offer here brings to further flower seeds that were sown in my earlier work on systematic theology, *GOD—The World's Future*. My constructive proposal comes in the form of a hypothesis, a suggestion for current theological exploration. It is offered not as dogma but rather in the mood of *theologia viatorum*—that is, theology on the way toward further constructive development. It presupposes that theology consists of the explication of the biblical symbols, an explication that seeks to clarify what scripture says in light of the intellectual context within which the theologian is working. In our own context, two ideas are particularly relevant to trinitarian explication, namely, the idea of person-in-relationship in social psychology and the idea of cosmological time in physics. As we proceed, I will try to cultivate an understanding of God as Trinity in light of these important contemporary concepts. Such attempts are ongoing, not subject to fixation or finalization. Hence, my thesis is a modest one, an attempt to add one voice to the present episode in the larger story of Trinity talk.

My research on the contemporary understanding of God as Trinity began with a close examination of the 1952 book *In This Name,* written by my colleague at the Graduate Theological Union, Professor and Dean Emeritus Claude Welch. What I found startling and edifying in this work was its near prophetic insight that the work of Karl Barth would become the wave of future trinitarian discussion. The last four decades have proved this to be the case. One of my tasks here is to report what has been said in order to show that the Welch prophecy has been fulfilled.

Yet it is also worth noting that the question on which today's trinitarian conversation focuses differs from that which prompted the debate when Welch wrote his book. At the middle of the twentieth century, the question was this: Which position is correct, Schleiermacher's method of *synthesis* that combines various utterances regarding our experience with God as one; or Barth's method of *analysis* of scriptural revelation that reports our primary experience of God in terms of Father, Son, and Holy Spirit? Barth seems to have won. Today's trinitarians seem to take it for granted that the primary scriptural witness comes to us already in the threefold form; therefore, we must rely upon the method of analysis or something akin to it. With this matter somewhat settled, the topic of Trinity talk has shifted. The question that prompts today's discussion represents a further stage in constructive development: What is the connection between the economic Trinity related to us in time and the immanent Trinity that is eternal? That the two are really one is the answer already sketched out by Barth. Subsequent Trinity talk has been filling out the picture, and in this volume I hope to contribute further detail.

With this sequence of events in mind, I would like to express my appreciation to Claude Welch, not only for his scholarly leadership both at midcentury and now nearing its end, but also for the collegial comradery we have enjoyed in Berkeley while discussing this and numerous other topics in historical and systematic theology.

Parts of Chapter 4 of this volume were prepared for a paper, "The Trinity In and Beyond Time," delivered at the Vatican Observatory near Rome in September 1991 at a conference on "Quantum Creation of the Universe and the Origin of the Laws of Nature." This work could not have been satisfactorily pursued without the critical review and constant encouragement by physicist-theologian Robert John Russell, my friend and colleague at the Center for Theology and the Natural Sciences in Berkeley. During the fall semester of 1990 Bob and I team-taught a seminar at the Graduate Theological Union on the doctrine of the Trinity, and the weekly interchange in and out of class sharpened my thinking on many issues. Such collegial conversation is a coveted commodity among scholars, and I feel I have been graced by the opportunity to work with Bob Russell on this and numerous other projects.

In addition, I would like to express gratitude to colleagues Timothy Lull, Durwood Foster, and Carol Voisin, as well as seminarian Margrethe S. C. Kleiber, for their critical reviews of an early draft of this work. I would also like to acknowledge my appreciation for the dialogue on this topic and the friendship I have shared with graduate students in Berkeley. Lou Ann Trost, Carol Tabler (who indexed this book), Wesley Wildman, and Duane Larson have directly and indirectly enriched my study of both Trinity and temporality. For these too I am grateful.

1. Introducing the Task of Trinity Talk

I bind unto myself the name,
The strong name of the Trinity
By invocation of the same,
The Three in One and One in Three.

Of whom all nature hath Creation,
Eternal Father, Spirit, Word.
Praise to the Lord of my salvation;
Salvation is of Christ the Lord!

—*Ascribed to St. Patrick*
(ca. 372–466)

How is it that Christians understand God? When we use the word "God" we do so ambiguously. In fact, it may have three or more overlapping references. First, we use the word "God" to refer to the general notion of divine reality as it can be found in most of the world's religions and, more specifically, to refer to Yahweh, the Holy Lord of Israel. Second, "God" may on occasion refer to the first person of the Trinity, to God the Father of Jesus. Third, we may speak of the entire Trinity—inclusive of Father, Son, and Holy Spirit—as the "Godhead" or simply as "God." Despite these three rather different uses, few people seem to be confused. We proceed to speak glibly of God as if we knew what we are talking about.

Yet we have considerable investment in trying to understand the nature of God, especially God's relationship to us and to our world. Christians believe the event of the death and resurrection of Jesus Christ has revealed to us the essential character of the divine life; or, perhaps even more dramatically, the Christ event actually comes to determine the very nature of the Godself. The affirmation follows, I think, that in this historical person from Nazareth the supreme divine reality has entered human history, thereby defining "God" in terms of differentiation and re-union. God ceases to be God—or, at least, what we might assume to be God—in order to become human and die; but in redefining humanity through the Easter resurrection, God takes what is human up into the divine reality itself. This forces Christians to think of God in terms of both oneness and differentiation, both unity and multiplicity, both eternity and temporality. The fundamental issue regarding the Trinity is not the so-called threeness of God. It is rather the dynamism of the divine life that can redefine itself by self-separating and reuniting, by dying and rising.

The Trinity Talk Task

The broad task of Trinity talk is to examine the Christian understanding of God as Trinity, to see why it is that we use the somewhat cumbersome language of three-in-one and one-in-three. Historically, there have been many reasons why the Christian church arrived at this formula. To trace this history in detail is not the task I have elected to pursue here. Rather, here I wish to test the constructive hypothesis that the trinitarian formula is a constructive answer to the question, How is God related to the world?

This question is a complicated one because the variety of ways in which it is formulated usually make answering it virtually impossible. For example, if God is absolute, how can God be related to anything? Or, if God is immutable and unchanging, how can God be related to a mutable world of change? Or, if God is eternal, how can God act and be acted upon in a world of time? What makes it so difficult to answer questions put this way is that they assume a radical disjunction between God and the world. To speak of God as absolute seems to include the assumption that absoluteness is the opposite of relationality. One cannot be both absolute and relational, it appears. Similarly, to speak of God as immutable implies that God can have no truck with that which is changing, deteriorating, or transforming. And, of course, if eternity is defined as timelessness, then an eternal God can only be isolated and divorced from the world of time. Hence, the question is posed with a disjunctive assumption that tells us immediately that this will be a very difficult question to answer satisfactorily.

The variant of the question to which we will grant the most attention in this volume is this: *How can our eternal God relate to our temporal world?* As we proceed toward a constructive answer, we will challenge the assumption that there exists a radical disjunction between time and eternity. If God is defined in terms of pure timelessness, then, of course, God could not be related to our world of passing time in any significant way. If eternity is timeless, then we would find it virtually impossible to understand God as creator and redeemer of our world. However, we need not define the divine eternity as disjointed from temporality. If we begin with the report of God's historical actions in the Bible, we find that the Hebrew and Christian experiences with the God of Israel have been temporal experiences. God acts within time. If one moves to the Trinity proper—and this is the thesis I propose—we find that God incarnate in Jesus Christ and present to us as the Holy Spirit places God within the spatial and temporal horizon of our experience. The trinitarian dynamics places God on both sides of the fence that divides eternity and time. God may be eternal, but God is temporal as well. Furthermore, that fence will not last forever. As we look forward to the promised everlasting kingdom of God, we look forward to a grand internalization of the world of time within the realm of eternity. The content of the eternal life of God will incorporate the temporal history of God's relationship to the creation. In sum, I try to answer the question by arguing that God is both eternal and temporal; and I argue as well that eternity—understood as that which transcends time—will be eschatologically inclusive of time.

En route to this proposed answer, we will take advantage of an important theme in the Trinity talk that has taken place—quietly but significantly—during the latter half of the twentieth century. It has to do with new insights regarding the tie between individuality and relationality. We have arrived at what might be a modern or emerging postmodern maxim: to be an individual person is to be in relationship. This derives from the observation that who we are as an individual is in a constant state of becoming. Our identity grows continually through interaction with other individuals and with the wider world around us. Gone is the image of the self-defined and autonomous individual, the island of personhood standing over against society. We now understand ourselves more interactively, recognizing how even our internal consciousness interacts with significant influences around us.

Relationality—a social-psychological concept so important for understanding human personality in our time—is becoming the key for unlocking newer understandings of the divine life. What has been happening is that the relational understanding of the human person is becoming a tool used by an increasing number of theologians for interpreting the relations of the three persons of the Trinity. The identity of Father, Son, and Holy Spirit is increasingly viewed as a relational identity, as an interdependent identity. And such relational identity implies dynamism, movement, change, and passage. So, we need to ask, Does it also imply time?

Also important, if not decisive, is the legacy of G. W. F. Hegel and the growing insight among a few theologians that Trinity and eschatology are inextricably linked. To understand the life of God as one in which the divine undergoes self-separation requires us to think about a reunion, an eschatological reunion. This reunion involves more than just Jesus alone, however. It involves us. It involves the whole of creation. The trinitarian life is itself the history of salvation. To put it most forcefully: the fullness of God as Trinity is a reality yet to be achieved in the eschatological consummation.

Some Misleading Assumptions

That a discussion of God as Trinity should follow this track may not be immediately obvious, because too frequently trinitarian discussion gets bogged down in pseudoissues. This cannot be helped if we rely upon misleading assumptions. In such cases, we end up trying to solve problems that are irrelevant to what is really at stake. Let me mention two such misleading assumptions that cannot but create pseudoissues: the idea that the doctrine of the Trinity is itself a mystery and the assumption that the basic problem has to do with the relationship between threeness and oneness. Focusing on either of these tends to lead trinitarian discussion on unnecessary detours.

The first detour begins with the frequently offered statement that the doctrine of the Trinity is a sublime mystery. Traditional textbooks in dogmatics typically sidetrack the reader by asserting that the doctrine of the Holy Trinity is absolutely incomprehensible to the human mind, that human reason cannot fathom or reconcile God's being as simultaneously threeness and oneness. It is alleged to be impossible to understand how one divine nature, which is simple and indivisible, can be possessed in its entirety by each of three persons. Because we allegedly cannot understand this, we customarily designate it a "mystery" of the divine reality.[1] To illustrate the problem, there is a story about a Bavarian parish priest on the Feast of the Trinity one year who announced to his congregation that because this was so great a mystery, of which he understood nothing, there would be no sermon.[2]

Thus, what we need here is a little honesty that will disclose a theological sleight of hand. The sleight of hand consists in covering over the difference between the authentic mystery of God with our doctrinal thinking about God. When Paul cries, "O the depth of the riches and wisdom and knowledge of God!" he is rightly acknowledging the mystery of the divine with God's "unsearchable" judgments and "inscrutable" ways (Rom. 11:33). Yet human reflection on the unsearchableness and inscrutability of God is just that, human reflection. The doctrine of the Trinity belongs in the latter category, and as a doctrine it can be made understandable if the theologians will work hard enough to make it understandable.[3] Because reflection upon the threefold nature of the divine mystery is admittedly difficult, the concept of the Trinity has led frequently to intellectual puzzles. The problem of becoming misled arises when we are tempted to cover over our puzzles and occasional lapses in clarity by ascribing them to the infinite mystery of the divine being itself. The sleight of hand consists in excusing doctrinal obscurity by appealing to divine mystery.

This pattern of referring to the trinitarian doctrine as a mystery probably goes back to the Cappadocian fathers working in that crucial period between the councils at Nicea and Constantinople, who affirmed on the one hand that each member of the Trinity was equally divine and of the same being *(ousia),* while on the other hand they granted clear priority to the Father, the "cause" from whom the other two persons are begotten and proceed.[4] Then, being aware of the confusion they were creating and to cover their inconsistency, they declared that what is common to the three and what is distinctive between them lay beyond speech and comprehension and therefore beyond analysis or conceptualization.[5] On the contemporary scene, theologians such as Karl Rahner insist that the doctrine of the Trinity will always remain mysterious, not because of the logical difficulties confronted by the doctrine but because the divine character itself is mystery. He says the mystery of the doctrine is "identical with the mystery of the self-communication of God to us in Christ and in the Spirit."[6] In short, because God is mysterious, so is the doctrine.

Such statements by Rahner worry me a bit. What is in truth mysterious is the being of the ineffable God. But the doctrine of the Trinity is just that, a doctrine. And like other doctrines, it is the analytic and synthetic construction of evangelical explication for the purpose of bringing faith to understanding, for the purpose of explaining the significance of what happened in the Christ event. That this particular path of explication has confronted frequent hurdles in logic gives it no right to claim divine ineffability as its own virtue.

The second sidetrack is a branch off the first one. It is the widely accepted assumption that the guiding theme of trinitarian thought has to do with arithmetic—that is, how to get one to equal three and three to equal one. The Trinity is often portrayed in terms of a polar argument between a unitary monotheism without distinction, on the one hand, and tritheism without unity, on the other. Do we have one god or three? Are Christians monotheists or polytheists? A recent treatise on the Trinity provides a good example. "The central problem of trinitarian doctrine is this: how to express the fact that the divine Three are one God. . . . How to equate trinity in unity and unity in trinity?"[7] Yet I contend that posing the issue this way is unnecessarily confusing.[8] It pictures Christian theologians trying to walk a middle road between two sides, as if seeking a *via media*.[9] But this is not the case. With regard to the first side, we must note that tritheism is never taken seriously as an option for Christian theology.[10] The church has never identified with polytheism. On the other side—the side of monotheism—Christians have always affirmed that they believe as do the Jews, namely, that God is one. Yet simple monotheism is too simple. The Christian position is not just one more form of garden variety monotheism, as if monotheism represents a religious club to which Christianity is seeking membership.

What, then, is the basic issue? I believe the real question has been, and still is, this: How do we understand the God of the gospel, the one creator of all things who raised Jesus on Easter and who is spiritually present to the believing community? Or, more abstractly put, just how is the transcendent creator and redeemer related to us, the redeemed creatures? The driving force of this concern is the assumption that God and God alone is able to accomplish full reconciliation between the Godself and fallen creation. No one less than God can do this. Yet the compact symbolism of the New Testament identifies Jesus Christ as the reconciling one. How then should we understand Jesus' relationship to divinity? These are the basic questions to which the idea of the Trinity is a proposed answer. Now, we must admit that the conception of three-in-one and one-in-three is a complicated conception. However, the complexity of the conception is no warrant for consigning the discussion to divine mystery or to redefine the question merely in terms of contradictory arithmetic.

The Beyond and the Intimate

Even though the doctrine of the Trinity is as rational and conceptual and philosophical as one can find in Christian theology, it is rooted in a fundamental religious sensibility. The idea of the Trinity is grounded in something much more basic than an idea; namely, it is grounded in an existential apprehension of the meaning of the divine symbols coming to articulation in scripture. The idea of the Trinity arises from the paradoxical sense that the God in whom we put our faith must be both *beyond* and *intimate*. As the Beyond One, God is ultimate. There can be no reality beyond God or to which God is subservient. God bows to nothing in time or space. The beyond lies beyond human concepts, beyond worldly perfections. God is transcendent, absolute, infinite, eternal, omnipotent, omnipresent, and neither matched nor exceeded by anything in glory.

Yet beyondness is not enough. God is also the Intimate One. The New Testament proffers emmanualism—that is, it reports the divine as Emmanuel, God with us. As the humble Christchild subject to the affections of his family and to the vicissitudes of growing up as an ordinary human being, God has joined the rest of us who belong to the human race. As the Holy Spirit, God becomes so inextricably tied to our own inner self that the line between the two sometimes seems to us blurred. We may even want to say with Augustine that God is nearer to me than I am to myself. It is the same God who created the universe and destined it for glory who fills our innermost soul with the ecstasy of divine love. And, most significantly, this paradoxical combination of beyondness and intimacy comes to definitive expression in the event of salvation, an event that catches up my most intimate self into the glorification of God throughout the whole of the cosmos.[11]

The Beyond and the Intimate—both belong to the experience of God as apprehended by the symbols of the Christian faith. When Christian theologians tend to favor one to the exclusion of the other, our religious sensibilities get restless until the two are brought back into their paradoxical yet complementary relation. It is this more fundamental sensibility, I think, that has been the driving force behind the formulation of so many of the conceptual problems involved in trinitarian thinking. It is the root of the logical problem of holding together God's absoluteness and God's relatedness.[12] And noting this will help us in part to see what is at stake with the variant of the problem we are addressing here, namely, holding together God's eternity and the world's temporality. To know God as only the eternal one beyond time is not enough. We need to know God also as intimate, and such intimacy as we experience it can only be time bound.

Perhaps time bound is too strong a way to put it. It might be better to say that in one or more respects the divine eternity has felt the impact of human temporality and, further, this impact has become internal to the trinitarian life of God. Eternity is affected by temporal contingency. This is indicated most dramatically in the relationship of the Father to the Son in the event of the cross. The Son surrenders himself totally to the Father's will, and this results in Jesus' suffering and death. The Father in turn suffers infinite pain out of his love for the dying Son. Jürgen Moltmann concludes forcefully: "What happens on Golgotha reaches into the very depths of the Godhead and therefore puts its impress on the trinitarian life of God in eternity."[13]

The Immanent Trinity and the Economic Trinity

One of the poignant places where the tension between the absoluteness and the relatedness of God comes to a head is in discussions of the relation between the immanent Trinity and the economic Trinity. Most traditional discussions of God as Trinity concern themselves with immanent relations, with what is sometimes called the "essential" or "ontological" Trinity—that is, the eternal perichoresis between Father, Son, and Spirit. Classical trinitarian thought seems to presume that this eternal perichoresis would continue unabated even if the creation had not come into existence. The coming into existence of the creation adds more. By extending the notion of economy *(oikonomia)* introduced earlier by Tertullian, post-Nicene theologians began to speak of an economic Trinity (or "Trinity of manifestation") in the created realm. This is the Trinity as manifested externally in the world through creation, redemption, and consummation. There is but one Trinity, of course. Yet classical trinitarianism has viewed it in two ways. One way is to view the Trinity in itself, in terms of its immanent relations. The other is to view it externally, as it relates to what is created, to what is not in itself divine.

Distinguishing between the two has some merit, but unfortunately the distinction has inadvertently produced some unwanted separations. This has been the case especially with regard to the second person. The cross of Jesus occurring within the stream of temporal history, it has been said, belongs to the economy of God's saving work but not within the eternal immanent Trinity. To that belongs only the eternal logos. Jesus Christ, in effect, is dubbed God's work *ad extra*.

Theologians in the Nicene-Chalcedonian period tended to split the eternal logos from the temporal Jesus Christ. They then asserted that attributes of the divine could be communicated to the human, but not the reverse. They spoke of the incarnate Jesus as one person (one: *hypostasis*) with two natures (two: *physis*). The one hypostasis is the divine hypostasis, not the human one. Jesus has a human nature but not a human hypostasis. All this was aimed at protecting the divine from vicissitudes of time, from suffering and death. Jesus could suffer and die in his human nature, but the divine nature would remain exempt. This helped to explicate what it meant to say that the economy of salvation through Christ was *ad extra*, external to the divine being proper.

What we end up with in this scheme is an eternal Son in eternal relationship to an eternal Father, rendering external the birth, teaching career, sufferings, and death of the historical Jesus. Despite sincere and authentic attempts to combat the docetic and gnostic challenges of the ancient Greco-Roman context, such trinitarian Christologies risked sacrificing the intimate God on the altar of the beyond.

On the one hand, the ancient theologians offer us much. Nicea has equipped us to say that it is the Trinity as such—not just the Father—that is God. In addition, the idea of the economic Trinity allows us to reaffirm the biblical insight that the entire Godhead—even God as Father—is related to the world. This is implied elegantly in Augustine's oft-repeated formula: the internal trinitarian operations are divided, the external trinitarian operations are undivided *(opera trinitatis ad intra sunt divisa, opera trinitatis ad extra sunt indivisa)*. It is God who relates to the world, Father included.

Yet, on the other hand, we must ask honestly if emmanuelism has been compromised by the immanent-economic distinction. Is the concept of the economic Trinity in effect merely a temporal image of a much more real and hence much more important eternal and unrelated Trinity? Instead of a single Trinity, are we presented with a double Trinity of six figures, three authentically eternal and three accidentally temporal? Do we not have here a subtle return of subordinationism—now that the temporal economic Trinity seems to be subordinated to the eternal immanent Trinity—the aim of which is to protect the divine absoluteness at the cost of relatedness?

Two moments in recent Trinity talk have begun moving us toward a much more satisfactory understanding of what is going on here. The first is Karl Barth's insistence that the incarnate history of Jesus Christ incorporates temporality into the divine experience.

The existence of the man Jesus means that God became man, the Creator a creature, eternity time. It means, therefore, that God takes and has time for us; that He Himself is temporal among us as we are. Yet He does this in a manner appropriate to Himself. He is temporal in unity and correspondence with His eternity.[14]

The second moment of note in recent Trinity talk has been to explore the hypothesis that the economic Trinity is the immanent Trinity, and vice versa.[15] This formula has been offered by Karl Rahner—we will call it Rahner's Rule—and it has been developed further by scholars such as Eberhard Jüngel and Jürgen Moltmann. This affirmation emerges from explication of the profound and thoroughgoing relatedness of emmanuelism reported in the gospel. Though going perhaps a bit further than Rahner might have intended, I offer this for consideration: the loving relationship between the Father and the Son within the Trinity *is* the loving relationship between the Father and Jesus. Relationships require otherness. Love posits and promotes otherness. What binds others in love is spirit. If this is the case, might we say that the Father's love for the Son and the Son's love for the Father actually take place within the texture of temporal history? Rather than a mere chimera of another love that takes place in some eternity divorced from time, could we say that when we look at Jesus we see the real thing? Might we say that this Father-Son relationship is immanent to the divine life? And, noting the relationship of the Son to the world as logos-creator-redeemer in combination with the Spirit as the power that binds all in love, might we go on to say that the whole history of creation and redemption is immanent to the divine life? If this is the economy of salvation, should it not affect the internal life of God? To what extent can we say that the economic Trinity is the immanent Trinity?

Before proceeding to construct a simple equation, we need to make note of one valuable contribution made by the immanent-economic distinction: it protects the freedom of God. A total collapse of the immanent Trinity into the economic Trinity might result in a finite God who is completely dependent for divine definition upon the world. The reaffirmation of intimate emmanuelism cannot be at the cost of the transcendent God who is beyond.

This presses on us the question, Have we arrived at a dilemma? On the one hand, to affirm the immanent-economic distinction risks subordinating the economic Trinity and hence protecting transcendent absoluteness at the cost of genuine relatedness to the world. But, on the other hand, to collapse the two together risks producing a God so dependent upon the world for self-definition that divine freedom and independence is lost.[16]

The search for a solution leads us into an even more exciting moment in the story of current trinitarian discussion. Over the last couple of decades, a handful of theologians have suggested that we look for the identity of the economic Trinity and the immanent Trinity in eschatology. Most helpful here is Robert Jenson, who tries to harvest seed insights from Hegel that have been cultivated further by Wolfhart Pannenberg and Jürgen Moltmann. Jenson contends that there has been a sort of Babylonian captivity of Christian theology in the intellectual prison camp of Hellenistic metaphysics, according to which timeless eternity is given ontological precedence over temporal history. This has misled us into thinking of the eternal Son as some sort of preexistent disincarnate logos *(logos asarkos)* just waiting up there in heaven for the moment to incarnate and become the historical and soteriological Jesus. Had the incarnation not taken place, there still would have been a Son ever "proceeding" from the Father, a "metaphysical double" for the Jesus we have come to know. Jenson proposes, in contrast, that we incorporate the dynamics of temporal movement into God's life proper and see Christ's deity not as a separate entity that always was in some far off eternity but rather as the final outcome of the divine intercourse with creation. Eternity, then, would incorporate the consummation of time into the eschaton, which is the reality of God. Between now and then the future is genuinely open, and God's freedom to act is maintained. The cross of Jesus constitutes one such free divine act, a divine act that will eschatologically result in the self-constitution of God as God. Thus, the actual saving events accomplished by the economic Trinity will ultimately be taken up into the eschatological transcendence of time and then become immanent.

> This "economic" Trinity is *eschatologically* God "himself," an "immanent" Trinity. And that assertion is no problem, for God *is* himself only *eschatologically,* since he is Spirit . . .

> As for God's freedom, only our proposal fully asserts it. The immanent Trinity of previous Western interpretation had but the spurious freedom of unaffectedness. Genuine freedom is the reality of possibility, is openness to the future.[17]

In similar fashion, Jürgen Moltmann exclaims:

> The economic Trinity completes and perfects itself to immanent Trinity
> when the history and experience of salvation are completed and perfect-
> ed. When everything is "in God" and "God is all in all", then the eco-
> nomic Trinity is raised into and transcended in the immanent Trinity.[18]

The eschatological proposal is sound, in my judgment. It issues from
sensitivity to the paradox of the beyond and the intimate. It expresses
the genuine desire to maintain the tension between divine absoluteness
and relatedness. It shows how eternity and temporality can be complementary rather than mutually exclusive. It also seeks to explicate adequately the gospel of Emmanuel, which implies relatedness within the
divine life as well as between God and the world. It encourages contemporary theologians such as Arthur Peacocke to make the connection
between eternity and time in the divine life.

> *God is not "timeless"; God is temporal in the sense that the Divine life is suc-
> cessive in its relation to us—God is temporally related to us; God creates
> and is present to each instant of the (physical and, derivatively, psychologi-
> cal) time of the created world; God transcends past and present created
> time: God is eternal,* in the sense that there is no time at which he did not
> exist nor will there be a future time at which he does not exist.[19]

Future Directions for Trinity Talk

A number of tentative conclusions can be drawn from the above discussion, conclusions that will help set the direction for continued Trinity
talk. First, it should seem obvious that in the construction of the doctrine of the Trinity there is no intrinsic interest in the number three.
What drives thought toward the trinitarian idea is the maintenance of
the paradox between the beyond and the intimate, a paradox in danger
of splitting apart without the uniting work of the Spirit.

Second, we need not assume that the three persons of the Trinity
are of the same kind or order. There is no warrant for coming up with
a definition of "person" and then applying it equally to all three persons so that they come out looking the same. We are not being driven
by a problem of securing democratic equality for each. This is not the
issue. Rather, we are looking for a way to conceptualize the actual
work of the one God as creator, redeemer, and sanctifier.

Third, our positing of a temporal dynamic within the divine eternity does not derive from a general metaphysical preference for becoming over being. This is not just one more attempt to motorize an otherwise stationary divine being. Rather, it arises from an analysis of what must be the case if the incarnation and consummation are taken seriously. It arises from the prophetic promise of a coming new creation that has already been realized in the resurrection of Jesus—who has been raised to eternity—and is slated for us as well. The Holy Spirit will make us one with Christ and, hence, one with God to live everlastingly in the kingdom of God. What is true about the Jesus of the past will become true for us in the future. By the power of the Holy Spirit, we will come to enjoy the relationship with the Father that Jesus enjoys. This is the eschatological promise, one implication of which is that what has been temporal will be taken up into the eternal.

Fourth, the trinitarian being of God is still open. God has a future in history as well as an eschatological future. The perichoresis of Father, Son, and Spirit is being carried out in time and through a history that is not done yet.

The utter seriousness with which we confront the temporality of the divine life will force us to ask about the nature of time. The nature of time is an enigma, a mystery in its own right. To affirm the temporality of God, ironically enough, adds a this-worldly mystery to the other-worldly mystery of eternity. Yet we must note that as soon as we ask about time, we alert ourselves to the fact that this is a topic of major proportion in twentieth-century science. To pursue the matter rightly, then, will require dialogue between theology and natural science. The theologian today ought to be cautious about making statements about time without some attempt to make consonance with the multiple meanings time has in the most fundamental of the sciences, physics. I will attempt this task in the final chapter.

In the meantime, I wish to affirm methodologically the that there is value for theologians in attending to what scientists say about the world in which we live. Pope John Paul II, who has an abiding interest here, advocates a "relational unity between science and religion," in which both retain their autonomy while working together. Because "theology has been defined as an effort of faith to achieve understanding, *as fides quaerens intellectum,*" he says, "it must be in vital interchange today with science just as it always has been with philosophy and other forms of learning."[20] So as we ask here about God's time, we will also ask about the nature of time discerned by the sciences.

Fifth, trinitarian thought is fluid. It must remain ongoing. It is *theologia viatorum*—that is, theology on-the-way—because it is aware that it points to, rather than possesses, the truth of a dynamic God. It is aware of what philosopher Eric Voegelin has objected to as the "hypostatization" of Christian dogma, a fixing that threatens to shut off further speculation.[21] The paradoxical nature of the initial problematic, combined with the ongoing work of the Holy Spirit, cannot leave us completely satisfied with past conceptualizations. New challenges are being raised by the modern and emerging postmodern mind that make us ask questions about relationality and temporality. We need to feel free to return on occasion to the drawing board. This volume is an attempt to do just this.

Sixth and finally, although the doctrine of the Trinity is just that, a doctrine, it need not be shelved as cold or irrelevant. It reports the gospel. It echoes the offer of grace. It invites us into the divine life of love. Patristics scholar Robert Wilken writes: "The doctrine of the Trinity reaches to the deepest recesses of the soul and helps us know the majesty of God's presence and the mystery of his love. Love is the most authentic mark of the Christian life, and love among humans, as within God, requires community with others and a sharing of the deepest kind."[22]

2. A Map of Contemporary Issues

Batter my heart, three person'd God; for you
As yet but knocke, breathe, shine, and seek to mend;
That I may rise, o'erthrow mee, and bend
Your force to breake, blowe, burn and make me new.

—*John Donne (1571?–1631),* Holy Sonnets, *14*

Not everyone touring trinitarian thinking is following exactly the same route. What I take to be the main highway will be the subject for Chapter 3. Here in Chapter 2 we will survey a number of issues that prompt current trinitarian discussion. Not all are of equal relevance. Some are entrance ramps onto the main route, whereas others are little more than parking lots for pet peeves.

We begin by raising the question of relevance, Is the doctrine of the Trinity so outmoded that contemporary theologians should debunk or avoid it? My own answer will be that it will seem outmoded only to those who do not make the effort to retrieve the essential nature of the gospel that is trying to come to articulation through it. Only if this is at least hypothetically granted can we justify serious consideration of further issues. As we travel, we will see that current debates such as those regarding the challenge to substantialist metaphysics or the nature of person-in-relationship will become feeder routes into the main artery of trinitarian traffic—the relationality and temporality of the divine life.

Is the Doctrine of the Trinity Outmoded?

The first in our list of issues is this: Is the doctrine of the Trinity outmoded, or is it conceptually viable today? Is the idea of the Trinity necessary dress for Christian faith, or have we outgrown it? Should we discard it or keep it? Philosopher of religion John Hick describes the

Trinity along with the incarnation as an "intellectual construction" that must be "left behind when the disciple of Jesus discards the cultural packaging in which Western Christianity has wrapped the gospel."[1]

Somewhere around midcentury, the idea of the Trinity had become a bit of an embarrassment. After all, skeptics said, it was formulated originally by some intellectually constipated Greeks and Latins in a bygone era to meet challenges that have long since disappeared. What we moderns have ended up with is a legacy of unnecessarily convoluted and unintelligible ideas. Cyril Richardson said that the Christian doctrine of the Trinity is crippled by "inherent confusions" because it is an "artificial construct."[2] To the question, What is the doctrine of the Trinity? Dorothy Sayers cites the average churchgoer's answer: "The Father incomprehensible, the Son incomprehensible, and the whole thing incomprehensible. Something put in by theologians to make it more difficult—nothing to do with daily life or ethics."[3] With such skepticisms in mind, Timothy Lull wrote recently that the Trinity should be subtitled "the guilt-producing doctrine," because we today cannot quite muster the theological enthusiasm of the ancient Athanasian Creed, according to which thinking about the Trinity is requisite for salvation.[4]

With apparent guiltlessness, the flamboyant Anglican bishop James A. Pike described the doctrine of the Trinity as "a heavy piece of luggage" that Christians should not have to tote along when pursuing the church's mission. Our trinitarian convictions are barriers to rapprochement with other groups such as Jews and Muslims. People who are vaguely theistic might listen to us if it were not for the triple personality we espouse. Hence, we should discard this excess luggage if we can. And we can, because the doctrine of the Trinity "is not essential to the Christian faith."[5]

What Pike advocated was a strict monotheism. So he ascribed the word "God" to the first person of the Trinity and then rethought its tie to the Holy Spirit and to Jesus Christ. He argued that all that can be said of the Holy Spirit can be said of God without attributing distinct personhood to the Spirit. All that has been said about the so-called third person was already said of the Spirit of God, the Wisdom of God, or the Spirit of Christ, in the Old Testament, the Apocrypha, and the New Testament before the councils declared the trinitarian formula. We do not need to think of the Spirit as a separate entity but rather as a particular way of God's relating to us, a way integral to God's very being. Pike denied that he was advocating Sabellianism or modalism here, because he believed he was simply describing the various ways in which we experience the one God.

Similarly, all that is affirmed as characteristic of the second person is also affirmable of God in general. God is the Word, or Logos (John 1:1). To speak of the Word independently is to add something extra yet unnecessary. The Word here does not refer to Jesus of Nazareth, of course, but rather to an eternal dimension of God's being. Thus, God can create and reveal without the second person. To dub the Logos a distinct person is to flirt with gnosticism. Thus, Pike concluded, "there is neither need for, nor plausibility in, this extra layer of operation."[6]

Pike was able to grant qualified praise to the doctrine of the Trinity, though, by describing it as "an earthen vessel" that organizes God in strictly human terms. But what is essential is that behind our ideas of the Trinity we must simply say "that God is . . . He just is."[7]

Not every theologian at midcentury was willing to accept this kind of embarrassment regarding the Trinity, however. In the 1952 publication of his dissertation *In This Name: The Doctrine of the Trinity in Contemporary Theology,* Claude Welch complained how trinitarian theology had fallen into disuse. It had dropped to secondary or tertiary importance. Too few people were even discussing it any more. Nevertheless, Welch predicted that the doctrine of the Trinity was about to become mainstream again. He argued on the basis of insights then being proffered by Karl Barth. Subsequent history, as we will see in Chapter 3, has confirmed Welch's forecast.

Welch believed that the root problem in the contemporary treatment of the doctrine of the Trinity is the question of its ground in revelation. By "revelation" he was referring to that to which the biblical symbols are pointing, namely, the God who is being revealed in Jesus Christ. More is being revealed than merely "he just is." There is built right into the original revelatory experience with God a "threefoldness." Welch turned to Karl Barth, maintaining that there is a threefold structure or pattern to all divine activity and, hence, to the being of God itself. What Barth was offering, said Welch, was an appropriate theological method—the method he dubbed "analysis"—that would explicate the "immediate implication of revelation" as found in scripture. The advantage of this analytical method is that it could bypass the many centuries of encrusted monotheistic metaphysics and even the convolutions of conciliar speculations. The net result is that the doctrine of the Trinity is much more essential to Christian faith than perhaps hitherto thought. "It is no longer possible to

accept the easy attitude that the doctrine of the Trinity is of only antiquar-
ian or historical interest," writes Welch. "*The doctrine of the Trinity comes
inevitably into a central place in the Christian understanding of God.*"[8]

By the time Robert Jenson published his book *God After God* in
1969, he had come to a place where he too could say that "Barth's doctrine of the *Trinity* [is] his great move into the future of theology." While
praising Barth, however, Jenson found it necessary to decry the likes of
Bishop Pike who, for whatever reason, could not find creative inspiration in the ancient trinitarian formula.

[The doctrine of the Trinity is] one of our most clearly moribund inheri-
tances from the past, moribund to the point where bishops can go about
denying it without so much as needing first to inform themselves about
what it says. In the piety even of most traditional churches and believers,
it is safe to say that the triune character of God plays no role at all.[9]

A quarter century later, the situation has all but turned completely
around. Today we find Catherine Mowry LaCugna unabashedly affirming a positive role to our understanding of God-as-Trinity. "Today trinitarian theology is being recovered as a fruitful and intelligible way to
articulate what it means to be 'saved by God through Christ in the power of the Holy Spirit.'"[10]

Where we find ourselves at the close of the twentieth century is in
the midst of a soft-spoken but profound conversation regarding the
unique understanding of God emerging from the gospel of Jesus Christ.
This conversation focuses on relationality. What the idea of the Trinity
does is impute the quality of relationality to the internal life of God as
well as to God's relationship to the world. This makes Trinity talk conceptually viable in a modern and emerging postmodern culture where
relationality is integral to our understanding of reality. This observation
brings us to the second in our list of issues, namely, the contrast between the substantialist metaphysics dominant at the time of the original
trinitarian formulations and today's way of thinking.

Is the Trinity Tied to Substantialist Metaphysics?

Do contemporary formulations of trinitarian theology require that we
embrace the substantialist metaphysics of the premodern era? Two se-
quential developments seem to threaten the credibility of the ancient
metaphysics of divine being: first, the Kantian critique, which seems to

forbid asserting any qualities of noumenal reality; and second, the post-Kantian metaphysics, which seems to emphasize becoming over being and relationality over substance. So we must ask, Is trinitarian thinking so tied to a substantialist worldview that if we change worldviews we risk throwing out the baby with the bathwater?

When the Niceno-Constantinopolitan Creed was formulated in A.D. 381 our theologians were quite confident that they could speak about the *being* of God. Whether speaking about the divine *ousia* in Greek or *substantia* in Latin, no one doubted that these terms referred to the divine reality itself. We can speak of God as the "very ocean of substance," Boethius would say, and acclaim God as the originating fount of all that is substantial. To speak of the divine substance was to refer to that which exists of itself, subordinating to it all other properties, accidents, deprivations, and relations. It was Tertullian who gave us the formula: one substance in three persons *(una substantia, tres personae)*.

> All are of One, by unity (that is) of substance; while the mystery of the dispensation *(oikonomia)* is still guarded, which distributes the Unity into a Trinity, placing in their order the three Persons—the Father, the Son, and the Holy Ghost: three, however, not in condition, but in degree; not in substance, but in form; not in power, but in aspect; yet of one substance *(substantiae)*, and of one condition, and of one power, inasmuch as He is one God.[11]

What it means for God to be understood in terms of divine substance was spelled out over time. Augustine described God as a substance that is invisible, unchangeable, and eternal. Thomas Aquinas identified God with the fullness of being, as pure act. This excludes such things as becoming and potency. Thus, God is immutable and cannot change, because change consists in the transition from potency to act. God in the Godself is unchanging and eternal. The world, in contrast, is temporal and constantly changing in relation to God.

Included in the substantialist presumptions was the distinction between absolute essence and relational attributes. The essence of an entity is absolute, remaining unchanged if identity is to be maintained. Relationality takes place through the attributes. What could not be countenanced is the notion that the divine essence is contingent upon the relational dimensions of its being.

Such classical commitments to a substantialist understanding of God's being have run into two major obstacles in modern thought: first, the denial that we could know God in the Godself, and second, the apparent incompatibility of an eternal unchanging God with the biblical view of a God in relationship to a world he loves.

First is the problem of knowing God. Although God had always appeared mysterious to Christian perceptions, God became even more mysterious and incomprehensible following Immanuel Kant's *Critique of Pure Reason* of 1787. Transcendent reality is just that, transcendent to human knowing. Hence, we do not have knowledge of God per se. When we speak of God's unchangeableness or necessity or such things, Kant says, we are giving voice to our human imagination, which seeks to pass beyond the limits of temporal finitude. We cannot know God in God's self. Applied to the issue at hand, this means among other things that we have no knowledge of the immanent Trinity.[12]

Second is the problem of God's relating to a temporally changing world. If God is not capable of change or becoming, it would seem that God could not be affected by the world. Even the suffering of its creatures could not elicit divine sympathy. God would be apathetic, unable to feel the pain of others. In addition, human freedom seems to be rendered superfluous because it would make no difference whether I love God or not. How, we might ask, can we reconcile the God of substantialist metaphysics with the portrait of God in Jesus' parable of the prodigal, as a grieving father who goes in search of his lost child? The scriptural story of salvation assumes that God responds to human conditions and actions, and to do so God must be affected by what happens in the world.[13]

Such considerations in recent times have led to an attack against the substantialist metaphysics that are presumed to underlie our idea of God as Trinity. This attack has been most vigorously launched by the process metaphysicians.[14] But their twentieth century arguments are not simply a reiteration of Kant's eighteenth-century prohibition against knowledge of things transcendent. Rather, they argue that the classical picture of God makes God look aloof, impersonal, unrelated to the world and hence uncaring. To speak of God as a divine substance that is immutable and existing independently of all other things seems to make it impossible for God to love us. To love, one must be affected by the beloved, perhaps even to suffer in loving. This implies change and mutability. Process thinkers, following Alfred North Whitehead, want to posit that God suffers with us as we suffer. Hence, we need to paint a picture of the divine life depicting it as dynamic and inextricably related to the life of the world. "As I see it," writes Joseph Bracken, S.J., "the nature of God is not a fixed state of being but an activity, namely, the activity of interrelating."[15]

Substantialist metaphysics appears reductive, whereas process metaphysics depicts itself as holistic. The classical Christian tradition prescinding from Plato and Aristotle found the identity of complex things in the simplicity of their underlying substance. Interactions are due to accident, not substance. In neoclassical or process thought, in contrast, the phases or parts of a process combine to create a single interactive reality bigger than themselves as parts, namely, a whole that exercises agency.[16] This interactivist or holistic thrust would seem to offer a most appropriate means for explicating the obvious dynamism inherent in the three-person trinitarian formula.

Process theism is post-Kantian in method, because it is not based upon supernatural or special revelations that allegedly come to this world from the transcendent world. Rather, it is based upon common human experience and human reflection, which leads to speculative metaphysics, which describes the phenomenal realm. It is constructive metaphysics based upon general, not special, revelation.[17] It is synthesis, not analysis. The biblical symbols of Father, Son, and Holy Spirit play at best a minimal role. The result is that process theologians, for the most part, find they can no longer embrace the Christian doctrine of the Trinity. If they keep a version of the Trinity, it is so transformed that it is scarcely recognizable. This is unfortunate, I think, because the process conceptuality with its emphasis on relationality could become an appropriate vehicle for trinitarian understanding. In sum, the advantage is that process theology proffers a dynamic and relational metaphysics that could very well help explicate the Trinity; the disadvantage is that the method of process theology builds upon common human experience rather than the special revelation of Father, Son and Spirit.

Process theologians are by no means the only contemporary critics of classical substantialism. Wolfhart Pannenberg argues that we have inherited an erroneous tendency to bind together individuality and substance in such a way as to cloud the distinction between person and substance. This makes inevitable the clouding of the relationship between person and subject.[18] We need to establish some distance over against classical substantialism, says the Munich theologian, if we are to find a way to affirm the singular subjectivity of God and the threefold personhood of the Trinity.

Thus, almost everyone, especially in the Protestant camp, tends to agree that the ancient ontology needs some reconceptualization. The key element in the current attempt to modify substantialist metaphysics—whether by process theologians or other thinkers—is the affirmation of the principle of relationality in contemporary thought. God must be reconceived in terms of relationality, it is commonly said. This brings us to the next in our list of issues: should "person" be thought of in essentially relational terms?

How Should "Person" Be Used in Trinitarian Discourse?

All parties to today's Trinity talk seem to agree that the definition of "person" has changed over the centuries. So the question arises: Can we still employ the formula "one being in three persons"? If we elect to use this formula, then which definition of "person" do we use, the ancient one or a more contemporary one? If we elect to abandon the ancient rendering, then what do we substitute for the word "person"?

Actually, what was meant by "person" in the fourth century is not all that clear. In antiquity, the key term behind our word "person" was *hypostasis,* a term with a stipulated reference employed so as to make a compromise between two schools of thought. The Cappadocian theologians had sharply distinguished between *hypostasis* and *ousia;* whereas Athanasius had used them interchangeably.[19] The Cappadocian theologians had placed the emphasis on the three persons and located the mystery in their unity; whereas Athanasius had emphasized the oneness of God whose mystery lies in threeness. The Cappadocians and their Orthodox heirs tended to give priority to person over essence or being, saying that the divine person determines the divine essence; whereas the emerging Latin tradition tended to give priority to divine essence.

At Constantinople in 381, the word *hypostasis* was chosen to refer to Father, Son, and Spirit because it could be interpreted to the advantage of both sides.[20] On the one hand, it could refer to the *ousia,* or essence of something, and be translated into Latin as *substantia.* On the other hand, it could be forced to refer to the face *(prosopon)* of God, the equivalent of *persona* in Tertullian's Latin formula, *una substantia, tres personae.* In sum, the term *hypostasis* equivocates.[21] This means, among other things, that it is of little or no help to try to discern its meaning by doing an etymological study of the word *prosopon* or a history of the relationship between masks, faces, and persons. Nor does it help to accept the further confusion created by Boethius, who defined a person as an individual substance of a rational nature *(persona est naturae rationabilis individua substantia)*, because this only further conflates the meanings of substance and person.[22] What we have to work with is the Niceno-Constantinopolitan word *hypostasis,* which we customarily render in English as "person," and it is simply up to us to argue theologically for one or another meaning of the term.

Be that as it may, the whole issue makes many twentieth-century theologians nervous. Karl Barth believes that the modern emphasis on human individuality requires that we cease referring to Father, Son, and Spirit as persons.[23] Robert Jenson is ready to substitute the word "identity" for "person."[24] Karl Rahner wants to hold on to the classical formulation, but he wants to define "person" as a "distinct manner of subsisting."[25] Leonardo Boff is happy with the word "person" *(persona)* because he believes it is equivalent to *hypostasis.*[26] Proposals vary. Yet all seem to operate with the assumption that contemporary understandings of personhood are relevant to trinitarian understanding. What is at stake here?

From the modern point of view—by modern we mean the eighteenth-century perspective that underlies such concepts as democracy, freedom, dignity, and human rights—we understand a person to be a unique individual who is a self-initiating and self-determining subject. Each person is a distinct seat of subjectivity and, hence, independent of other persons and things. One's personhood signals one's autonomy. If, then, we were to apply without qualification the modern understanding of person to the trinitarian formula of "one substance in three persons," we could not avoid positing three distinct subjectivities only tenuously tied together. It would constitute a thinly veiled tritheism.

In order to avoid the appearance of tritheism, modern theologians have for the most part placed the seat of divine subjectivity in the unity rather than in the persons. This is what Karl Barth does. The result, however, is that the meaning of "person" when applied to Father, Son, and Holy Spirit seems vacuous. Barth dubs them "modes" or "ways" *(Seinsweise)* of divine being, a move that deprives the persons of their distinctiveness and tends toward modalism.[27] In sum, the modern notion of person seems to import too much individuality and independence for the traditional trinitarian formula to work.

But there is also emerging a postmodern point of view, one that emphasizes relationality. Its relevant axiom is that persons are always interpersonal. No one can be personal except in relation with other persons.

Who we are as individuals is dependent in part on our ongoing interaction with other individuals. Whatever distinctiveness or autonomy we enjoy is due to the context of relations in which we find ourselves.[28]

J. D. Zizioulas, for example, argues that personhood implies the "openness of being," and even more than that, the *ekstasis* of being. To be a person, then, one must be open toward communion. A person is a self in the process of transcending the boundaries of the self, and this self-transcendence is the root of freedom. *Ekstasis* is *hypostasis*, says Zizioulas. On the one hand, a person is an integrated unity, to be sure; yet on the other hand, a person who fulfills personhood is ecstatically open for communion.[29] In short, persons are interpersonal by definition. The being of a person is a being-in-relationship.

This notion of interpersonal personhood is becoming a dominant theme in the central discussion of the Trinity—that is, in the work of such scholars as Eberhard Jüngel, Jürgen Moltmann, Leonardo Boff, Catherine Mowry LaCugna, and Wolfhart Pannenberg. Through a principle such as analogy or correspondence, what we understand to constitute human personhood-in-relation is applied to the inner life of God. The Son can be identified as Son only by virtue of his relationship to the Father, and vice versa. The Spirit is Spirit by virtue of its interaction with the other two, not as an independent substance. The relations are constitutive of each person's identity. Boff presses the interactive model all the way to a social doctrine of the Trinity, proposing a correlation between the divine society and human society. He writes, "Seeing people as image and likeness of the Trinity implies always setting them in open relationship with others; it is only through being with others, understanding themselves as others see them, being through others, that they can build their own identities."[30]

The issue regarding personhood prescinds from the issue of substantialist metaphysics. If we follow the classical pattern and think of a person as a substance, then every community including the Trinity is a mere aggregate of individuals. But if we turn to more recent metaphysical notions such as process and holism, then we might think of an interpersonal community as a whole that is greater than the sum of its parts. According to Joseph Bracken, for example, the unity of God is not a unity of substance but rather the unity of community. Community and person are correlative. Neither is prior. Each requires the other. Hence, in one and the same moment all of the three divine persons are constituted as individual existents, and God as Trinity is constituted as a divine community.[31] Although not everyone embraces the holistic principle that the communal whole is greater than the sum of its constituting parts, the idea of person-in-relationship seems to be nearly universally assumed.[32] "Person indicates relationship," writes Catherine Mowry LaCugna. "Trinitarian doctrine is therefore inescapably a theology of personhood, regardless of how this is formulated."[33]

In sum, for current Trinity talk it is inconceivable that we would have a single person existing in total isolation. When applied to the Trinity, then, we could posit a postmodern or relational understanding of person to Father, Son, and Spirit and hold together both the unity and diversity. What we could not do is apply the postmodern concept of person to God in a singular sense—that is, in a brute monotheistic sense. This observation leads us to the next issue in current Trinity talk, namely, to what extent should Christians affirm monotheism?

Are Christians Monotheists?

Let us restate the previous issue: Does God have one personality or three? Does God have one subjectivity or three? Where do we find God's self, in the unity or the plurality? If we move in the direction of attributing personhood to the Father, Son, and Spirit, are we giving up on monotheism? Does monotheism constitute a club in which Christians want to hold membership?

For most of the last two millennia, Christians have more or less assumed monotheism. Norman Pittenger articulates it in a familiar way: "The Christian is indeed a monotheist, but his monotheism is enriched by the belief that in the mystery of the divine Reality there are distinctions or relationships, so that it may properly be said that sociality as well as personality are to be ascribed to deity."[34] The Christian affirmation is monotheistic, to be sure; but it is an internally textured and dynamic understanding of the one God as Father, Son, and Holy Spirit.[35]

Not everyone is convinced that trinitarianism makes orthodox Christianity eligible for membership in the monotheistic club. First Jews and then later Muslims found the role ascribed to Jesus Christ as Son to compromise the oneness of God. New voices of criticism were added in the wake of the Protestant Reformation with the rise of unitarianism. Reiteration of the unipersonality of God was voiced in Poland and Hungary in the sixteenth century, moving to England in the seventeenth, and to America in the eighteenth. William Ellery Channing's sermon of

1819 and manifesto for "Unitarian Christianity" holds that the unity of God cannot be reconciled with the doctrine of the Trinity.[36] The orthodox distinctions between being and person have produced a formula of three divine beings, having different consciousness, different wills, and different perceptions, performing different acts, and sustaining different relations. This is both unscriptural and irrational, complained Channing. The unity of God cannot be compromised, he insisted; and trinitarian theology makes such a compromise.[37]

Even within the camp committed to orthodox trinitarianism, the classical commitment is being reexamined. To illustrate, I suggest that we think of three basic positions on the contemporary continuum, locating Schleiermacher's strict monotheism at one end and Moltmann's social trinitarianism at the other with Barth in the middle. Let us look at them in turn.

Schleiermacher's method begins with the human experience of absolute dependence, and this leads directly to a corresponding emphasis on divine unity. The consciousness that we are absolutely dependent can be described only in terms of monotheism, he says.[38] The primary utterances of the Christian faith refer us to the one God. What we know as trinitarian discourse is secondary. What we say about the Trinity is a combination or synthesis of more basic utterances that reflect our experience with the divine unity.[39] Thus, Schleiermacher is assuming that there is no real distinction between the presence of God in Christ and the presence of God in the Spirit. With a bow to Sabellius, he says the distinctions between Father, Son, and Spirit have to do with God's external relations to the world, with the spheres of divine operation. In the divine self, however, there is only unity; and this unity is the principle of monotheism.[40] Christianity, he contends, is one of the three great monotheistic communions. Judaism and Islam are the other two.[41] Because of his emphasis on divine unity in monotheistic terms, Schleiermacher dropped the doctrine of the Trinity to a near appendix at the end of his systematic theology, *The Christian Faith*.[42]

In deliberate contrast to Schleiermacher, Barth places the doctrine of the Trinity right at the beginning—in the prolegomena—of his systematic theology, *Church Dogmatics*. He argues that the trinitarian distinctions belong to the primary utterances of the Christian experience with God. Our most primitive experience with God is as Father or as Son or as Spirit. The Trinitarian nature of God belongs to the original revelation proper. It is not constructed by combining or synthesizing prior utterances of divine unity. God is revealed as Trinity, and our task as theologians is to analyze this revelation.

One implication is this: Christian trinitarianism is not a subspecies within monotheism. Barth is not applying for a membership card to join a club in which Judaism and Islam are members. Christian theology, he says, does not measure its understanding of God by the broader idea of monotheism.[43] Nevertheless, this by no means implies a loss of divine unity. Barth emphasizes divine oneness. There is one single essence to God that is not tripled by the doctrine of the Trinity.[44] God is a single personal self in three modes of being.

Moltmann follows Barth's lead and goes further, even to the extent of pitting monotheism against trinitarianism. He repudiates the former and affirms the latter; but in doing so, he denies that trinitarianism is tritheism or polytheism. Rather than multiple gods, Moltmann says that the one God has alienated himself from himself in the cross and is returning to union through the Spirit. God's love for the world has precipitated a division within God's being. It is this internal diremption of the divine being that distinguishes the Christian revelation from what others know as monotheism.

Moltmann has a clear preference for the Cappadocians over Athanasius, beginning with the plurality and working back toward unity. He emphasizes the three persons as three subjects, as three loci of activity. He then attacks Karl Barth for thinking of God as a single subject. This, he complains, is capitulating to monotheism.[45]

Perhaps we should pause to ask why Moltmann follows this course. He says he does so because the God of monotheism is cold and uninvolved in human suffering. The God who is a single simple unity is an absolute individual, incapable of relationship. The trinitarian God, however, is fully present in the sufferings of Jesus Christ on the cross and, hence, in the sufferings of oppressed peoples everywhere. This realization shatters our monotheistic idea of God. It splits it apart in trinitarian fashion.

Moltmann adds to this an argument that he believes befits the agenda of liberation theology. He puts it forcefully: "Monotheism is monarchism."[46] The problem with monotheism is a political one, namely, the notion of a divine monarchy in heaven justifies earthly domination. Kings create hierarchies and then dominate with a "holy rule." The idea of the almighty ruler of the universe legitimates a corresponding hierarchical power structure that oppresses human society. "Monotheism and monarchism are only the names for two sides of the same thing," he writes.[47] The trinitarian understanding of God, in contrast, is nonhierarchical and inspires identification with the oppressed in society. This leads Moltmann to distance himself from Islam and demand that Christianity repudiate monotheism.

> Strict monotheism has to be theocratically conceived and implemented. . . . The strict notion of the One God really makes theological christology impossible, for the One can neither be parted nor imparted. It is ineffable. The Christian church was therefore right to see monotheism as the severest inner danger, even though it tried on the other hand to take over the monarchical notion of the divine lordship.[48]

Moltmann's contention is worth considering for a moment. Let us ask the question, Just what can he mean by saying that monotheism is monarchism? The statement is either false or, if true, then trivial. If he means it in the strong sense that monotheism is the source of monarchism, then we could falsify it by finding one monarchy that is polytheistic. This is easy to do. Nearly all the known societies of antiquity were polytheistic and came with kings and hierarchies. For example, the pharaoh in ancient Egypt was the embodiment of one of the many Egyptian gods and goddesses. And the king in Babylonia represented Marduk, one of the pantheon. These houses of royalty or emperorship did not find their source in monotheism.

Perhaps Moltmann is attacking the monotheistic divinity of Aristotle. Aristotle, after all, was a philosophical monotheist. He founded no religion, as far as we know. Aristotle happened to be the teacher of Alexander the Great, a great monarch. Did Aristotle's monotheism give birth to Alexander's monarchy? No. The idea of establishing an empire with a single throne to rule the world was the idea of Alexander's father, Philip of Macedon. Alexander's concept of the world monarch probably came from his father, not Aristotle. Did Aristotle have any subsequent influence on monarchy? Perhaps for a short time. Aristotle's political philosophy affirmed monarchy as a sane form of government. Yet it is interesting to note that upon Alexander's death in 323 B.C. the unified Greek empire divided itself into three parts.

It appears that Moltmann cannot sustain the thesis that "monotheism is monarchism" in the strong sense. So, perhaps Moltmann means to use this assertion in a weak sense: given monarchy, then monotheism can be exploited to support the monarch's power. If it is in this weak sense that Moltmann intends his proposition to be used, then it is trivial.

In fact, the monarch may use anything—the military, the economy, religious symbols, advertising, campaign slogans, whatever—in order to consolidate his power. He can even use polytheistic theology for this purpose, as has been demonstrated. There is nothing intrinsic to the nature of monotheism as such that makes it monarchical.

This leads to a second question, To what does Moltmann refer when using the term "monotheism"? If we look at the monotheism of the Bible, we find no support for the oppressive use of power by monarchs. Recall the significant precedent set by the Samuel cycle in the Deuteronomic history. The confederacy of Israel's twelve tribes seemed to the people to be unable to withstand the attacks from their enemies, especially the Philistines. So the people asked Samuel the prophet if they could have a king just as other nations have kings. Samuel objected, saying that God alone rules Israel and that any human king might usurp illegitimate power. Finally, at God's advice, Samuel yielded and granted permission for the Israelites to have a king. But there was a difference. Israel's understanding of the king did not duplicate that of other nations. In Israel, the charisma formerly belonging to the judges was now divided into two parts: the king received the power of political leadership, but the prophet received the spirit of God. In short, the monarch was secularized. All through the Deuteronomic history of 1 and 2 Samuel and 1 and 2 Kings, the prophet stands as God's appointed critic against the king for misusing his dominion. The theological point is clear: God alone has dominion, and the human king is God's steward. Belief in the one God of Israel provides the very critical leverage needed to release us from the grip of the monarch's "holy rule." So, we ask, does Moltmann have the God of Israel in mind when he equates monotheism with monarchism? This would surely be a mistake.

Mention of the God of Israel alerts us to another problem, namely, Moltmann's avowed dependence upon the Jewish understanding of God. He does not begin his search for God's involvement in human suffering by going to the Christian understanding of the Trinity. He goes rather to Jewish scholars such as Abraham Heschel and Franz Rosenzweig. The God of the Hebrews was passionate and capable of suffering, Moltmann says, whereas the God of Aristotle was not. What he opposes is the "apathetic God of the philosophers."[49] From this it looks like the monotheism Moltmann is attacking is that of the philosophers, not that of Judaism or Islam. Does this then put Judaism and Islam into the trinitarian camp? No. These two are still monotheisms. So we have to ask, If Moltmann can affirm divine passion and divine involvement in human suffering already within the context of Hebrew monotheism, is this divine passion and involvement in itself sufficient grounds for abandoning monotheism in favor of trinitarianism? Is monotheism per se the culprit, or is it simply the Greek version of monotheism? Is Moltmann confused?

In his dialogue with Rabbi Pinchas Lapide, the rabbi is less than convinced by Moltmann's argument. As a Jew, Lapide cannot give up the shema: "Hear, O Israel: The LORD our God is one LORD" (Deut. 6:4; RSV). To Lapide, Moltmann's Trinity appears at best like a heavenly triumvirate and, at worst, like a tritheism that is reminiscent of a lapse into paganism.[50]

In sum, Moltmann's attempt to drive a sharp wedge between monotheism and trinitarianism creates confusion upon confusion. It denies while affirming continuity between the Hebrew and Christian apprehensions of God. The concept of monotheism is so undefined one cannot tell for certain what it refers to. And the vitriolic rhetoric against human hierarchy only veils the vague if not equivocal equation of monotheism and monarchism, an equation that offers no analytical advantage. Until a better argument can be mustered, for the time being it appears that Christians should assume that their trinitarianism and monotheism go hand in hand.

A better argument has come along. Wolfhart Pannenberg begins with Moltmann's most cherished commitments to a loving God who has become involved with the suffering of the world. The intratrinitarian relations, argues Pannenberg, are characterized by love. In fact, the phrase "God is love" should be understood as the comprehensive expression of the fellowship between Father, Son, and Spirit. This love is the essence of the divine life, an essence that binds the three into one. This leads Pannenberg to argue that the trinitarian understanding of the one God makes it a fuller expression of monotheism. He writes, "Christian theology can even maintain, in response to Judaism and Islam, that only the trinitarian God, who, in his infiniteness, not only transcends the world but is also immanent in it, can be conceived in a consistently monotheistic fashion."[51]

To Whom Should We Pray?

To whom should we address our prayers? To Jesus Christ? To God the Father only? These questions are being asked by some contemporary theologians who have some reservations about praying directly to God the Son. What is not a hot topic in the current debate, curiously enough, is whether we should be praying directly to the Holy Spirit. The issue seems to focus on the first and second persons of the Trinity.[52]

Christians have addressed prayers to Jesus Christ as well as through him right from the beginning of New Testament times— Stephen at his martyrdom (Acts 7:59) and the biblical call for maranatha, "our Lord come"—and this was one of the practices both before and after the composition of the Nicene Creed. There never has been a time in the history of Christian worship when this was not the case. If we presume a relationship between *lex orandi* and *lex credendi*—between the rule of prayer and the rule of belief—then we find the creedal trinitarian formula consistent with worship practice. To pray to Jesus Christ is to pray to God.

In our own generation, however, this is being challenged. Prayer, when properly addressed, the challengers say, should be directed only to God; and God is to be understood here as God the Father. Prayer may be addressed *through* Jesus Christ as mediator, but *not to* Jesus as the Son.

This challenge argument follows two steps. First, the theological language that asserts that Jesus Christ is the Son of God is deliteralized. John Hick and Maurice Wiles, for example, argue that although the assertion that Jesus is the Son of God was taken as literally and metaphysically true in the time of Nicea, we today can do so no longer. We should think of it as a mythological story without metaphysical reference. "That Jesus was God the Son incarnate is not literally true," writes Hick.[53] Rather, sonship is a mythical or poetic way of imagining Jesus' relationship to God as that of a prince to a king. It models true humanity and, hence, mediates to us an image of how we should relate to God.

The second step is to appeal to a unitary understanding of God that mysteriously transcends all human language about God. Because the word "God" refers us to mystery, we must think of our language about God as a construction of human imagination. In worship, says Wiles, we want our theological language and our vox orandi to evoke the mystery of the divine. This means we need to be careful. There is but one God, and prayer to Christ without reference to the Father suggests multiplicity in God. "The Trinitarian cannot allow that prayer is ever offered to Christ to the exclusion of the other persons of the Trinity," writes Wiles, "for God is one and is the only proper object of all

Christian prayer or worship."[54] Wiles does not actually recommend that
we eliminate prayers directed to Christ. Rather, when prayed, he thinks,
we need to maintain a constant awareness that they refer not to Christ
per se but to the one God, which transcends the reference to Christ in
the prayer.

We find a variant of this argument in the work of Geoffrey Wainwright.
Wainwright is critical of Hick and Wiles on a couple of counts. First, he
challenges their assumed split between the metaphysical truth claims of
trinitarian theology and the relegating of the language of worship to that
of myth and poetry. If there is to be a genuine relationship between lex
orandi and lex credendi, both need to be grounded in truth claims and
not in mere expressive language. Second, Wainwright accuses Hick and
Wiles of conceptual unitarianism while permitting liturgical trinitarianism.
Again, there should be consistency between what happens in liturgy and
what we assert in reflective theology.[55]

Like Hick and Wiles, however, Wainwright believes that we should
pray to God the Father in the name of Jesus Christ; but we should not
pray to Jesus Christ. Why? He begins with a mediator Christology. The
two primary terms in his theological scheme are God and the world. He
puts Christ between the two, mediating a proper understanding of the
already existing divine-human relationship. This is not unitarianism,
however, because in Wainwright's case the mediating Son comes from
God proper. "The Christian understanding is that he mediates actively
by assuming our imperfect worship into his perfect service of the
Father."[56]

Wainwright then notes that the person to whom we address our
prayer becomes, in effect, our Lord. To address prayer to Jesus Christ is
to treat him as our Lord. Inexhaustible lordship, however, belongs only
to the Father. God is ultimate, whereas Christ is penultimate. Worship
should be viewed stereoscopically: it is directed toward God the Father
as its ultimate focus, but it passes through Christ. Therefore, Wainwright
argues, we should pray to the Father through the Son. This clearly commits him to a subordinationist trinitarianism.

In support of his position, Wainwright appeals to Origen, who argued that prayer may go through the Son but only to the Father. Origen
distinguished between prayer in the strict sense of the term (kyriolexia),
which should be offered to the Father, and a secondary form (kat-
achrestikos), to Christ the high priest who will convey it to the Father.
Such a scheme presumes that the Father is God in the absolute sense,

whereas the Son may have divine qualities but is God only in a derived or relative sense. This subordinationist position was hardened by Arius into a view that made the Son a creature of the Father, a position rejected at Nicea. Wainwright embraces Origen, but he says he does not want to embrace Arius.

What is wrong with Arianism? Wainwright says the cardinal error of Arianism is that it makes us worshipers of a creature. How do we avoid worshiping a creature? There are two ways. One way is to affirm that Christ is fully God and continue to worship Christ. This is the option taken by Athanasius and the Niceno-Constantinopolitan Creed. The other way is to affirm that Christ is something less than God and then worship not Christ but strictly God himself. Wainwright, along with Hick and Wiles, advocates taking the second option.

Yet one must ask, How can Wainwright side both with Origen and with Athanasius? How can he be both subordinationist and Nicene? His answer is this:

> To take the ontological risk: I myself go for subordinationism. I understand that the Son is *God as self-given* (the divine self-giving takes incarnate form in Christ), while the Father is *God as inexhaustibly self-giving*. This may not be so far removed from Athanasius' position that the Son is God in all things, except that he is not the Father.[57]

Christ the mediator, according to Wainwright, is both human and divine, but his divinity is a contingent or borrowed divinity. It depends completely on the divinity of the Father. The Father's divinity, in contrast, is independent. The Father's divinity is the source of the Son's divinity, but not the reverse. This, as we will see later in this volume, is one of the points where contemporary trinitarian theology is engaged in the most fundamental rethinking. The relational understanding of personhood is leading some theologians to suggest that divinity is derived from the interpersonal dynamics of Father, Son, and Spirit. This will turn out to be an antisubordinationist trinitarianism, because the divinity of the Father will be as dependent upon the Son as the reverse. This is the direction I recommend we take.

To posit a relational unity of three identities is still to posit a unity; and, in a sense, this permits partial agreement with Wainwright that we would not designate Jesus Christ as God apart from the Father and Spirit. Here, with some modification, we might follow John Calvin, who already follows Augustine in thinking this way: Christ with respect to us is called God; with respect to the Father, Son. Again, the Father with respect to us is called God; with respect to the Son, Father. Finally, the Spirit in respect to us is called God; with respect to the other two persons, Spirit.[58] What this means for our worship and prayer life, then, is that we treat each of the three persons as fully God. We do not direct our religious affections toward an allegedly mysterious divine nature, which these identifiable persons allegedly hold in common or, worse, which allegedly lies beyond them. Rather, when our thoughts, feelings, and worship are directed toward either the Father, the Son, or the Spirit, we can assume they are directed toward God proper.

Is Trinitarian Language Hopelessly Sexist?

Does the use of the traditional rendering "Father, Son, and Holy Spirit" deify male appellations? Does the trinitarian formula so serve the interests of patriarchal oppression that contemporary Christians should abandon it? Should we speak of the Holy Spirit as feminine in order to balance out the masculine dominance of the Father and Son? Should we create the image of an androgynous God or God/ess? Should we in our liturgical practice substitute a nongender rendering such as "Creator, Redeemer, and Sanctifier"? Or "the Parent, the Christ, the Transformer"? Or "Abba, Servant, and Paraclete"? These are the questions being asked as feminist theology increases its impact on the life of the church in our time. The heat these questions generate is indicated in the following probably apocryphal interchange.

> Layperson: "My pastor baptized my baby in the name of the Creator, Redeemer, and Sanctifier. Will my baby go to hell?"
>
> Theologian: "No, but the pastor will."

Perhaps the issue could be formulated with less heat and more precision so as to discriminate the various contemporary positions if we orient the discussion around this question: *Is trinitarian language sexist and, if sexist, does this warrant its abandonment in favor of inclusive substitutes?* At one end of the spectrum, we find feminists who answer yes to both, saying the Father-Son imagery is hopelessly patriarchal and, hence, oppressive; therefore, it must be exchanged for images that evoke human gender equality. I will call this the substitution argument. This argument makes the assumption that the terms "Father" and "Son" are metaphors and, therefore, exchangeable with other metaphors. At the other end of the spectrum we find those who say no to both, arguing that the trinitarian formula of Father-Son-Spirit, along with Abba, constitutes God's proper name and, hence, is nonexchangeable. I will call this the nonsubstitution argument. In the middle we find at least two mediating positions, both of which accept the assumption regarding the metaphorical nature of the divine appellations yet argue for keeping the Father-Son-Spirit terminology on the grounds that it is nonexchangeable. One variant in the middle accepts that the original trinitarian formulation has in fact been patriarchal and oppressive, but a proper interpretation of it can overcome the sexism. The other closely related variant is slower to admit the inherent sexism of the traditional language—taking a patriarchal, nonoppressive position, to the extent that it is discernible. Yet it also argues for nonexchangeability on the grounds that the symbolic nature of the divine appellations is what provides access to the God revealed in Jesus Christ. Here we will look at samples of these arguments in a bit more detail.

The extreme substitution argument for modifying or replacing the traditional trinitarian language begins with the assumption made by Hick and Wiles described above, namely: God is mysterious and unknowable, therefore, all human speech about God consists of metaphorical creations of the human imagination. The divine has no name, no essence that can be discerned in human discourse. We cannot speak literally about God's reality. All descriptions of God, therefore, are said to be based upon analogies drawn from human experience. To speak of God as Father, as has been the Christian custom, is to describe God in terms of a human father. It would be idolatrous, however, to speak of God *literally* as our Father. This would deify human maleness. Yet this is what the Christian tradition has allegedly done. This literalism and its accompanying idolatry, then, must be combated. The way to combat it is to alter our language for God—that is, to speak of God androgynously or in gender-free terms. This warrants creating new metaphors and talking about the God of Christian faith as "God/ess" or "Mother" or "Liberator."[59]

The substitution argument assumes a second premise: the existing language for God functions to support the social oppression of women. Trinitarian language was born in a period of patriarchal culture and, if continued in our own day, will function to promote the same patriarchy. The value of shifting to androgynous or gender-free appellations for God is that they will contribute to the establishment of social equality. It is the socially transformative power of language that is important here. Once we assume that there is no privileged set of linguistic symbols that grant us access to God, then our words for God can be evaluated according to a social calculus. Hence, the value of a phrase such as "Creator, Redeemer, and Sanctifier" is that it contributes to the equality of male and female roles in society.

A good example of this argument can be found in the work of Roberta C. Bondi. She contends that the trinitarian language of the Nicene Creed—its imagery of God as Father and the incarnation of the Son—is patriarchal. This is due to the cultural context of patriarchy within which the creed was written. She surmises that the language of the creed could not be otherwise. Nevertheless, Bondi says, we today need not be bound by that language. Why not? Because "all language about God is metaphorical."[60] We may take from the Nicene Creed the meaning it intended to express, and we may do so without taking its wording. We may affirm its theology without affirming its terminology.

Bondi is well aware that her opponents will argue that the fundamental reason for retaining the "Father, Son, Spirit" rendering is that it is the scriptural language. Here she makes a most interesting move. She observes two things. First, the Arians used scriptural language just as much as the orthodox did. From the point of view of Athanasius and the Nicene fathers, the problem with the Arians was not their use of scriptural language but rather the way they twisted the meaning of that language. Then, second, the Nicene fathers employed a nonbiblical term to differentiate their position from Arius. They introduced the phrase *homoousion to patri* in order to fix the meaning of the otherwise shared terminology. On the basis of this precedent, Bondi argues, we today should be able to alter our language for God and employ nonbiblical terms in order to convey the same faith the creed intended to summarize and express.

Bondi does not limit her argument to following this interesting precedent, however. She appeals as well to biblical allusions to God that employ feminine imagery, such as the womb. She appeals also to explicit New Testament statements regarding the equality of men and women. She summarizes her position:

> The needs of today's church with respect to the status of women are pressing. The character of the tradition as I understand it in fourth-century

terms lies in its content, rather than its language. Again and again what is affirmed is the unknowability of God, with our inability to lay hold of God in words or concepts. Yet the way in which we hold to the titles "Father" and "Son" suggests that we are, indeed, often filling those words with inappropriate images of masculine power, strength, or honor. I recommend that in the Creed we avoid all names for God that are gender-linked.[61]

Deborah Malacky Belonick disagrees. Representing one variant of the middle between the two ends of the spectrum, she says there is no evidence that the masculine gender of the Nicene terminology ascribes maleness to the divine or contributes to the oppression of women. Patriarchal speech does not necessarily entail oppression. For her, the symbols "Father, Son, and Holy Spirit" constitute our access to the God of Jesus Christ and, hence, are unexchangeable.

Belonick grants in part the working assumption that God is mysterious and unknowable. Yet she points out that this protection of the divine mystery from literalistic speech was already a significant component in the arguments of the church fathers during the framing of the Niceno-Constantinopolitan Creed. She cites Gregory of Nyssa on God's divinity and our "inability to give expression to such unutterable things."[62]

More directly, Belonick offers a careful analysis of the role played by terms such as "Father" and "Son" in the fourth-century deliberations. The historical documents seem to indicate that the framers of the creed were not attempting to ascribe masculine or fatherly qualities to God on the basis of analogy to human experience. They were not trying to deify maleness. In fact, they were attempting just the opposite. This becomes clear in the argument between Athanasius and the Arians, an argument that looks astonishingly parallel to the issue we face today.

The Arians contended that we should call the first person of the Trinity "Creator" and not "Father." They argued that Jesus Christ was not the divine Son, but merely a superior creature. Because Jesus was not Son, then God could not be Father. Therefore, a term other than "Father" was called for.

Athanasius opposed the Arians by stressing the importance of the biblical divine names "Father, Son, and Holy Spirit." No other terms count as equivalent substitutes.[63] Then he gave two arguments, one logical and one theological. The substitution of "Creator" for "Father" entails a logical problem. This would make God dependent upon the existence of creatures. One cannot be a creator without something created. If creation did not exist, he asked, would this "Creator-God" cease to be? No, of course not. God is *a se,* independent as well as unoriginate. Hence, the word "Creator" fails as a substitute.

Theologically, it would be wrong to attribute the creative work to only the first person of the Trinity. According to scripture, all of the members of the Trinity act in concert. In fact, all three activities—creating, saving, and sanctifying—apply to all three persons in the Trinity (Gen. 1:1–2; John 1:1–3; 5:21; Acts 2:24; Rom. 1:4; Eph. 5:26; 1 Thess. 5:23). In sum, God's being is much more than just that of a creator. When we call God "Father," we mean something higher than God's relation to us creatures.

In a fashion similar to Athanasius, Gregory of Nyssa contends that we call God "Father" because of the reciprocal relationship between the first person of the Trinity and the incarnate Son, Jesus Christ. The terms "Father" and "Son" identify a dynamic within the divine life. Gregory is aware that such words are metaphors, to be sure; but they "contain a deeper meaning than the obvious one."[64] The divine Father is as different from, and transcendent to, earthly fathers as the divine is different from, and transcendent to, the human. Gregory holds that it is through the terms "Father, Son, and Holy Spirit" that women and men can enter into the divine abyss, somewhat equipped to understand the inner relationships and persons of the Trinity.

After a review of the Nicene theologians, Belonick concludes:

> In the theology of the early Church, the traditional trinitarian terms are precise theological terms. Therefore these terms are not exchangeable. Through them humanity encounters the persons of the Trinity, and through them relationships among members of the Godhead are defined. . . . There is no historical evidence that the terms "Father, Son, and Holy Spirit" were products of a patriarchal structure, "male" theology, or a hierarchical Church.[65]

Catherine Mowry LaCugna and Patricia Wilson-Kastner offer similar arguments. Although Belonick denies the inherent oppressiveness of the terms "Father, Son, and Holy Spirit," LaCugna grants that the male terminology has had deleterious social impact. "The trinitarian tradition, like the Bible," she says, "is *both* the source of revelatory truth about the mystery of God *and* a powerful resource for patriarchal culture."[66] Yet the same trinitarian theology, rightly understood, can combat what is so reprehensible about patriarchy, namely, distant domination. How? Because essential to trinitarian theology going back to the Cappadocian fathers has been the principle of relationality. The kenotic entrance of God into human life through Jesus Christ repudiates a unitarian or monarchical monotheism, because the trinitarian God is personal and relational both within and without. The Father-Son imagery makes this point vividly. The issue is not the sex of God, because no one in Christian theological history would ever seriously think of God as male. The issue is rather the relational component to the divine life. Wilson-Kastner makes the same point. "Trinity is more supportive of feminist values than is a strict monotheism. . . . Put very simply, if one imagines God as three persons, it encourages one to focus on interrelationship as the core of divine reality, rather than on a single personal reality, almost always imagined as male."[67] In sum, whether one grants the assumption that the classic trinitarian terminology was historically patriarchal-oppressive or not, these two mediating positions use a Cappadocian inspired emphasis on the personal and relational quality in the divine life to justify continued employment of "Father, Son, and Holy Spirit."

At the nonsubstitution end of the spectrum, arguing in defense of the nonsexist origin and nonexchangeability of the biblical symbols, we find some theologians asserting that "Father, Son, and Holy Spirit" constitute God's "proper name." Robert Jenson does. Our access to salvation depends upon our unambiguous identification of the God of Israel, the God who raised Jesus from the dead on Easter. The triune name "Father, Son, and Holy Spirit" occupies the place in the life of the church occupied by "Yahweh" in Israel. When Jesus addressed Yahweh of Israel as *abba,* he settled for us the issue of naming the divine. To be initiated into the new life of Jesus Christ in baptism is to be initiated into the name of the Father and Son through the Holy Spirit.

Jenson's nonsubstitution argument is based solely on the place the trinitarian formula enjoys in scripture. It is tied to the event of revelation and salvation. Jenson's argument is not based upon a general principle of describing an otherwise unknowable God in terms analogous to human experience. His method is not one of projection for purposes of social change. In fact, he repudiates the notion that we are deprived of human equality just because our gender is not represented in the divine being, and he repudiates as well the plan to achieve social equality by projecting our own human qualities in equal measure upon God.

The assumption that it is a deprivation not to address God in one's very own gender is a case of humankind's general religious assumption of direct analogy from human perfections to divine qualities. In the faith of the Bible, this direct line is, for our salvation, broken. Indeed, Christianity's entire soteriological message can be put so: God's self-identification with the Crucified One frees us from having to find God by projection of our own perfections. Therefore no argument that depends on the assumption of unbroken analogy from human worth to divine characteristic can have any place in the church.[68]

What we know about God is not the result of projecting human images onto a divine screen. Rather, we know God because God in Godself has come to us and identified with us in the Crucified One.

What Jenson has done here is attempt to shift the formulation of the issue. The issue is not one of obtaining knowledge of an otherwise unknowable God. Nor is it one of constructing imaginative metaphors for God in the struggle for women's liberation in society. Rather, the issue is one of identity. How do we identify God? How do we identify the divine reality that has come to us in the saving activity of Jesus Christ? The only way to identify this God, Jenson argues, is to use the proper name "Father, Son, and Holy Spirit."[69]

In a controversy within the Evangelical Lutheran Church in America that broke out in 1990, the question was raised: Are baptisms performed in the name of the Creator, Redeemer, and Sanctifier valid? The issue was addressed in a document, *Guidelines for Inclusive Use of the English Language.* After repeating the above mentioned assumption regarding the mystery or unknowability of God—"all language ultimately fails to represent God fully"[70]—the Guidelines state that "'Creator, Redeemer, and Sanctifier' is not a synonym for the traditional Trinitarian baptismal formula of 'Father, Son, and Holy Spirit.' "[71] This, argues Carl Braaten, settles the issue: "Baptism in any other name than Father, Son, and Holy Spirit is not valid Christian baptism."[72]

Catherine Mowry LaCugna goes beyond the question of validity to add what baptism bestows. The event of baptism changes our relationship before God. By the power of the Spirit we now live in Christ, so we begin to relate to God as Jesus did. By the Spirit we become part of God's family, so to speak. We address God intimately as *abba* (Rom. 8:15; Gal. 4:6). What Father-Son-Spirit language does is communicate to us our participation within the dynamic of divine relationality. It is living language.

Is trinitarian language hopelessly sexist?[73] After examining the arguments, I believe I stand somewhere between the two ends of the spectrum. On the one hand, it seems plain that the terms "Father" and "Son" when ascribed to God are in fact metaphors. "Holy Spirit" probably is as well. We begin with Jesus Christ as the Son and then liken his relationship with the God of Israel to that of a son with a father. We do this in part because Jesus himself set the precedent in the Lord's Prayer by saying, "abba Father." The metaphorical structure of the trinitarian language is obvious, even if one were to assert that Jesus Christ is literally the divine Son, because God would be Father not literally but on analogy with human fathers.

Therefore, to say that the trinitarian formula is God's proper name is to say too much. To liken it to *Yahweh* in the Old Testament is to say too much. The terms "Father, Son, and Holy Spirit" are primarily titles used in address. Titles can be distinguished from proper names. Titles are typically translated from language to language, whereas proper names are normally transliterated. The trinitarian formula "Father, Son, and Holy Spirit" is routinely translated, and nobody feels any loss. The only proper name given to us is the historical name of the Son, Jesus, and this is routinely transliterated. And, we note, this proper name does not even find a place in the trinitarian formula.

I am reluctant to grant that "Father, Son, and Holy Spirit" constitute the proper name of the divine on the basis of another observation as well. In the New Testament, we find many words by which we may address the divine, such as "God" or, of most importance, "Lord." The term "Lord" has a sort of preeminence. It was an Old Testament custom to substitute the "Lord" *(adonai)* for the tetragrammaton *(YHWH)* so as to avoid risk of violating its holiness. It referred to God by virtually naming God. That the title "Lord" *(kyrios)* is used in the New Testament to refer to Jesus Christ is of decisive importance. Christ is identified with that which is most holy and which commands our total allegiance. One might easily go so far as to say, as does Karl Barth, that "Lord" is the root of any appellation or name we might use when referring to God.[74] If God actually has a name, then "Lord" should receive first consideration. Yet even this term, "Lord," is but one of the many designations that sit side by side in the New Testament. So, if the words "Father, Son, and Holy Spirit" are absent, there is little worry that we will fail to recognize who the biblical writer is talking about. The same God is intended regardless of word choice, as long as the chosen words come from

the recognizable biblical collection. The trinitarian set of terms constitutes a family of symbols within a larger clan of biblical symbols we use
to identify the God of Christian faith. We use the specifically trinitarian
symbols on those occasions when we want to call the Trinity to mind.

On the other hand, to recognize the metaphorical dimension to
"Father, Son, and Holy Spirit" does not in itself make these symbols exchangeable with other terms. It does not follow that just because the divine Father-Son relationship is grasped on analogy with human
father-son relationships that we can substitute another set of imaginative
metaphors. There is only one trinitarian formula: Father, Son, and Holy
Spirit. This is because it is tied inextricably to the event of revelation
and salvation itself. In conjunction with other New Testament symbols,
it identifies the God in whom we put our faith as Christians. To bypass
the biblical terms in favor of some substitutes is to identify with a God
other than that of Jesus Christ.

In addition, the substitution argument in behalf of the exchangeability
of trinitarian formulas implicitly denies the trinitarian doctrine itself.
The argument proposed by Arius, recall, began with an unoriginate
creator. Jesus Christ, the redeemer, was dubbed an originate creature.
Whether knowingly or unknowingly, the contemporary substitution argument retrieves the Arian position when employing the "Creator,
Redeemer, Sanctifier" formula,[75] and for more than mere terminological
reasons. The major assumption, as mentioned above, is that God is alleged to be so mysterious and unknowable that all language about
God consists of human attempts to create imaginative metaphors to describe the divine reality. What we have here is infinite transcendence
with no finite presence. This implicitly denies the event of incarnation
and revelation, placing all the responsibility for knowing God on the
shoulders of the metaphor-makers. The claim made by trinitarian theology, in contrast, is that God has taken flesh in the person of Jesus and
become a historical event.

Or, to put it a bit differently, the substitution of "Creator, Redeemer,
Sanctifier" for "Father, Son, Holy Spirit" confuses the persons of the
Trinity with the functions. It arbitrarily assigns creation to the first person, redemption to the second, and sanctification to the third. This denies the coinherence of the three persons and tends toward
monarchianism, the view that distinguishes departments of divine activity
in the world without reference to the internal divine life. Against this we
find Augustine's rule, *opera trinitatis ad extra sunt indivisa,* stipulating

that God's actions in the world are undivided yet fully present in each person. This means that the Father, for example, is not merely the creator; he is also redeemer and sanctifier. The same could be said of the Son and Spirit. The classic trinitarian formula refers to the structure of the divine in being and in act, not merely to types of action carried out by an alleged mysterious divinity that transcends all distinction.[76] When exchanging the original trinitarian language for functional substitutes, we inadvertently (or purposely?) posit a transcendent deity that is not fully present as God in the event of incarnation. In the worthwhile attempt to avoid sexism, something essential to the Christian faith becomes discarded. Is this too high a price to pay?

In sum, the event of Jesus is not simply a metaphor to describe an otherwise separate or absent divine mystery. The event of Jesus has to do with God proper. It is God present to us under the conditions of finite history and under the conditions of human language. Hence, to know Jesus Christ is to know God—not just to know about God but to know God in the Godself. The transcendent divine being remains mysterious, to be sure. But we are not left in a situation where we know nothing literally. We are not left to the pure arbitrariness of an infinite field of competing human metaphors. The phrase "Father, Son, and Holy Spirit" may not be a proper name, yet it specifically identifies the one God who has become finitely present in Jesus Christ and who now binds us and our world to the divine destiny.

Does "Trinity" Mean Bomb?

The next item is more of a potential rather than an actual issue. It prescinds from the previous discussion regarding the possible deleterious social effects of the patriarchal language belonging to the doctrine of the Trinity. It has to do with the associative power of symbols. We might ask, If a religious symbol is associated with a negative human experience, will it either warp an existing faith or even discourage a person from having faith? An affirmative answer is frequently assumed in anti-patriarchal arguments: if a young woman grows up with an abusive father, then, allegedly, she will be repulsed by the symbol of God as Father in church. The way to overcome this, at least according to scholars such as Sallie McFague, is to employ a plurality of metaphors for God, including many feminine metaphors.[77] Evidently, the abuse associated with one metaphor can be offset if alternatives are available. This appears to be a form of the divide and conquer method, or, perhaps better, multiply and divert.

David Tracy may hint at an alternative method, namely, a hermeneutical retrieval of a symbol's meaning in a mutually critical dialectic with contemporary experience.[78] Rather than divide and conquer or multiply and divert, Tracy is suggesting that we attend to the meaning in the Christian tradition of the symbol in question. The attempt to retrieve the traditional meaning necessarily involves a double critique. Beginning with the hermeneutic of suspicion in our contemporary situation, we critique the tradition asking, What social structures has a particular symbol supported? In the case of God as Father, we would ask if it supports an all-male priesthood in church or child abuse in Christian homes. Reversing the direction, we employ what Christians have intended their symbols to mean in order to analyze the present situation. In the case of God as Father, again, the Christian emphasis on fatherly love would seem to negate justification of male oppression of women and children. Might Tracy's method offer us something regarding the Trinity?

I raise this prospect because of a potential issue regarding the Trinity that arises from an association that parallels the association of God as Father with sexism and child abuse. It is the association of the Trinity with nuclear weaponry. If feminists are correct that the symbol of God as Father is compromised by negative experiences women have with human fathers, then might this apply as well to the symbol of God as Trinity for those who fear the devastation that nuclear war might bring? Can the saving significance of the Trinity be retrieved for those who associate the Trinity with the bomb? Let me explain how such questions arise.

In March 1944, scientists on the Manhattan Project began planning for what would become the test detonation of the first atomic bomb. Robert Oppenheimer, director of the project at Los Alamos, New Mexico, proposed the code name for the test. He was well aware that the first nuclear explosion would be a historic event, and its designation might become a name that history would remember. He chose the word "Trinity." "Why I chose the name is not clear," he said when later reflecting on these events; "but I know what thoughts were in my mind. There is a poem of John Donne, written just before his death, which I know and love." Oppenheimer could quickly quote these lines of "Hymne to God my God, In My Sicknesse":

As West and East
In all flatt Maps—and I am one—are one,
So death doth touch the Resurrection.

What is important here is the paradoxical tension between death and resurrection, between destruction and renewal. In the fourteenth of Donne's Holy Sonnets, we find the theme of redemption through destruction and the allusion to the Trinity that Oppenheimer referenced.

Batter my heart, three person'd God; for you
As yet but knocke, breathe, shine, and seek to mend;
That I may rise, o'erthrow mee, and bend
Your force to breake, blowe, burn and make me new.

What physicist Oppenheimer found in Donne's poetry was something reminiscent of Niels Bohr's principle of complementarity. During the political debates that led to the Manhattan Project, Niels Bohr had argued relentlessly against military secrecy and in favor of the free flow of scientific information as well as international control of nuclear weapons. Bohr was seeking an open world modeled on the republic of science. The shocking knowledge of the atomic bomb combined with international control could prevent an arms race, thought Bohr, and perhaps even usher in an era of world peace. Oppenheimer was influenced by Bohr's thinking and, even though he had given himself over to military secrecy, he was hoping that the development of the most destructive weapon in history would produce not war but peace.

Oppenheimer worried that he might be remembered and perhaps even reviled as the person who led the work of bringing to humankind the means of its own destruction. Richard Rhodes comments, saying that Oppenheimer "cherished the complementary compensation of knowing that the hard riddle the bomb would pose had two answers, two outcomes, one of them transcendent. Such understanding justified the work at Los Alamos if anything did, and the work in turn healed the split between self and overweening conscience that hurt him."[79]

Although a conscience-stricken and religious person, Oppenheimer did not normally draw strength from symbols of the Christian tradition. His own spiritual meditation usually turned in the direction of the Bhagavad Gita. Following the first test explosion at 5:30 A.M. on July 16, 1945, after the light and the blast and the wind had passed, Oppenheimer referred his colleagues to Vishnu's words in the Gita,

"Now I am become death, the destroyer of worlds." Kenneth Bainbridge slapped Oppenheimer on the back and said, "Now we are all sons of bitches." Oppenheimer later reported that Bainbridge's words were the most appropriate spoken that day. The successful test at the Trinity site in New Mexico led to the immediate production of the atomic weapons that were loaded aboard B-29 bombers and then dropped on the Japanese cities of Hiroshima and Nagasaki.

Trinity and mass death: it is an association drawn by guilt trying to cover its own tracks, by a conscience in a feeble attempt to hide. Yet the world must live hereafter with the association.

The association of Trinity with mass death has already been exploited by feminist writer Mary Grey. The problem, as Grey sees it, is with God's transcendence. She believes the Trinity teaches a God beyond but not a God intimate. Transcendence, it is assumed here, justifies rape and other sorts of violence against women. So she cites the blistering critique of Mary Daly.

> The circle of destruction generated by the Most Unholy Trinity and re-flected in the Unwhole Trinitarian symbol of Christianity will be broken when women, who are by patriarchal definition objects of rape, exter-nalise and internalise a new self-definition whose compelling power is rooted in the power of being. The casting out of the demonic Trinities is female becoming.[80]

Having set the stage, Grey proceeds to ask rhetorically, "Was it a complete accident that the atomic bomb research programme—which culminated in the destruction of Hiroshima in 1945—was code-named Trinity?" Grey goes on to attack John Donne's sonnet that had inspired Oppenheimer. "Here is the transcendent God battering from the out-side, invited to take the poet by force: this is the model of Christian love—which uses the language of rape and seduction!"[81] Grey's concern here is not death but rather to depict women as victims of rape and to critique symbols that encourage rape. This leads her to capitalize on the negative association of Trinity with the bomb.

So, we ask, Can the symbol of the Trinity survive the association with mass death? Yes, I think so. Its tensive strength is already exhib-ited in Oppenheimer's somewhat inchoate reasons for choosing it. Yes, of course there is the obvious reference to God's force breaking, blowing, and burning. Yet there is much more. Of particular value is the portent of death followed by resurrection and both caught up in the comprehensive unity of the one three-person'd God. And there is the conscience conflict of the battered heart, and the faint hope that as Oppenheimer himself enters the vestibule of death he will be ushered through its halls to resurrection beyond, at least to resurrection understood as public exoneration for his attempt to turn the bomb into a missile for world peace. Of most importance, perhaps, is Oppenheimer's assumption—even though he was not a committed Christian believer—that the Trinity symbolizes something widely associated with what is good and true. He wanted to paint the sepulcher of dark death white, and the Trinity became his paint.

Hence, even before we begin to apply Tracy's method of mutually critical correlation, we find that the symbol of the Trinity is already incipiently at work as prophetic critic of the Manhattan Project. Its choice by Oppenheimer brings to articulation the double mindedness, the moral ambivalence that was present among the scientists. It is another way of saying, "We are all sons of bitches." So, should the issue of whether or not the Trinity means bomb arise in theological debate, we will have to pose crisscrossing questions. First, on the basis of the hermeneutic of suspicion, we will ask whether this symbol is so hopelessly tied to weapons development that—like Moltmann's equation of monotheism and monarchism—it can only serve the interests of the superpowers who want to dominate the world through nuclear terror. Then, second, we will ask if the meaning of the Trinity with its eternal perichoresis of divine love has sufficient internal strength to render a critique against those who would use it to cover over the absence of human love. If we answer yes to the second question, then this might imply a no to the first. Inherent in the symbol of the Trinity is more meaning than we can say and, like a beneficent Trojan horse, it may for generations yet continue a quiet witness to transcendent love within the citadel of nuclear death.

What Really Was Going On with Arius?

Turning from the contemporary back to the traditional, we note that considerable ferment and excitement have broken out recently in patristic studies. During the last decade, scholars have begun challenging the received tradition regarding the triumph of Nicene orthodoxy over the rampant Arian heresy. The received tradition views the turbulence of the fourth century from the perspective of the victors, or, perhaps more accurately, from the perspective of the settlement at Constantinople in 381. From this standard textbook perspective, it looks as though the Athanasian forces of orthodox doctrine won a close but significant victory over the attacking Arian heretics. The citadel of truth successfully defended itself from the siege of heterodoxy. The common assumption seems to be that prior to the Nicene crisis in 325 such a thing as an orthodox trinitarian theology existed and that Arius posed a threat to its role as guide and authority for church life. At least, this seems to be the officially received tradition regarding what took place during the Constantinian era. Yet this is being challenged now by scholars who do not want to receive the tradition just this way. The challenge comes from the kind of question a historian would ask, namely, What really happened?

Let us remind ourselves of the standard textbook version of what happened. It goes like this. In Alexandria during the second decade of the fourth century, Arius began to preach that the Son of God is a creature, that the Son does not share the same *ousia* with God. Bishop Alexander of Alexandria condemned Arius' teaching at a synod in 318. Arius then withdrew to Asia Minor and converted many to his heterodox doctrines. The Council of Nicea in 325 condemned the Arian position when propounding *homoousion* as the proper articulation of the orthodox position. The Eastern bishops, however, continued to espouse Arian views in increasingly subtler forms until the year 360 when, as Jerome put it, "the whole world groaned, and was astonished to find itself Arian."[82] The resistance to the Arian threat came primarily from Athanasius of Alexandria who, despite persecution and exile, indefatigably defended Nicene orthodoxy. Eventually, the three Cappadocian fathers picked up the baton and carried it to the finish line at Constantinople in 381, where the final triumph of orthodoxy could be proclaimed.[83]

The challenge to the standard view begins between 1979 and 1981 with a handful of new book-length studies, especially the publication of *Early Arianism: A View of Salvation* by historians Robert Gregg and Dennis Groh. Prior to that, modern treatments of Arianism assumed, first, that orthodoxy already existed before Arius came on the scene and, second, that what was at stake in the fourth-century controversy was ontology or cosmology, questions about the being of God and the world. This emphasis on ontology came from Bishops Athanasius and Alexander, who had described the situation this way. They described Arius as aiming to protect the singularity and monarchy of God at all

costs, and this allegedly warranted demoting the Son to creaturely status. Alexander and Athanasius could then attack Arius for attacking
Christ. Alexander described the Arians as soldiers standing in battle formation against the divinity of the Son, a cloud-raising pack of brutes
howling against Christ. Athanasius, similarly, could classify Arius with
those who advocate a radical oneness of God, such as Jews, and then
go further to attack Arius for inspiring "hatred" toward Christ.[84] As long
as we take the word of Alexander and Athanasius, we will assume that
Arius was motivated by a strict monotheism and wanted to sidetrack
Jesus Christ in order to focus on the one truly sublime God.

Gregg and Groh, in contrast, although not denying the divine ontology, locate the driving motive of the Arians elsewhere, namely, in soteriology. The thesis is this:

> Early Arianism is most intelligible when viewed as a scheme of salvation.
> Soteriological concerns dominate the texts and inform every major aspect
> of the controversy. At the center of the Arian soteriology was a redeemer,
> obedient to his Creator's will, whose life of virtue modeled perfect crea-
> turehood and hence the path of salvation for all Christians.[85]

Far from inspiring antagonism against the person of Christ, the Arians
revered him and devoted themselves to him, because in Christ they
found the path to salvation.[86] In Christ they found the model which, if
we fulfill in our own lives, will merit our becoming adopted into divine
sonship just as Jesus Christ was so adopted. Whereas for Athanasius and
what became the orthodox position—note the assumption here that the
orthodox position was still in the process of being formulated—the Son
is the precise image of the Father. For Arius, in contrast, the Son is precisely a creature as we are, and the Son's creatureliness is just what is
necessary to make his saving work effective. Salvation for Arius is by
imitation. Jesus conformed his will totally to that of the Father, and we
can follow Jesus by conforming our wills to that of God. Christ's eleva-
tion to sonship was a reward for performance, and this performance is
within the capacity of those who believe in him.[87] What is "common to
us and the Son," argues Arius, is adoption, and in this we find the basis
for Christian hope.

> The Arian hermeneutic cannot be misconstrued: what is predicated of the
> redeemer must be predicated of the redeemed. . . . [T]he central point in
> the Arian system is that Christ gains and holds his sonship in the same

way as other creatures. Arius' doctrine that Christ was advanced to God by adoption contains the ground and definition of the faith and hope of believers. The early Arians portrayed Christ as they did because the advo-cacy of this Christology gave fullest expression to their understanding of the content and dynamic of salvation.[88]

At least in part, the repudiation of Arius by the orthodox shared the motivation of Augustine in repudiating Pelagius nearly a century later, namely, to remind us that our salvation is a gift of God's grace and not the product of human achievement. Gregg and Groh describe the con-test as a "choice between an orthodoxy in which grace had come to be the entry into a stabilized order of redeemed creation and an Arianism in which grace empowered people for moral advance in a transactional universe."[89]

What emerged as the point of conflict between the Arians and the anti-Arians during the fourth century was competition between two dis-tinctly different frameworks for conceiving theology, one based on will and the other on being. The Arians emphasized will. God willed to have a Son. It was a free divine choice. Prior to so willing, there was only God. Once a Son was willed, then God became a Father. Athanasius, in contrast, argued that God did not will to have a Son. Rather, the Father generated the Son from his own divine being, and because this genera-tion took place in eternity there never was a time when God was not also Father. Deity by nature is generative, though God's involuntary gen-eration can be distinguished from his voluntary will to create the world.

No doubt, theologians prior to this period concerned themselves with matters of being and willing. But Gregg and Groh contend that a new note is being sounded here.[90] What became clear for the first time is that will and being each provided a paradigmatic framework for con-ceiving the *ordo salutis*. Hence, for us today to depict the fourth-century controversy as one centered around the being of God and the being of the Son is to presume wrongly that Athanasius had defined the frame-work for argument.[91]

In sum, what we take to be Nicene orthodoxy was not already in place prior to the rise of Arian teachings. In fact, it was the prompting by Arius that stimulated the theological construction that led eventually to what we now know as the orthodox position. The controversy itself was creative, and we need to be reminded that Christian doctrine consists of constructive growth that carries us conceptually well beyond the roots.

What About *Filioque*?

Although the issue of *filioque* by no means appears at center stage of current trinitarian discussion, its faint echoes from the wings can be heard. Reconsideration of *filioque* is being prompted today by ecumenical concerns, of course, but even more so by the attempt to import—or, perhaps better, to recognize—the relational understanding of personhood in the divine life. This is the case because relational personhood implies that the Holy Spirit is in dialectical relation with the Son as well as the Father.

The question is, What is the mode of the Spirit's origin? Does it proceed from both the Father and the Son *(ex Patre Filioque)* or from just the Father alone? The Niceno-Constantinopolitan Creed of 381 stated simply that the "Spirit proceeds from the Father," but, in pondering a remark by Hilary of Poitiers, Augustine began to think in terms of a double procession. The Hippo bishop thought of the Holy Spirit as the mutual love of Father and Son, the communal bond that unites them. The Holy Spirit, then, cannot be the Spirit of just one but rather of the two in relationship. The Father is the author of the Spirit's procession because he begot the Son, yet it is the begetting of the Son and the resulting relationship that warrants the procession of the Spirit.

This is a systematic argument. There is also a biblical argument. Augustine said that the procession of the Spirit from the other two persons is taught in scripture because the Bible speaks of the Spirit of the Son and also the Spirit of the Father. The Father and the Son must then be a single principle in relation to the Holy Spirit. With this in mind, might we then affirm that the Holy Spirit proceeds from the Son as well as the Father?[92] The product of this line of thinking became the doctrine of the *filioque,* a Latin term referring to procession also from the Son.

There was no intention at this early date to use the *filioque* as a polemical attack against the Eastern church. Its aim, like that of evangelical explication in general, was to explain the trinitarian symbols more clearly. Be that as it may, this interpretation became intertwined with ecclesiastical politics and was employed as a weapon in the Latin fight for papal dominance over the church. The concept of the Spirit's double procession surfaced at the Synods of Toledo in 447 and 589 and was later promoted for popular usage by Charlemagne among the Franks. Rome and Constantinople were competing for influence in newly Christianized areas of Europe such as Bulgaria, so Charlemagne in

809 asked Pope Leo III to rewrite the Nicene Creed with the *filioque* added. Leo III refused on the grounds that such a unilateral move on his part would violate the authority of the first ecumenical Council of Constantinople. The bishops of Rome subsequent to Leo III saw things differently, however, and the *filioque* eventually slipped into Western creedal usage, finding papal approval for use during the Mass by 1014. The practice grew and came to a church-dividing climax in 1054 when Pope Leo IX excommunicated the patriarch of Constantinople, Cerularius, on the grounds that the Eastern Orthodox were omitting the *filioque* from the Nicene Creed.

In the ninth century, Photios, the patriarch of Constantinople who became a political football in the game of power between East and West, lashed out at these Latin "blasphemies." Photios advanced three arguments against the addition of *filioque,* one ecclesiastical and two theological. The ecclesiastical argument is clear and forceful: when an ecumenical council representing the whole Christian church establishes a statement of faith, as was done at Constantinople in 381, then only a similar council has the right to amend or alter it. The unilateral action taken by the bishops at Rome must be considered arbitrary if not scandalous.

The first of Photios' theological arguments is exegetical. Appealing to the Bible, he underscores what Jesus says in the very important passage (John 15:26), namely, that the Spirit comes "from the Father." Photios asks rhetorically, If the Spirit comes from both the Father and the Son, then why did Jesus not add "and from me"? If "from the Father" was good enough for Jesus, then it ought to be good enough for the church.[93]

The second of Photios' theological arguments is systematic, focusing on the destruction of the concept of the Trinity, which he believes is entailed in the concept of *filioque.* The idea of *filioque* seems to imply that the Spirit is inferior to the first two persons of the Trinity, because the Spirit is produced by them but they are not similarly produced by the Spirit. This means the three persons lose their equality. It leaves us with a dyadic God made up of Father and Son. And even worse, if we think of the Son as generated from the Father prior to the Spirit's proceeding from the two of them, we may end up with a Father monarch and a Son prince as a mere intermediary. Photios accuses the West of flirting with Sabellianism because *filioque* points to a series of successions leading from the Father to the Son and then, lastly, to the Spirit. He worries that if Christ is the Father's Son, then the Spirit must be his "grandson."[94] *Filioque,* it seems to Photios, cannot help but shortchange the Spirit's divinity.

For contemporary Orthodox theologians such as Kallistos (Timothy) Ware, the battle over *filioque* today is being fought on essentially the same field as it was in the patristic period. Ware begins by emphasizing that the first person of the Trinity, the Father, is the cause or source of the Godhead. The Father is the principle, or *archē,* of unity among the three; and it is in this sense that Orthodoxy speaks of the "monarchy" of the first person. The other two persons trace their origin to the Father and are defined in terms of their relation to him. It follows that Christ, then, underwent two births: one eternal and one in time. The Logos was born of the Father before all ages and also born of the Virgin Mary in the days of Herod, King of Judea. Similarly, a firm distinction must be drawn between the eternal procession of the Holy Spirit and the temporal mission. The first concerns the relations within the Godhead and the relation between God and creation. The second concerns the sending of the Spirit into the world.

This leads Bishop Ware to accuse the Latin West of di-theism and semi-Sabellianism. To say that the Spirit proceeds from both the Father and the Son is to imply that there are two independent sources, two separate principles of origination in the Trinity. Is this not tantamount to belief in two gods? To be charitable, Ware could concede that the Latin West rejects the idea of two gods. To reject di-theism while affirming filioque, however, is only to jump from the frying pan into the fire. This requires the fusion of the Father and the Son into a single principle of origination, or *archē.* And what else is this, complains Ware, than the rebirth of Sabellius or some similar Sabellian monster?[95]

It is my judgment that the ecclesiastical argument raised by Orthodox spokespersons such as Photios should carry the day. The insertion of *filioque* in the Western version of the Nicene Creed was an act of unwarranted authority and certainly not done in the interest of church unity. The value of an ecumenical council is found in its attempt to decide matters as a whole. For Western Christians to ignore such a conciliar decision and to operate as if the East and its concerns did not exist reveals at minimum a lack of integrity and at maximum a divisive spirit. Should the Holy Spirit at some point in the future lead us further toward a new level of ecumenical unity, I would hope that Christians in the West would apologize for their renegade ancestors and seek forgiveness from their Eastern sisters and brothers.[96]

When we turn to the specifically theological import of *filioque,* however, I must say that there is much to commend the Western position. If we think of theology as an ongoing process of evangelical explication, then we need not assume that what was somewhat hastily decided at Constantinople in 381 should remain fixed as the last word regarding the Holy Spirit. Continued exploration into the matter and drawing out further the implications of the basic Christian symbols could in principle lead to new insights. *Filioque* is one such insight.

In makes sense on a couple of counts to think of the Spirit as proceeding from the Son as well as the Father. The concepts of relationality and communality help make this clear. In the first place, with regard to the life of faith, *filioque* ties the Holy Spirit closely to the resurrected Christ. It is the Easter Christ who is present to us in faith, and it is the Spirit that is responsible for this presence. The Spirit is this presence. In this work of transcending and applying the historical event of Jesus Christ to our personal lives, we must think of the Spirit as proceeding from Jesus Christ.

In the second place, within the divine life proper, whether conceived as the immanent or economic Trinity, the Spirit—not the Father—is the principle of relationship and unity. The separation that takes place between Father and Son—the separation that defines the Father as Father and the Son as Son—is healed by the Spirit. It is the Spirit that maintains unity in difference.[97] There is a sort of constitutional dependency of the Spirit upon the twoness or doubleness within the divine life. This is not to posit a temporal priority, as in a modalistic program of three successive stages of divine development. The dependency is rather a logical one. The principle of relationship depends upon having two persons to relate.

The Spirit is everlasting or eternal in the same sense that the triune Godhead is. As the principle of relationship within the immanent Trinity, it is always due to the work of the Spirit that the Father is the Father in relation to the Son and, conversely, the Son is who he is due to a corresponding relationship. The Western picture is not the way Photios so humorously describes it, where God the Father generates the Son and then subsequently produces a grandchild Spirit. The Spirit is the condition whereby the generation of the Son is made possible, yet without the Son to whom the Father relates there would be no divine Spirit.

Is the Holy Spirit the Mutual Love of Father and Son?

The traditional controversy over *filioque* is pregnant with a possible offspring, namely, the question as to whether the Holy Spirit should be understood as the love between the Father and Son. Both come from Augustine. Both imply each other. Although *filioque* does not command center stage in current trinitarian discussion, it may eventually be drawn into the drama as increased attention is given to pneumatology. Some contemporary theologians, notably Wolfhart Pannenberg, build upon Augustine's insight here because it fits so well with the relational understanding of perichoresis.

Augustine describes the Holy Spirit in terms of gift, communion, and love. The Spirit is gift in the sense that it comes to the Son from the Father and to the Father from the Son. It also comes to us, the beneficiaries of the work of salvation, as a gift from the Father and as a gift from the Son. The reciprocity of gift exchange indicates a communion.

> The Holy Spirit is a certain unutterable communion of the Father and the Son. . . . [B]oth the Father is a spirit and the Son a spirit, both the Father is holy and the Son holy. In order, therefore, that the communion of both may be signified from a name which is suitable to both, the Holy Spirit is called the gift of both.[98]

This unutterable communion is also known as love.

> Therefore, the Holy Spirit, whatever it is, is something common both to the Father and Son. But that communion itself is consubstantial and co-eternal; and if it may fitly be called friendship, let it be so called; but it is more aptly called love.[99]

The import of Augustine's point here is that the Holy Spirit is itself the relationship between the Father and the Son.[100] The Spirit is not an additional entity that sponsors a relationship as if in itself it were independent of the relationship. If this were the case, then we would have a quaternity rather than a Trinity—that is, a Father, Son, and Spirit, plus the relationship that ties them together.[101] Rather, as the communion of love itself, the Spirit—the giving and the binding power of reciprocity in relationship—is itself the presence of God.

Is this understanding of the Holy Spirit as the mutual love of Father and Son scriptural? David Coffey believes it is, and he has sought to support it exegetically. On the one hand, he says the Holy Spirit as the

Father's love for Jesus is emphasized in the synoptic theology. In the an-
nunciation, the Holy Spirit comes upon Mary so that her child will become the Son of God (Matt. 1:18–25; Luke 1:26–38). In Jesus' baptism,
similarly, the Spirit of the Father descends to commission his Son. Coffey
points out how the text does not say merely "Son" but "beloved Son," indicating that the Spirit is of love. Further, it is the Spirit of the Father that
makes possible the fulfillment of Jesus' destiny as the Suffering Servant
and as our Savior. In sum, Coffey says the bestowing of the Spirit by the
Father establishes Jesus as the Son and inspires him to obedience to the
Father's will and the fulfillment of his appointed destiny.

Similarly, though a bit more difficult to show, the Holy Spirit constitutes Jesus' love for the Father. Coffey notes how for some texts (Phil.
2:8; Heb. 5:8–9; 2:10) the Spirit enables Jesus to be obedient to suffering
and that suffering purifies him so that, eventually, in death it makes him
perfect—that is, Jesus became ever more completely and perfectly the
Son of God. This is not the case in the Johannine material, however, because its strong concept of preexistence and incarnation would pre-
clude such a growth process. Jesus arrives already perfect. In the
Gospel of John, the Spirit "remains" on Jesus, so that Jesus' baptism becomes a source of the Spirit for others (John 1:33). What Coffey calls
the "sacramentalism" of John indicates that the flesh of Jesus is the divinely appointed means whereby men and women penetrate by faith to
the dimension of Spirit (John 6:53–57, 63; 19:30; 1 John 4:2; 5:6–8).
Then the key passage (John 19:30): on the cross Jesus "bowed his head
and gave up his Spirit." In its "higher meaning," says Coffey, this text
means that Jesus gave up "his own" spirit and, because it is the gift
freely given by the Son to the Father, it is the Holy Spirit.

Also relevant here is that Jesus gives the Spirit to others. The Holy
Spirit is sent upon his followers by Jesus (John 4:14; 7:37–39; 15:26;
20:22; Luke 24:49; Acts 2:33; 1 Cor. 15:45). In such instances, the Holy
Spirit has become "the Spirit of Jesus," or "the Spirit of Christ," or the
"other Paraclete." This means the Holy Spirit is now impregnated with
the personality of Jesus, and indeed precisely in his orientation to the
Father, so that the Spirit is now the mode of Christ's saving presence
among us today. The content of the experience of the Spirit is now
Christ himself. Thus, the internal love within the Godhead and the external love that incorporates us the beloved creatures share continuity
by the work of the one Spirit. Coffey writes:

[Jesus] relates to the Father in the Spirit received originally from the Father but made his own. And if the Spirit is also the vehicle of God's love as the NT reveals it to be, then we must conclude that the Spirit is more than just the bond of love between the Father and Jesus His Son, as it is with us: it is their mutual love. When we say that Jesus sends the Spirit as his own upon the Church, we are expressing the fact that in the Spirit he gives himself to the Church. This is precisely what he does vis-à-vis God in the course of his life and on the cross: in the Spirit he gives himself to the Father. Each of these actions is love.[102]

When we put this in terms of the "facing" of each of the three *prosopa,* we can say that the Son faces the Father as well as faces away from him. As he faces away from the Father, he proceeds from the Father and is sent into the world. Here he also constitutes with the Father the coprinciple of the Spirit's procession—that is, he is the cosender of the Holy Spirit into the Church. But as the Son faces the Father, he is joined to him in a mutual love that is identical with the Holy Spirit. As we are caught up with the Son in this relationship, we are drawn up into this eternal communion of love within the life of God.

Coffey reiterates that this mutual-love theory reaffirms *filioque.* Will this only drive Western theology further away from the Eastern Orthodox? Coffey hopes not. In fact, Coffey hopes the mutual-love theory will play an important part in reconciling East and West on the doctrine of the Trinity. What may make it acceptable to the Orthodox is the observation that the Holy Spirit here issues ultimately from the Father alone, in that the Father's love for the Son produces the Spirit that the Son returns to the Father. But if the East balks at this, Coffey then plans to respond with the challenging question, What is to be made of the scriptural fact that Jesus appropriates the Spirit? This appeal to the New Testament should work, Coffey thinks, because it begins with the economy of salvation and properly moves toward our understanding of the immanent Trinity; and the latter should be dependent upon the former.

Yet Coffey's view is not completely satisfactory, in my judgment, especially when he speaks of the Spirit as gift. Coffey finds he can argue in the following way: "If Jesus can return the Spirit as his own and as his love to the Father, and bestow the same Spirit, again as his own and as his love, on his fellow human beings, then this shows that Jesus, like the Father, is divine."[103] Now, I do not fault his conclusion. But I do question his assumption regarding the nature of the Spirit. He treats the Spirit as if it were a thing that can be possessed and then distributed around. He assumes that the Spirit is a kind of divine football that can be carried or passed. Could it be that Coffey is still working with substantialist assumptions that have "over-thingified" the divine hypostases?

This is where recent trinitarian discussion that emphasizes relationality becomes important. In the appropriation of Augustine by Wolfhart Pannenberg, for example, the relationship—in this case, the Holy Spirit—almost takes priority over the terms of the relationship—in this case, the Father and the Son. It is the communion of love that makes possible the divinity and the precise character of the first two persons of the Trinity. The love of the Father for the Son, who is other, is requisite for God to be Father at all. It is the love of the Son expressed through obedience, for example, that makes it possible for God to be Lord. The mutually defining power of the otherness of the Father and the otherness of the Son could not effect divinity except through the loving communion that is the Holy Spirit. Pannenberg even goes to the extreme of describing the Spirit in terms of a dynamic force field within which the Father and Son become concrete expressions of a previously unutterable communion of love.[104]

Before leaving this topic, perhaps we should address one more question: Are we cheating the Holy Spirit out of equality with the Father and Son here? If the Holy Spirit is just a relationship, is it not just the third party in this divine ménage à trois?

This is part of a larger, enduring question. It is frequently thought that the Holy Spirit receives inadequate attention. Already in the days of Augustine it was common fare to say that the Holy Spirit does not receive the "same fullness and care" given to the other two persons.[105] Yet there may be a misunderstanding at work here due to a confusion regarding the task of trinitarian thinking. The task of trinitarian theology is to explicate the biblical symbols in such a way as to gain an increasingly adequate set of ideas for conceiving of God's creative and redemptive work. There is no inherent reason for assuming that the three persons have to be identical or equal in nature. There is no reason to think that trinitarianism must constitute a civil rights movement for the Holy Spirit. The notion of one being in three persons is simply a conceptual device for trying to understand the drama of salvation that is taking place in Jesus Christ. It does not imply that each of the three persons is the same in every way. Karl Rahner reminds us that "the concept of hypostasis, applied to God, cannot be a universal concept, applying to each of the three persons in the same way."[106]

Can the Orthodox East and the Latin West Agree?

Whether the great streams flowing from sources in the Orthodox East and the Latin West will ever converge completely into a single flow of thought is impossible to predict. In contemporary Trinity talk, however, we find a spring of refreshing ideas in the work of Catherine Mowry LaCugna. One of those ideas, the parabolic model of the Trinity, has potential for guiding the flow of East-West conversation. It also has potential for contributing to the the notion of temporal relationality I am trying to develop here.

Recent Trinity talk in both East and West affirms the need to speak about God in terms of personhood, to unite person and being, and to define a person not as an isolated individual but in relationship. Orthodox theologian J. D. Zizioulas defines personhood in terms of *ek-stasis*—that is, in terms of one's openness toward communion. In doing so, he identifies person with *hypostasis* and over against substance. A self-existent substance, especially as understood in terms of Aristotelian ontology, is a being determined by its own boundaries. But persons are persons and not substances by the very fact that they transcend their own boundaries. "Since 'hypostasis' is identical with personhood and not with substance," he writes, "it is not in its 'self-existence' but in *communion* that this being is *itself* and thus *is at all*. Thus communion does not threaten personal particularity; it is constitutive of it."[107] Zizioulas is not shrinking from ontology here. Rather, the ontology that speaks of the divine *ousia* or *esse* is constructed from the divine person-hood that comes prior. The being of the divine persons is constituted by the relationships they enjoy. To understand the Trinity in terms of person-in-relationship has emerged as the aim of Trinity talking between East and West.

Spokespersons for the Orthodox East contend that this aim can be achieved only by stressing that the Son is begotten from the person—not simply the being—of the Father; so the Father is affirmed as the sole source *(archē)* and cause *(aitia)* of both the divine essence *(ousia)* and the persons of the Son and the Holy Spirit. So also the creation of the world that follows. By contrast, spokespersons for the Latin West are likely to contend that personhood can be affirmed as ultimate only if the one divine *ousia* is understood in terms of a coinherence of rela-tionships that is affirmed as itself *archē* and *aitia*. This makes the Son begotten from the divine being or nature, not the person, of the

Father.[108] Vladimir Lossky emphasizes that the first person is the source from which divinity and the other two persons emanate. "The Greek Fathers always maintained that the principle of unity in the Trinity is the person of the Father. As Principle of the other two persons, the Father is at the same time the Source of the relations whence the hypostases receive their distinctive characteristics."[109]

Karl Rahner tries to explain the different positions by saying that the Latin begins with a unity in nature, whereas the Greek begins with the three persons who share a single divine nature, and this divine nature is a consequence of the fact that the Father has communicated his whole nature.[110] In short, the Latin West thinks of the persons as a mode of a more fundamental nature or essence; whereas the Greek East thinks of nature or essence as the content of the first person.

Turning from the immanent to the economic Trinity and God's relation to the world, we must acknowledge a fine distinction drawn by Greek theologians, at least since Gregory Palamas in the fourteenth century, among *ousia, hypostasis,* and *energia.* The reality of God has three emanating and descending aspects: (1) the permanently unnameable and imparticipable divine essence; (2) the three hypostases, or persons; and (3) the uncreated energies that provide the mode for God's unmediated union with what is created. The created world participates in the divine energies, but not in the divine essence. The created world may enter into communion with the divine energies, but not the divine persons. Even if the energies are enhypostasized—that is, even if the energies express what the person is—the three persons are a step removed from the economy of salvation.[111]

With these things in mind, contemporary Roman Catholic Catherine Mowry LaCugna contrasts Eastern and Western trinitarian models. She depicts the Eastern emanation model as a descending sequence, as a series of arrows from the Father to the Son to the Spirit and finally to the world. Over against this, she sets the Western model, which she depicts as a circle enclosing all three persons of the Trinity; then the circle in its entirety emits an arrow to the world. This image captures Augustine's principle that the trinitarian works of God in the world are undivided. Then, in a move toward reconciliation, LaCugna offers her own proposed synthesis—the parabolic or chiastic model. Capitalizing on the meaning of parabola, to throw outward, she draws a single arrow beginning from God the Father and descending through the Son and Spirit to the world; but then the single arrow continues and makes an upward ascent through the Spirit and the Son ending finally with the Father. The LaCugna image expresses the one ecstatic movement of God from whom all things originate and to whom all things return, *a Patre ad Patrem,* from the Father to the Father. Incorporated into the divine life proper is the economy of incarnation and deification. Rather than freezing at any one point in time, the movement as a whole is what counts. Thus, Christology is no more prominent than pneumatology. Nor is the immanent Trinity thought to be separate from the economy of salvation. United here are *theologia,* the mystery of God, and *oikonomia,* the mystery of redemption. The strength of this model, she argues, is that it avoids the separation between God *in se* and God "for us."[112]

Whether Orthodox theologians will warm up to the LaCugna proposal remains to be seen. What I find of decisive value are two things. The first is LaCugna's insistence that the economy of salvation belongs intrinsically to our understanding of God as Trinity. The second is her understanding of the ecstatic character of the divine movement in the creation and incarnation and consummation. God is both beyond and intimate, both eternal and temporal. The divine self-definition takes place through a divine movement that includes the history of the world. It includes relationality. But does it include temporality? We will pose this question again in Chapter 3.

Is the Trinity Interreligious?

Is the understanding of God as Trinity the private possession of Christianity, or is it the common property of the various world religions? The argument that trinitarian thinking belongs to many or all the world's religions usually takes as its premise something like Augustine's *vestigia trinitatis.*[113] It assumes that the trinitarian structure resides in the human psyche; and because it resides in everyone's psyche, one can think of it as universal. If the trinitarian structure of thought is universal, then one would expect to find it everywhere.

"Wherever there is life there is the mystery of three-in-oneness," writes Nicholas Berdyaev. "The meeting of one with another is always resolved in a third."[114] Triadic thinking is universal. Similarly, Paul Tillich operates with the generic category of the "history of religious experience" and argues that trinitarian thinking has a *fundamentum in re,* a foundation in reality. Three factors lead him to see threeness as a universal structure: first, the tension between the absolute and the concrete element in our ultimate concern; second, the symbolic application of the concept of life to the divine; and third, the threefold manifestation of God as creative power, as saving love, and as ecstatic transformation. Why does the number three seem to persist here? Tillich answers that the number "three corresponds to the intrinsic dialectics of experienced life and is, therefore, most adequate to symbolize the Divine Life."[115]

Building on theological assertions such as these, contemporary commentator David L. Miller identifies the Trinity with what is "human," or the "all too human." Threeness seems to structure the human self. This observation permits him to construct a nonexclusive method of religious study wherein he can look for trinitarian images in the myths of various religious traditions and in secular poetry or drama.[116] "A theology of trinity is not unique to Christianity," he says.[117]

"The Trinity," says Raimundo (Raimon) Panikkar, "may be considered as a junction where the authentic spiritual dimensions of all religions meet."[118] The goal of Panikkar's method is the universalization of Christianity, to develop its theology and spirituality so as to take this one religion beyond its sectarian borders and ally it with non-Christian traditions.[119] So Panikkar identifies the Father of the Christian Trinity with the absolute *Brahman* of Hinduism and *Tao* in Taoism. As such, the Father is the transcendent truth beyond every name, the unnameable. The Father begets the Son, and this is a total generation in which the Father gives himself totally to the Son—that is, the Father empties himself *(kenosis)* into the Son; and Panikkar labels this "the Cross of the Trinity" or "the integral immolation of God."[120] The Father, then, has no being; the Son is his being. The kenosis of absolute being leads Panikkar to identify it with the Buddhist experience of *nirvana* and of *sunya* (emptiness). The corresponding devotional practice leads to total apophatism, a spiritual movement toward no place, a prayer that is always open. With whom then do we as spiritual human beings relate? To the Son. "The God of theism, thus, is the Son; the God with whom we can speak, establish a dialogue, enter into communication."[121] The Christ is the link between the infinite and the finite that makes the absolute relative to us. In affirming this, Panikkar does not have in mind the historical Jesus of Nazareth. Rather, it is the Christ as the universal Logos he affirms here. As the universal Logos, Panikkar can find Christ manifest as a mysterious mediator between the eternal and the temporal within other religious traditions. He names the Hindu *Isvara,* the Buddhist *Tathagata,* and even the Hebrew *Jahweh* and the Muslim

Allah as examples of this Logos-mediator between the absolute and the personal.

The Spirit, according to Panikkar, is the communion of Father and Son. In some manner, the Spirit passes from Father to Son and back again at the same time. Just as the Father empties himself into the Son, the Son holds nothing back from the Father. The kenotic cycle is completed and consummated through the Spirit. The result is that there is no divine *self* in the reflexive sense. The self of the Father is the Son. The Son has no self beyond being the "Thou" of the Father. Similarly, one cannot say "in himself" regarding the Spirit. There is only the Spirit of God, the Spirit of the Father and the Son. At this point, Panikkar invokes the Vedanta notion of Advaita, or nonduality, to help Christians explain what they mean. "If the Father and the Son are not two, they are not one either: the Spirit both unites and distinguishes them."[122]

What motivates Panikkar to follow this method is his desire to expand the horizon of Christian thinking to include consciousness of the world's religions. Further, he wants to promote breakthroughs in interreligious dialogue. Not only does he want to enrich each religious tradition separately, he also wants to add an element of synthetic merging. He believes that "it is in the trinitarian possibilities of the world religions, in the striving of each in its own fashion towards a synthesis of these spiritual attitudes, that the meeting of religions—the *kairos* of our time—finds its deepest inspiration and most certain hope."[123]

A close look at Panikkar's method will show that he is not in fact looking for multiple trinities, one for each religious tradition. Nor is he assuming that religious experience is always threefold in character, so that variants of the one Trinity should appear in different traditions. Rather, what in effect he is doing is explicating the Christian understanding of Trinity in light of non-Christian terminology and conceptuality. It is my observation that this is a more precise formulation of the actual task systematic theologians concerned about the world religions have set for themselves.

Ninian Smart and Steven Konstantine, for example, have set out down this path. Assuming that Christian experience is in continuity with all other religious experience, they argue that Christian theology must be pursued in a world context—that is, in the context of the world's religions. Before tackling the Christian apprehension of God as Trinity, they acknowledge the wide variety of concepts of the divine: *Brahman* as impersonal being; *Isvara* as personal Lord; *Tao* as a monistic quasiprinciple; and emptiness experienced as *nirvana*. These differ quite significantly from one another. To help sort them out, Smart and Konstantine adopt what they call a "two aspect theory of truth" borrowed from Mahayana Buddhism and Advaita Vedanta, according to which they presume there is a glittering other world from which come the rays that suffuse this world's saints with light.[124]

To track the light back to its source, they begin by examining the experience of Jesus and the experience of Jesus' disciples that eventually led to the formulation of the doctrine of the Trinity. Jesus' reference to God the Father as *abba* is treated here in terms of the Hindu notions of *bhakti* and *dhyana*, intimate devotion and love to God. The exterior witness of the disciples to the resurrected Jesus combined with the interior witness of the Holy Spirit provides the power by which the Spirit transforms the Christian person into the image of Christ.[125] This leads to worship, and worship is said here to precede doctrinal construction. More specifically, in sacramental worship such as the Eucharist, the Son and the Spirit are prayed to directly; and in Baptism the threefold trinitarian formula is recited.[126] These religious experiences evidently constitute the light rays that lead back to their source, the source we doctrinally refer to as the Trinity.

When referring to the Nicean version of the Trinity, Smart and Konstantine say "Brahman is composed of three hypostases."[127] The way they formulate this is noteworthy. One might think that the task of explicating the Christian understanding of Trinity in dialogue with Hinduism would take us immediately to the existing doctrine of triple divine manifestation in Brahma, Shiva, and Vishnu. But this is not where Smart and Konstantine go, because these three Hindu gods are united by a "different logic that reflects three different modes of divine operation rather than an abiding Trinity."[128] These scholars go instead to the concept of Brahman. Father, Son, and Spirit, they argue, point to the threefoldness in the inner or immanent nature of Brahman, not merely to three modes or phases of divine self-manifestation. The eternal Brahman is triple, and its threefoldness is not dependent upon Brahman's relation to the world. It is an immanent Trinity prior to its modes of economic manifestation. Smart and Konstantine are opposed to modalism and sharply reject, among others, Karl Barth as a modalist. The threefold relationality is eternal, they say, having no origin in time. What this does to the concept of Brahman, I think, is significant. It imports differentiation into what is usually thought to be the undifferentiated ground of being.

In a manner somewhat akin to that of Smart and Konstantine, Munich theologian Michael von Brück offers a subtle yet dramatic argument in behalf of employing the Advaita tradition within Hinduism for the purpose of expanding the Christian understanding of God as Trinity. He employs a cross-cultural mirror method. By placing the symbols and thought forms of the two different traditions together so that they mirror one another, their ideas become mutually clarifying without losing their individual identity. The von Brück method is a version of interreligious dialogue that does not seek a synthesis of the Hindu and Christian notions of the divine into a third or higher view; rather, it seeks to make "a contribution to Christian theology by means of an advaitic notion of the trinity."[129]

By Advaita we refer to the philosophy of nonduality propounded by Sankara (c. A.D. 800) and the contemporary Vedanta Society which, von Brück insists, is not a form of monism. Rather, as nonduality, it refers to a level of meditative consciousness in which the duality of subject and object and the duality of God and the world are overcome. The ultimate ground of reality is *Brahman*—Brahman is everything and in everything—and as such simply cannot be encountered as something over against us. It can only be realized experientially in the overcoming of duality. The philosophical question of the relation between the one and the many is solved through inducing an experience of nonduality. This experience is *satcitananda* (sat = being; cit = consciousness; ananda=bliss).

It may help to note how von Brück is motivated here by a strong desire to transcend not just duality but fragmentation. He assumes that the meaning of life is dependent on the unity of reality, and this unity must include—more than include, be established by—subjectivity. He writes: "If reality is to remain shattered and broken up into discrete parts, contingently determined and thus threatened by meaninglessness—which would also imply fragmentation in our lives—we need to speak of a subjectivity which includes everything."[130] The methodological value of employing Advaita to help clarify trinitarian thinking is to aid us in focusing on the goal, namely, the unity of reality.

For this reason, von Brück believes he gains ground by pointing out parallels between Advaita and Augustine's doctrine of the Trinity. Augustine emphasized divine unity. God is one being and one will and one subject in relationship to the world—*inseparabilia sunt opera trinitatis*. The whole Trinity is incarnate. The whole is present in each of the persons. The one God is generating subject, self-generated object, and, in the constant exchange of these two, one God. This unity in God of subject and object transcends rational knowledge. This means that despite Augustine's long list of analogies and *vestigia trinitatis,* God cannot be finally understood in terms of analogies. Thus, in von Brück's judgment, Augustine arrives at an impasse: he cannot explain satisfactorily how three persons can have their own identity while still being the whole. If Augustine turns from rational knowing to contemplation of divine oneness under its three aspects, which are not properties but relational moments by which the whole becomes present in each of the particular notions, then we can perceive a parallel in *satcitananda.* "Consciousness is one and identical with itself insofar as it comprehends a multitude of contents."[131]

Von Brück follows a similar trail in explicating Hegel. But with Hegel, the trinitarian God is a becoming God. Temporality enters the picture. The threeness brings forth and makes present particular moments of the process. The first determination, identified with the Father, is the unmoved silence of God prior to the creation of the world. The second determination, the realm of the Son, refers to God as creator of the world of division and distinction; and it refers to the appearance of incarnate divinity as a particular within this world of duality. God denies being in and for itself and enters the world of appearances, which is itself an appearance when it is thought of as an other alongside God. The third determination or realm of the Spirit is the negation and overcoming of particularity. Particularity is sublated within the Spirit's integrated unity, within the divine consciousness that overcomes the division between God and the world. The positive parallels between Hegel's sublated Trinity and Vedanta's Advaita seemed outweighed, however, by the negative contrast. For Hegel, nonduality is the result of a temporal process, whereas for Sankara, nonduality is the experience of what is eternal. The historical process of overcoming duality by the integrating power of the divine Spirit cannot be reconciled with the Asian vision of lifting the veil on timeless eternity and rendering illusory dualistic ways of appearing and viewing.[132]

In his own constructive work, von Brück identifies the Father with Sankara's notion of *nirguna Brahman,* as impersonal undifferentiated being. The Father is the "whence" of being, the indivisible origin of the multiplicity of created things. As Father, God is perfectly simple. The first person of the Trinity is simple being, *sat.* In relation to the Father, creation comes from nothing, *creatio ex nihilo.*

"The Son is being, realized."[133] The Son is the "where" of being. The Son is the mediator of creation, the divine participating in creative self-realization, in *creatio in participatione*. This realization through differentiation in creation cannot take place apart from its origin, yet the origin does not exist apart from its realization in created particularity. The two permeate one another. The Son, therefore, is fully God. Corresponding to Sankara's *saguna Brahman,* the Son is personal and particular being. The second person of the Trinity is *cit,* or consciousness. As such, he is nothing added to *sat,* but rather a determination of the Father that is comprehended and constituted by and in the other. Then the cross signifying kenotic self-sacrifice is the event that overcomes the separation of the particular from the whole.

The Spirit is the "whither" of being. The Spirit is "God in all," God as immanent in the life-producing energy that drives the creation. The Spirit is *actus participationis* in the ongoing creative activity of the world. Through the Spirit, each being participates in the dynamism of God's ongoing trinitarian life. In this way, the Spirit makes possible the unity of the many in return to the paternal source, through the reality of the Son. To experience this is to experience bliss, *ananda*. In bliss, time is overcome. In the Spirit, the particularity of the Christ event is "released from its historical limits in order to attain its essential universality."[134]

The problem of historical time is a knotty one for von Brück. This is because "God's revelation in the incarnation, cross and resurrection describes a concrete historical event. This means that Christian revelational theology must reflect on the historicity of revelation. The world cannot be regarded as an illusion." This brings us to the limits of a method that parallels Trinity with Advaita. The role of world history in Christian trinitarian theology cannot be identified with the Sanskrit maya, the creative and manifest power of *Brahman,* which creates the illusion of many when in fact being is one. The unity of being cannot be ascertained by dubbing temporal change and multiplicity as illusory. Rather, unity must be found by incorporating time and by integrating the many into one. Showing the influence of Hegel, von Brück foresees that the world's fragmentation and sufferings will be overcome when world history is sublated into God's trinitarian unity. "Christian revelation demands that the advaitic relationality of one reality be regarded as a mediated process which integrates history. History then becomes salvation history."[135] Temporality and relationality belong to the divine life proper.

In this chapter, we have mapped the topography of Trinity talk by identifying and formulating the issues occupying current discussion. We have organized what we observe by locating and isolating the points and viewpoints under debate. As we turn to the next chapter, we will cover some of the same ground. But we will organize it differently. We will travel a single highway of conversation that winds its way from Karl Barth down through decades of theological discussion to the present. In the final chapter, we will forecast where that road might take us in the future.

3. Trinity Talk in the Last Half of the Twentieth Century

He was made human so that we might be made divine
—*Athanasius,* Incarnation of the Word, *54*

T hings have changed since Claude Welch wrote his book on the Trinity, *In This Name,* in 1952. The problem at that time as Welch saw it was that too few people were paying attention to the doctrine of the triune God. It had fallen into widespread disuse, being treated at best as a secondary speculation. It was not playing the important and integrative role in Christian thinking that it had in the past. The Enlightenment appeared to have cut contemporary theology off from its ancient roots, and the classical doctrine of the Trinity was withering on the vine. So Welch began a search for a theological method that would rejuvenate trinitarian thinking. What he found was the method of revelation-analysis used by Karl Barth. A Barthian approach, he believed, would provide the fertile soil that, if tilled further, would bring a harvest of trinitarian thought.

What has changed is that trinitarian thinking four decades later is flourishing. It is now a major topic on most theological agendas, and it is thought to be so integral that the idea of the Trinity is being used to sharpen the distinction between general notions of God and the unique Christian commitment. The concept of the Trinity has become a weapon in the contemporary war against classical metaphysics—that is, against the classical philosopher's deity that is *a se,* immutable and unrelated to the world. What characterizes the Christian view, many contemporary theologians seem to agree, is that the God of Jesus Christ is inextricably and passionately involved in the affairs of human history and that this involvement is constitutive of the trinitarian life proper. The current agenda is how to make this comprehensible.

This is not where Welch himself is today. Curiously enough, Welch himself has changed. His own constructive commitment has shifted away from Barth's christological starting point and moved closer to that of Ernst Troeltsch or H. Richard Niebuhr. He now prefers to begin with our more general experience of the fundamental mystery of the whole. Nevertheless, for our purposes here, Welch's early work is most valuable. Where Welch seems to have been on prophetic target is his suggestion that the work of Karl Barth would become important, that it would point the way. This seems to be just what has happened in the second half of the twentieth century. The major contributors to the contemporary rethinking of the doctrine of the Trinity either extend principles already proffered by Barth or else follow lines of thought that parallel his *Church Dogmatics*. Most specifically, they rely upon the priority of revelation-analysis and Barth's belief that the historical event of Jesus Christ belongs to the becoming of God proper.

What I intend to do here is take us back to 1952 and to the insightful assessment offered then by Claude Welch. We will subsequently turn our attention to more recent developments in Christian thinking, showing especially how Barthian shoots have begun to blossom in the work of Eberhard Jüngel, Karl Rahner, Jürgen Moltmann, Robert Jenson, Wolfhart Pannenberg, and to some extent Catherine Mowry LaCugna. In passing we will note the quite different (and less productive) direction taken by Leonardo Boff and the process theologians. Where we will end up is the contemporary problematic: How do we conceive of God's essential being as constituted by the relations between the persons? Because theologians of our period seem dedicated to overcoming the substance metaphysics of classical thought, the problem becomes how to construct a concept of a unitary divine life constituted by the relations between the three persons. Our suggested solution will be to conceive of God as in the process of self-constitution, a process that includes God's saving relationship to the world right in the definition of who God is.

Claude Welch's Forecast: There's a Barth in Our Future

The central question of Claude Welch's book *In This Name* was this: How should contemporary theology orient itself with regard to what has traditionally been called the distinctively Christian conception of God, namely, the Trinity?[1] This question was about to become mainstream in the twentieth century, Welch predicted, because it was being fed by multiple streams of nineteenth-century thought.

These streams are still pouring over a watershed. That watershed is the challenge of the Enlightenment that seems to render trinitarian speculation either impossible or superfluous. Modern liberal theologians in the wake of Immanuel Kant found it presumptuous to think they could speak speculatively or metaphysically about the secret life of the immanent Trinity. The inner dynamics of the divine being belong to the noumenal realm, whereas human cognition is strictly limited to the phenomenal realm. Kant opened the nineteenth century by diking off the flow of trinitarian speculation. What followed were three responses, and these three have trickled into our own century: (1) some theologians follow Schleiermacher, who denies that the doctrine of the Trinity is essential to the expression of the Christian faith, thereby relegating it to the status of a second-rank doctrine; (2) those who follow Hegel affirm a version of the Trinity that is the equivalent of a metaphysical truth that can be established more or less independently of the Christian revelation; (3) conservative spokespersons for orthodox Christianity continue to hold the classical position because it is held to be a direct and unmistakable deliverance of an authoritative scripture or a tradition rooted in scripture and interpreted by an infallible church. These three streams, each in its own way, have been dammed up by false assumptions and misleading agendas so as to leave what Welch considers serious trinitarian thinking high and dry.[2] Welch wants to open the gates and release the flow once again.

What constitutes serious trinitarian thinking for Welch begins with commitment to "the affirmation that God has indeed revealed himself in Christ." It is due to this revelation that there has arisen "the conception of God as in his very Being (that is, ontologically or essentially) Triune—one God, the Father, the Son and the Holy Spirit."[3] This Christ-centered and revelation-grounded trinitarianism is what Welch wants to see become mainstream. But how?

It cannot be accomplished by following the currents of the Hegelian stream. For Hegel, the Christian Trinity is nothing more than a pictorial illustration of an otherwise discoverable philosophical truth. The Hegelian interpretation is simply unwilling to rest its case for the doctrine on the basis of revelation and Christian experience.[4] In contrast to the *philosophical trinitarianism* of Hegel, Welch contends that we need a *trinitarian philosophizing* that would begin with the trinitarian conception as we find it already in divine self-revelation; we would then see if this conception illuminates a variety of aspects of finite existence. This is more than working out analogies as Augustine did for the purpose of illustrating the Trinity. Welch here assumes that what has been revealed to us in the Trinity has to do with ultimate reality, with the structure of being itself. Therefore, the revealed Trinity should be illuminating for understanding the reality in which we daily live.

If the Hegelian current is unsatisfactory, what about the conservative or orthodox stream? Claude Welch is also dissatisfied with the methods of fundamentalism and Roman Catholic theology. This is because they rely upon an outdated authoritarianism. Both of these schools of thought assume that the doctrine of the Trinity is a direct revelation. It is considered a deposit of faith which, according to the conservative Protestants, appears intact in the divinely inspired scriptures; and the Roman Catholics (pre-Vatican II) add that it is infallibly explicated by the councils of the church. Although Catholic theology is more subtle and elaborate, comments Welch, both are "incorrigibly obdurate" in their attitude to biblical criticism. Welch sides with the objection of liberal Protestants that the doctrine of the Trinity cannot be justified on the basis of biblical literalism and the method of proof-text together with the fragmental and propositional view of revelation that it implies.[5]

A distinctively modern method for developing trinitarian thinking must presuppose that revelation is not to be identified with the biblical texts but with that to which those texts point. It must presuppose a theory of revelation in act, rather than in proposition. Hence, "the doctrine of the Trinity is not developed simply by piecing together trinitarian proof-texts, understood as divinely given truths, but is constructed as a consequence of the gospel taken as a whole." It is Welch's contention that "all Christian doctrine must continually be recreated out of the faith of the community, not on the basis of infallible deliverances of scripture but looking to the revelation of God in the concrete historical events to which the scriptures bear (finite and fallible) witness."[6] To put it more succinctly: our doctrine of the Trinity should be a contemporary construction based upon an analysis of ancient revelation and experience.

Would then the liberal Protestant stream flow in the direction Welch wants to take us? No, not quite. Welch refers us repeatedly to the founder of liberal Protestantism, Schleiermacher, for whom the trinitarian distinctions within God are not "an immediate utterance concerning the Christian self-consciousness but only a combination of several such utterances."[7] Thus, trinitarian thinking for Schleiermacher is the product of synthetic construction. What is key here is that Schleiermacher assumes that the basic Christian experience and hence the basic Christian symbols refer us to a single God, the God of monotheism. Hence, trinitarianism is a synthesis of the variety of faith utterances that produce the concept of the Trinity only after the fact. In other words, the threefoldness of God is not a part of the primary witness of faith, but is strictly the result of an attempt to put together, or synthesize, various elements of the primitive revelation.

So Schleiermacher only illustrates for us the very problem that Welch is addressing. If we follow Schleiermacher too far and affirm with him that the doctrine of the Trinity does not stand on a par with primary symbols such as God as Creator, the divinity of Christ, or the deity of the Spirit, then it is quite understandable why the Trinity becomes demoted to secondary importance. The assumption that the doctrine is a synthesis of otherwise random convictions regarding a more fundamental monotheism renders the Trinity systematically superfluous. The triune nature of God is removed from the center of our faith affirmations.

What Welch wants to consider is how the doctrine of the Trinity is rooted in the revelation at the primary level and, further, how it could even in our modern period become a source of illumination for all the other Christian doctrines. The presuppositions of the indirect or synthetic method prevents the doctrine of the Trinity from occupying central place, from serving as a genuine *archē,* or first principle, of Christian thought. "The synthetic view of doctrine tends inevitably to suggest that it is essentially a kind of defensive doctrine, somewhat further removed from the life of faith than those affirmations which it is supposed to bring together." The synthetic approach seems to assume that we begin with monotheism, whether Jewish or Greek, and then try to reconcile it with the New Testament claims that Jesus is divine or that the Spirit is divine. The Trinity becomes the product of this synthetic reconciliation of otherwise contradictory ideas. "The ultimate objection is that this approach to the doctrine rests on a false and misleading separation of the elements of the Christian revelation. . . . This must be judged untrue to the language of the New Testament."[8]

What Welch is doing here is making the assumption that trinitarian language is already embedded in the primary symbolic utterances of the New Testament. Furthermore, this trinitarian language in no way repudiates monotheism. Monotheism is most explicitly affirmed by the New Testament right where Christ and the Holy Spirit are being affirmed. Hence, there is no tension to be resolved, no conflict to be reconciled through extrabiblical synthetic construction.

"The root problem in contemporary reconstruction of the doctrine of the Trinity is," according to Welch, "the question of its ground in revelation." Welch is searching for a way of looking at the doctrine of the Trinity as an "immediate implication of revelation, and therefore as essentially identical with the content of revelation."[9] Karl Barth provides the most helpful solution. For Barth, the ground, or "root," of the doctrine of the Trinity is found explicitly stated in scripture. The history of dogma has watched this root grow, and the form it has taken is presumed to be nascent already in the original text. For Barth, then, trinitarian thought consists of an explication of the original revelation. It is an analysis of what is already there; it is not a synthesis or reconciliation of several elements that results in the construction of something new. In short, Barth's method consists in an analytical development of the central fact of revelation.[10]

Barth finds the root of the Trinity in two places: first, in the formal structure of revelation and, second, in the primary utterances of Father, Son, and Holy Spirit. With regard to the formal structure of the event of revelation, Barth analyzes sentences such as "God speaks" *(Deus dixit)* or "I show myself." Assuming that God's word is identical with the Godself,[11] Barth sees God as the subject, object, and predicate of the revelatory act. The word "God" applies to all three: the revealing God, the event of revelation, and even its effect upon us who receive the revelation. "Thus, to the same God who in unimpaired unity is Revealer, Revelation, and Revealedness is also ascribed in unimpaired variety in Himself precisely this threefold mode of being."[12] This formal analysis of the grammar of revelatory speech does not produce the Trinity itself; rather, Barth says it "brings us in a preliminary way into proximity with the problem of the doctrine of the Trinity."[13]

The second location of the revelatory root that eventually branches out into the church's doctrine of the Trinity, according to Barth, is found in the substantive biblical utterances regarding what is revealed about God. What is revealed in scripture is that God as creator is our eternal Father, that God as our reconciler is the eternal Son, and God as the redeemer who sets us free is the Holy Spirit. These identities—what Barth calls "modes of being"—are sufficiently discrete as to remain distinguished when positing the unity of the one God. In sum, an analysis of the content of revelation leads to the trinitarian formula of threeness in oneness.

Rather than follow Schleiermacher's method of synthesis, then, Welch suggests that we follow Barth's method of analysis. By analyzing the scriptural utterances, we find the doctrine of the Trinity emerging almost by logical necessity. The affirmation that God has reconciled the world to himself through Jesus Christ inevitably entails a trinitarian understanding. The content of the affirmation that God is triune is not different from the simple scriptural confession that "Jesus is Lord." "The threefoldness indicated by the terms Father, Son, and Spirit is a threefoldness in the structure or pattern of the one act of God in Christ and therefore the structure of all divine activity and of the Being of God."[14] The Trinity is already buried there in the biblical revelation. Theology as analysis digs it out and makes it visible.

Thus, Welch is following the trail blazed by Barth, acknowledging that Barth already embraces the classical Christian position regarding the Trinity. What Barth has added, and what Welch appreciates, is the poignant way in which Barth grounds the doctrine in scriptural revelation. God is not known as trinitarian apart from what is revealed in the Christ event. Although Welch by no means denies the contribution of general revelation or Hebrew monotheism,[15] he follows Barth in asserting that we do not start with a generic monotheism and then add a Christology. Rather, we begin with the Son, on the basis of which we apprehend God as Father. The Christian conception of God is not equivalent to any other conception of God, even that of the Old Testament. Here Welch parts a bit from Barth and Calvin too regarding the uniformity of the biblical witness. "The Father, in the Trinitarian sense of the term, is not known except as the Father of the Son," and the Son is known to us solely through the New Testament witness.[16] According to Welch, the doctrine of the Trinity

is precisely in itself a primary affirmation of faith, a doctrine which follows directly from and is an immediate explication of the confession that God has revealed himself to us in Jesus Christ. . . . [I]t is an immediate consequence of the gospel, because the revelation on which everything depends cannot be stated except in trinitarian terms. The doctrine of the Trinity is of all-embracing importance because it is the objective expression, the crystallization of the gospel itself. It is not just one part of the doctrine of God, but is integral to every aspect of the doctrine of God and to every other doctrine as well.[17]

In sum, Welch's proposal assumes that the primary Christian experience is already trinitarian in form. He does not actually argue the case against Schleiermacher. Rather, he simply posits it as a logically necessary ingredient in the experience of Jesus Christ as Lord. This approach to trinitarian doctrine avoids splitting up what has come to us already together. It not only prevents us from identifying God simply with a Creator-God of nature and natural theology, thus falling into a "unitarianism of the Father," but it also makes impossible a Christology that is not wholly theocentric or a pneumatology that is not genuinely Christocentric and theocentric.[18] This doctrine is a "revealed doctrine," not, of course, in the sense that propositions about the Trinity have been given word for word by God, but in the sense that this doctrine gives genuine expression to the experience of those who stand in the situation of revelation.

Must these be exclusive of one another? Must we choose between synthesis and analysis? It is my contention that theological explication in the form of trinitarian thinking is both synthetic and analytic, although my use of these terms is not precisely that of Schleiermacher and Barth. In defining the theological task as explicating the biblical symbols, I assume with Schleiermacher that there exists within the scriptural witness a variety of primary utterances, which when combined lead toward the Trinity, to be sure; but they do not automatically entail just the view of the Trinity we have inherited. That is to say, the particular form that the development of trinitarian doctrine took in the first four centuries is due in part to the accidents of history. The doctrine of the Trinity we have inherited is due at least in part to the intellectual challenges endemic to the context of life in the cultural milieu of the Roman Empire. The resulting doctrine, then, is undeniably a synthesis. It is synthetic in multiple ways. It represents an internal synthesis of various biblical symbols, and it also represents a synthesis of biblical patterns of thinking with Hellenistic philosophical speculation. It is synthetic, finally, in the sense that constructive trinitarian thinking must continue in our own time because of our constantly changing intellectual context.

Nevertheless, constructive trinitarian thinking could not be authentic if it did not take to heart the intention behind Barth's analysis. What I prefer to call *evangelical explication* seeks to explicate what is genuinely there in the original symbolization. It does not seek a second root for our belief in God, a root outside or beside the scriptural witness. We must test what we say theologically to see if it is entailed by what the scripture says. Therefore, I must disagree with Schleiermacher to the extent that he makes the doctrine of the Trinity an expendable appendix to monotheism. The method of analysis shows, I think, that the Trinity is essential to the Christian understanding of God.

More could be said about methodology here. Theology is constructive. It builds. It grows beyond its roots. As it grows it is nourished and sometimes retarded by its surrounding atmosphere.

Analysis and synthesis are internal to theology. As internal, they have to do with the revelatory root, the Bible. Yet there are external sources and forces as well. The contextual atmosphere within which theological construction is pursued inevitably plays a role, hidden or acknowledged. When acknowledged, constructive theological thinking invokes the principles of contextualization and engagement. It seeks to formulate Christian commitment so as to be intelligible within its contemporary intellectual context. The Greco-Roman context within which the definitive trinitarian formulas were hammered out included, among other things, highly sophisticated challenges from competing religions and philosophies that so exalted the divine that incarnation seemed preposterous. Docetists and gnostics spoke of the beyond as so far beyond that intimacy in the flesh seemed repulsive. Irenaeus and other apologists found themselves interpreting and engaging such belief systems, emphasizing that the sublime beyond had indeed become one with us in the body and blood of Jesus. The need to emphasize the enfleshment seemed to grow as the contextual challenge grew.

In our own contemporary context, the modern and emerging postmodern intellectual milieu influences our understanding of topics relevant to trinitarian discussion. From the social sciences and humanities, we are developing a new appreciation for the dynamic of mutuality in relationships. The concept of person is undergoing change as we move from a more individualist point of view toward a sense that personhood is dependent upon one's nexus of relations. Also relevant to our discussion are the natural sciences, especially the twentieth-century discoveries regarding the nature of time. So, when we speak of one God in three persons or of an eternal Trinity, to be intelligible we will have to consider the contemporary context and then offer constructive concepts.

With analysis, synthesis, and the constructive task of theology in mind, let us return to our story of the Trinity talk in the last half of the twentieth century. Our real concern here with Claude Welch's appropriation of Karl Barth has less to do with the method of analysis itself than with the stream it releases that continues to flow in the decades to follow, namely, further exploration into the relationship between the economic and immanent dimensions of the Trinity. If we take Barth seriously that the Word of God in revelation is not just a word *about* God but rather *is* God in the Godself, then we find God on both sides of the revelatory equation. God is also on both sides of the eternity-time equation. Barth makes this crystal clear: "Without ceasing to be God, He has made Himself a worldly, human, temporal God in relation to this work of His."[19]

God is similarly on both sides of the experience equation. Our experience of Jesus in history and the Holy Spirit in the church is an experience of God actually present. To turn it around, our experience of God is countered with God's experience of us. The divine-human intercourse belongs as much to the divine life as it does to ours. The event of salvation consists *inter alia* in the incorporation of an alienated creation history into the divine life proper. The divine life comes to be understood as relational, and there is a tie posited between God's relations to the world and the relational dynamics within the divine life itself. What happens to God *ad extra* becomes constitutive of God *ad intra*. The tie between the economic and immanent dimensions of the Trinity becomes a knot.

Eberhard Jüngel and the Principle of Correspondence

Claude Welch is not the only one to have foreseen the value of Barth for trinitarian thinking in light of the modern problematic. So has Tübingen theologian Eberhard Jüngel. Jüngel accepts as axiomatic that trinitarian thinking begins with an analysis of the revelation bequeathed to us through the biblical symbols. He then proceeds to describe our post-Enlightenment context as one in which the concepts of becoming and relatedness take precedence over being and unrelatedness. It is this that gives his trinitarian reconstruction its distinctive character.

The significance of the doctrine of the Trinity for Eberhard Jüngel's work is that he believes that it resolves the dilemma between the aseity of God and the relationality of God. Jüngel formulates the dilemma amidst a critique of Helmut Gollwitzer and resolves it by offering a commentary on the work of Karl Barth. To his book *The Doctrine of the Trinity,* Jüngel appends the subtitle "God's Being Is in Becoming," which immediately suggests that he is positing a dynamic relationality already within the divine life proper. This is just what he does.

The current problematic begins with our desire to affirm that God is personal, because to be personal means necessarily that one is in relationship with other persons. So we must ask, Just what is the status of God's relationality? The dilemma that arises when we try to answer is this: If, on the one hand, we insist that God is independent—that is, that God is *a se*—and not in any way dependent upon the creation, then it seems that we must deny that relationality is essential to the divine being. On the other hand, if we insist that God's relationship to the creation is constitutive of God's own being, then we make God dependent upon something outside God and hence lose divine aseity.[20] The solution to the dilemma that Jüngel proposes is to affirm that relationality already exists within the divine being, already within the immanent Trinity.

Jüngel affirms that in principle God could be involved in personal relationships even had God never created a world. Where this takes us is to Jüngel's thesis: God's relationship to the world *ad extra* corresponds to the interpersonal relationality within the divine life *ad intra.* This solves the dilemma by preserving God's aseity while still affirming the personal dimension of God's relationship to the world. In short, the dilemma is solved because there exists a correspondence between the inner life of God and God's external relationship to the creation.[21]

Axiomatic to Jüngel's argument is the priority of special revelation. Like Barth before him, Jüngel insists that we begin not with general philosophical speculation but with God's act of self-interpretation within temporal history—that is, with the person of Jesus Christ.[22] In other words, what we say about God must be christologically grounded. This yields a startling consequence: the finitude, the historicity, the humanity, the subjection to suffering and death, which characterize the life of Jesus, are now considered attributes of God's being proper. "Jesus Christ is that man in whom God has defined himself as a human God."[23] However we define God, we must include the experience of the human Jesus in the definition. And because the human Jesus represents the incarnation—that is, God in the world—one would expect that God's relationship to the world would become constitutive of God's being, or better, becoming.

In pursuing this line of thinking further, let us digress a moment to note that Jüngel finds it difficult to reconcile his position with Luther's concept of the paradox embedded in the theology of the cross. For Luther, who distinguishes between the revealed God and the concealed God, God is revealed under his opposite—that is, God's power is revealed in Jesus' weakness and God's glory is revealed in Jesus' humanity. This is the paradox. Now Jüngel, like Barth before him, affirms a theology of the cross. But the difference from Luther is this: Barth and Jüngel proceed to remove the paradoxical element. The paradox is removed by denying that God is revealed under his opposite. Jesus' weakness and humility are not said to be opposed to divinity. Rather, they are constitutive of divinity.[24] Because God has taken unto Godself the conditions of finite historical life through his incarnate activity, we must acknowledge that God in God's own being is historical. God is in the process of becoming Godself through relationship with the temporal creation.

Nevertheless, proceeds Jüngel, God's being could not be self-constituting in relation to temporal events if it was not already so in eternity. Jüngel's thesis is that God's relationality to the temporal world *corresponds* to the relationality that already exists within the eternal divine life. Jüngel assumes that God could not be nonrelational within God's own being and then become relational through mutual interaction with the creation. God could not be simple in Godself and then become interactive. God must have been interactive all along. There must exist a correspondence between God's life with the world and what goes on within the divine life apart from the world.

So let us ask, What goes on within the divine life? Answer: the eternal *perichoresis* or *circumincessio* in which each person of the Trinity distinguishes itself from the others while participating in the being of the others. "Through this reciprocal participation the three modes of being *become* concretely united. In this concrete unity they *are* God." The three persons are constantly "passing into one another, through which trespass of one mode of being against another is impossible."[25]

Jüngel here reiterates Barth's driving emphasis on the oneness of God. Barth repeats again and again the classical axiom, *opera trinitatis ad extra sunt indivisa,* that the external acts of the Trinity are undivided. The unity of God cannot be broken. Nevertheless, the unity of God is not a simple unity. It is not an undifferentiated unity. Rather, as Jüngel explicates it, it is closer to a unification. It is an eternal process of becoming unified, "a becoming one." And because God's essence and work are not twofold but one, it would follow that God's relationship to the world is one of becoming one with the world. This becoming one with the world accomplishes our salvation, the taking up of human life into the event of God's being.[26]

This is what can be said ontologically regarding the being of God and the divine relationality both *ad intra* and *ad extra*. When we turn to epistemology, Jüngel's argument is parallel. He asserts that objectivity already exists within God; therefore, through the principle of correspondence, we creatures may gain genuine objective knowledge of our creator. God "assigns to himself his being as Father, as Son and as Spirit and so corresponds to himself." Each person of the Trinity can know the other objectively. (Barth had earlier posited that objective knowledge exists within God's life proper, though it is an immediate objectivity in contrast to our human or mediated objectivity.) God reveals himself as such. Because God himself reveals himself as an object of human thinking, we can therefore objectify God in our thinking. And the way we objectify God as Father, as Son, and as Spirit corresponds to the way God really is.[27]

Jüngel's assumption and assertion is that because God is self-related, God can be world-related. The peculiarity of God's being as becoming is that it can reiterate itself. "The reiteration as God's relation to us is the correspondence to God's relatedness: *analogia relationis*." In sum, here is Jüngel's thesis:

> One will have to understand God's being essentially as *double* relational being. This means that God can enter into relationship *(ad extra)* with another being (and just in this relationship his being can exist ontically *without* thereby being ontologically dependent on this other being), because God's being *(ad intra)* is a being *related to itself*. The doctrine of the Trinity is an attempt to think out the self-relatedness of God's being.[28]

Jüngel's thesis depends upon the credibility of the concept of correspondence. Evidently, according to Jüngel, if God were not self-related, God could not be world-related. It also seems to be assumed that the way in which God is related to the world cannot be different from the way in which God is self-related. If God could relate to the world in a way different from that by which God relates to himself, then we would not need a principle of correspondence. And if we did not need a principle of correspondence, then it would be logically possible to have a non–self-related God relate to the world. Jüngel's very formulation of the dilemma implies the necessity for such a principle of correspondence. To put it in traditional terms, Jüngel requires that what is true for the economic Trinity must be true—via the principle of correspondence—for the immanent Trinity.

If we press beyond the general thesis to examine in a bit more detail just what corresponds, however, a problem emerges. The problem has to do with the ambiguity in the word "person." Although Jüngel does not spend time defining and developing this important concept, he gives us a hint of how he understands it when formulating the dilemma vis à vis Gollwitzer. In Gollwitzer's words: "Personal being means being in relationship! It must be emphatically maintained that person is a concept expressing relationship . . . and not as a concept of substance expressing the nature of a magnitude existing for itself."[29] It is the association here of person with relationship that makes the issue an issue—that is, to be personal one must be in relationship. It seems to follow that one's own personalness is necessarily dependent upon someone else to whom one relates. One cannot be personal all by oneself. The question is, Is God personal? This is where the ambiguity begins.

Here we need to return to Barth for a moment. Barth, along with almost every theologian of the modern period, acknowledges that the definition of the term "person" has changed through the centuries. With the advent of the idea of personality and its quality of independent self-consciousness, we can no longer apply it without qualification to the three hypostases of Father, Son, and Spirit. "The Christian Church has never taught that there are in God three persons and therefore three personalities in the sense of a threefold ego, a threefold subject. This would be tritheism."[30] In order to avoid tritheism, Barth suggests that we think of the Godhead in its entirety as the divine person and the three hypostases as "modes of being" *(Seinsweise).* Thinking of the patristic formulation *(mia ousia, treis hypostases; una substantia, tres personae)* then, Barth finds it better in our modern situation to identify the person of God with the *ousia* or *substantia* than with the *hypostasis* or *persona.*[31]

Now returning to Jüngel, what does this do to the thesis regarding God's self-relatedness? How closely does Jüngel wish to tie together the concepts of person and relationality? If, on the one hand, he were to follow Barth and affirm that God is personal in the divine unity, in the divine substance, then God would have only one person. To whom would this one divine person be related? The world? Whom else? If God is a single person, and if relationship requires more than one person, then God would lose the correspondence between the being of God *ad intra* and God's relation to the world *ad extra*.

If, on the other hand, Jüngel were to apply the dimension of personhood to each of the three hypostases, then the inner being of God could be described as a community of terms defined by their relations. The correspondence between God's relationship *ad intra* and God's relationship to us *ad extra* would be established. But then Jüngel would risk Barth's accusation of tritheism. So we have simply returned to the dilemma in a new form: to identify the personhood of God with the divine substance would deny the principle of correspondence, but to identify the personhood of God with the three *personae* would deny the divine unity.

To my reading, Jüngel does not commit himself in *The Doctrine of the Trinity* in either direction, leaving us with an additional dilemma. If, on the one hand, he would continue to refrain from committing himself, he would leave us with an unsatisfying ambiguity. If, on the other hand, Jüngel were to make such a commitment in either direction, then his thesis regarding the *analogia relationis* would dissolve.

One might also ask if the original dilemma was not a pseudoproblem right from the beginning. Jüngel had already committed himself to limiting his understanding of God to special revelation, to interpreting the event of Jesus Christ. He was following Barth in denying the relevance of the philosopher's deity, the deity produced at the end of a chain of natural reasoning that is usually characterized as being simple, transcendent, immutable, eternal, *a se*—in short, a God who is in-and-for-himself. In other words, the God in-and-for-himself whom Jüngel puts on one horn of the dilemma does not belong there. The philospher's God is not the God who is in-relation-to-us. This God is by definition not the God revealed to us in the Christ event. If this is the case, then why does Jüngel feel he needs to reconcile the revealed God who in his own "being as becoming" is in-relation-to-us with the deity of philosophical speculation whose being is not in relation to us? Why not just go all the way and affirm a God whose personhood is itself being constituted through God's ongoing relation to the creation? If we grant Jüngel's assumptions and restrict ourselves to the relational God of revelation and part company with the *a se* deity of the philosophers, then why would we have such a dilemma in the first place?

Furthermore, why would we need a principle of correspondence? Why is it necessary that God be related to himself *ad intra* before becoming related to the world *ad extra?* Why does Jüngel feel constrained to depict God in terms of unrelated relatedness? As long as we have a God whose being is in his becoming, why not explore the possibility that God becomes personal through relationship with the other just as we do? Or, conversely, what is the warrant for requiring that God be personal all by himself without someone else around to be personal with? If Jüngel is really serious when he says that the historical event of Jesus Christ means that "God has defined himself as a human God," then why not make God's incarnate intercourse with the world part of that ongoing process of divine self-definition?

That Jüngel may finally have to give up his grip on a God of unrelated relatedness is indicated by a commitment he makes in his later book, *God as the Mystery of the World.* Here he gives unqualified agreement to what we refer to as Rahner's Rule: the economic Trinity is the immanent Trinity and the immanent Trinity is the economic Trinity.[32] What this implies is that the relationality God experiences through Christ's saving relationship to the world is constitutive of trinitarian relations proper. God's relations *ad extra* become God's relations *ad intra.* Insofar as we bridge the distance between these two, we remove the need for any *analogia relationis.* This has a devastating impact on Jüngel's thesis, for once we have established unity between the immanent Trinity and the economic Trinity, we no longer need correspondence.

Perhaps we should turn now to the author of Rahner's Rule and mark the next step on the way from Barth to the contemporary conversation.

Karl Rahner and Rahner's Rule

It is Rahner's Rule—that the economic Trinity is the immanent Trinity and the immanent Trinity is the economic Trinity—that marks the new stage at which trinitarian discussion has arrived.[33] Rahner proposes this rule in order to advance his thesis that it is God as one or another of the divine persons who relates to the world; it is not God as the unity of the divine being. The way we experience God is through God's saving activity within history—through the economy of salvation—and here we know God as the redeeming word in Christ and as uniting love in the Spirit. We do not know God in general. We experience God first in the economy of salvation, and Rahner believes we can trust this experience. In the economy of salvation, God is communicating the Godself. God is actually internally just the way we experience the divine in relation to us, namely, as Father, Son, and Spirit. An implication that Rahner himself does not yet draw, but which Jürgen Moltmann and Robert Jenson later do, is that the eternal or immanent Trinity finds its very identity in the economy of temporal salvation events. Yet, despite what might seem to be a conflation or equation of the economic and immanent dimensions of the Trinity, Rahner persists in the classical insistence that God's eternity is independent of historical self-constitution.

What is significant to Rahner's Rule here is that the way God relates to the world is discerned in terms of each of the three hypostases, not in terms of God as a unity. Each one of the three divine persons communicates itself to humanity

> in gratuitous grace in his own personal particularity and diversity. . . . It is God's indwelling, uncreated grace. . . . In other words: these three self-communications are the self-communications of the one God in the three relative ways in which God subsists. . . . God relates to us in a threefold manner, and this threefold, free, and gratuitous relation to us is not merely a copy or an analogy of the inner Trinity, but this Trinity itself, albeit as freely and gratuitously communicated.[34]

Rahner is here opening the door to the possible identity of God in Godself and God in relationship to others. The threefold manner by which God relates to us is not "merely a copy or an analogy" of God's internal threefold relatedness. Rather, it is that relationship proper. On this point, Rahner seems to be going a step beyond Jüngel, for whom there was only a correspondence between the two. Rahner is on the brink of saying that God relates to the Godself through relating to us in the economy of salvation.

With regard to methodology, Rahner looks like he is closer to Welch, Barth, and Jüngel than he is to Schleiermacher. Rahner assumes that the immanent Trinity is actually given to us already in the experience of grace. "The Trinity is not for us a reality which can only be expressed as a doctrine. The Trinity itself is with us."[35] Rahner believes he must make such an assumption, otherwise, the proof from scripture would unavoidably begin to look like a method that, by the use of subtle dialectical tricks, tries to draw conclusions from a few scattered statements, putting them together in a system about which we cannot help wondering whether God has really revealed to us such abstruse and obscure things that need so many complicated explanations. Or, more briefly, Rahner's method is one of analysis rather than synthesis.

Rather than Welch's term "analysis," however, Rahner's near equivalent term is "logical explanation." Rahner contrasts this with "ontic explanation." A logical explanation clarifies a statement by making it more precise. It does not use one state of affairs to explain another one. All the concepts used to explain that one statement can be derived from it. An ontic explanation, in contrast, is one that takes account of another state of affairs in such a way that this helps us to understand what is being explained.[36] The issue as Rahner sees it is this: everyone wants to say exactly what the scripture says, yet he or she cannot simply repeat the words of scripture. The restatements in different epochs of the life of the church constitute logical explanations—not ontic explanations—of scripture. They are analytical extensions. They always refer back to the origin from which they came, namely, the experience of faith that assures us that the incomprehensible God is really, as God is in the Godself, given to us in the twofold reality of Christ and his Spirit.

What is the role of the already official logical explanation bequeathed us by the postscriptural tradition in the form of the doctrine of the magisterium? On the one hand, Rahner seems to grant decisive authority to unchanging dogma. "An authentically personal and at the same time theologically justified act of faith," he writes, "is not possible through a mere recital of the explicit doctrine of the magisterium, since every act of faith occurs unavoidably and necessarily under some theology. Yet in order to make sure that this theology is the theology of the Church, we must from the start mold it after the doctrine of the magisterium."[37] On the other hand, Rahner seems to be open to change due to the challenges of our new context. "The Church and its official proclamation stand ever again before a new task, because the fitness and intelligibility of a given concept with regard to a certain reality may change, and because the Church, which must speak as intelligibly as possible for concrete man, cannot prevent such change."[38] One wonders here just how Claude Welch would judge Rahner's method. Would he put it in the category of the "incorrigibly obdurate" along with other Roman Catholics and fundamentalists or in the category of analysis along with Barth? My own interpretation is that Rahner belongs predominantly in the latter category, but he is not without a hint of the former.

Where Rahner wants to take his "logical explanation" is toward the argument that the unique role Jesus Christ plays in human history is the same role he plays within the divine life proper. When we talk about the economy of salvation, the role of redeemer could be played by only the second person of the Trinity, not by either of the other two nor by the Godhead in its entirety. Only the Logos could have become incarnate, he argues. We need to ask "what it means for the Logos, precisely as Logos, as distinct from the other divine persons, to have become man." He objects to the tradition of Christian theology, saying that "starting from Augustine, and as opposed to the older tradition, it has been among theologians a more or less foregone conclusion that each of the divine persons (if God freely so decided) could have become man, so that the incarnation of precisely this person can tell us nothing about the peculiar features of this person within divinity."[39]

The problem with what seems to have become acceptable since Augustine is the notion that the Spirit could exist without the incarnation and that each divine person could in principle become human. What this implies, Rahner fears, is that the mode of divine relations with the world is arbitrary and that our experience with the economy of grace does not accurately report what goes on within God's life. For Rahner, in contrast, if by the incarnation we mean God's Word has truly become flesh, then it follows that the Logos alone is the one who begins and can begin human history. If indeed God's way of owning the world is that the world is not only his work, a work distinct from him, but becomes God's own reality, then it could well be that one only understands the incarnation when one knows what precisely *Word* of God is. And one only understands well enough what *Word* of God is when one knows what incarnation is.

Jesus is not simply God in general, but specifically the Son. The second divine person, the Logos, becomes human, and only he becomes human. There is one mission, one presence in the world, one reality of salvation history that is not merely appropriated to some or any divine person, but which is proper only to him. It belongs to the Logos alone. It belongs to the history of one of the divine persons and not to the other two. This makes false the statement that there is nothing in the economy of salvation history that cannot equally be said of the triune God as a whole and of each person in particular.[40]

Similarly, we must conclude that it is precisely the Spirit that sanctifies. It is not God in general. If we fail to assume this, then what we learn from the economic Trinity has no warrant for applying to the immanent Trinity—that is, a genuine revelation of God has not taken place. Rahner, therefore, opposes the idea that God has wrapped himself in the disguise of a human nature or a spiritual nature that only clings to him exteriorly and has come to this earth to set things right because they could not be managed well enough from heaven.

The intended effect of this line of argument is to give us confidence that the divine hypostasis we experience within history corresponds to the same hypostasis within the Godhead proper. Now, should we call each of the three hypostases "persons"? Rahner says "yes." He disagrees with Barth's reluctance to use the term "person" just because modern connotations make it ill adapted to express the intended reality; and he denies that it should be replaced in ecclesiastical terminology by another word that produces fewer misunderstandings.[41] After all, says Rahner, the word "person" has been around for fifteen hundred years. This consecrates it. There really is no better word, therefore, that can be understood by all and would give rise to fewer misunderstandings.

If, however, we were to replace the term "person" with something else, then Rahner recommends the phrase "distinct manner of subsisting" as superior to Barth's "manner of being."[42] In explicating this, Rahner believes he can speak of three subjectivities, one for each person, as long as we keep away from the modern notion of person. They are not three individuals. In reference to God, we may not speak of three persons in the same way that we do elsewhere. They still share one common essence. Rahner has no desire to abandon the classical substantialist ontology here. This leads him to an interesting distinction regarding subjectivity: each person as concrete possesses a self-consciousness, yet in essence this self-consciousness does not distinguish one person from the other. The result is a position quite close to that of Barth: there is one divine subject. We should not believe "that there exist in God three distinct consciousnesses, spiritual vitalities, centers of activity, and so on. . . . There is only one real consciousness in God, which is shared by Father, Son, and Spirit, by each in his own proper way."[43]

The ontological possibility that God could create the creation and become incarnate *ad extra* is based upon the prior derivation of the Logos, or Son, within the Trinity. This position seems quite close to that of Jüngel regarding the *analogia relationis*. But I wonder if there might be a fallacy here. The assumption seems to be that God could not create and become incarnate (Rahner) or be related (Jüngel) to the creation *ad extra* unless there were already within the divine reality *ad intra* some sort of creative relationality. Only after the divine life has attained this status can it then create or relate to the world *ad extra*. But again, what is the warrant for this? Is Rahner, like Jüngel, slipping in the unnecessary assumption that we are dealing with the *a se* deity of the philosophers again? If so, then we can recognize the problem—the pseudoproblem—again: How is it that a simple God enters into a complex relationship with the external world? What these theologians are doing is arguing that the simple God has previously become complex *ad intra*. But does this help? It only pushes the dilemma back to a previous level. Instead of asking how a simple God became complex when relating to the world in trinitarian fashion, we now ask how God, while still unrelated to the world, could make the transition from simple to complex. What really is the gain? The hidden agenda, it seems, is to keep the unrelated God unrelated.

That this is the actual effect of the argument is supported by the way Rahner formulates the problem: How can an immutable God change so as to make sense of the phrase "the Word of God has *become* flesh"? Rahner insists that we cannot give up our assumption that God is unchanging and that this unchangingness is a perfection. Yet he also affirms that the Logos *became* a man and that the changing history of this human reality is his own divine history, that our time has become the time of the eternal, that our death has become the death of the immortal God himself. Rahner's proposed solution to the above dilemma is to distinguish between internal and external change. "Since God is unchangeable, we must say that God who is unchangeable in himself can change in another (can in fact become man). But this 'changing in another' must neither be taken as denying the immutability of God in himself nor simply be reduced to a changement of the other. . . . The mystery of the incarnation must lie in God himself: in the fact that he, though unchangeable 'in himself,' can become something 'in another.'"[44]

Now has Rahner actually resolved the dilemma or only shrouded it in neologisms? Has he eliminated the paradox that the unchangeable changes? I do not think so. The introduction of terms such as "internal change" and "external change" simply relocates the problem: How can a God who does not change internally actually change externally? All Rahner has done is stipulate two definitions and then consign the whole matter to the mystery of the divine being. The real issue we need to raise with Rahner, just as we did with Jüngel, is why we must work with the premise that God is immutable? If we take the revelation reported in scripture as seriously as these scholars ask that we do, then perhaps the exalted attributes of Greek philosophical speculation simply need not have univocal application to the God who became manifest in Jesus.

Be that as it may, we note in summary that Karl Rahner has advanced the discussion.[45] He may even have advanced the discussion further than he intended. What we are calling Rahner's Rule—the economic Trinity is the immanent Trinity and vice versa—marks a decisive watershed in twentieth-century trinitarian thinking. Its ramifications are yet to be fully worked out. As we work them out, Walter Kasper warns us against possible misinterpretations. First, says Kasper, we would misinterpret Rahner's identification if we understand the economic as a mere temporal manifestation of an eternal immanent Trinity. History counts. The second person incarnate in Jesus of Nazareth means God exists in the world in a new way. The incarnation implies that God really does become.

Second, Kasper warns us against the opposite misinterpretation—taking the identification to mean that the immanent Trinity is dissolved in the economic, as though the eternal Trinity first came into existence in and through history. In its extreme form, this mistake is exacerbated when the immanent Trinity is pushed completely out of the picture and we limit ourself to the Trinity in the economy of salvation. Such a course, complains Kasper, would deprive the economic Trinity of all meaning and significance. For it has meaning and significance only if God is present in the history of salvation as the one who he is from eternity. So, in an attempt to avoid this misinterpretation, Kasper reformulates Rahner's Rule: "In the economic self-communication the intra-trinitarian self-communication is present in the world in a new way, namely, under the veil of historical words, signs, and actions, and ultimately in the figure of the man Jesus of Nazareth."[46]

But does this actually solve anything? Kasper seems to assume that the internal relations of the immanent Trinity are already fixed in eternity, so that what is new is merely their manifestation under the "veil" of history; that is, the meaning and significance of the Trinity in history is due solely to its being a manifestation of the Trinity in eternity. In the last analysis, then, Kasper avoids the second misinterpretation only by retreating to the first misinterpretation.

There may be a third way, namely, to reconceive the relationship between time and eternity so that what happens in the history of salvation becomes constitutive of the content of eternal life. The problem with classical formulations is that when God is described as eternal it is assumed that the immanent Trinity is somehow fixed and immutable before entering history through the incarnation. The presuming of prehistorical or extrahistorical intactness of the trinitarian relations in eternity cannot but treat the incarnation in Jesus docetically, as a mere apparition pointing to a transcendent rather than an embodied divine reality. By identifying the immanent with the economic relations, Rahner opens Barth's door a bit wider so that we might consider how the history of the incarnation as history becomes internal to the divine perichoresis itself. And along with the incarnate Son comes the world that he was destined to save, so that the whole of temporal creation enters into the eternity of God's self-relatedness. With this in mind, we turn to the work of Jürgen Moltmann, who opens the door even further to this kind of consideration.

Jürgen Moltmann's Open Trinity

What we get with Jürgen Moltmann is perhaps the biggest step yet away from the substantialist unity of God toward a relational unity in which the divine threeness is given priority. Moltmann goes so far as to draw a line between monotheism and trinitarianism, denying that Christianity should be monotheistic at all. In saying this, he is not recommending polytheism in the form of tritheism, however. He acknowledges correctly that tritheism has never been a genuine temptation for Christian faith. Trinitarianism is neither monotheism nor polytheism, he argues. It is rather something unique on its own account. It is the peculiar product of the Christian experience with the God who suffered in the cross of Jesus.

"God suffers with us—God suffers from us—God suffers for us: it is this experience of God that reveals the triune God."[47] Amidst the suffering of the cross, Jesus experiences the agony of being forsaken by the Father. The Father in turn experiences the anguish of being separated from the Son. Yet in the surrender to suffering for the sake of sinful humanity, Jesus and the Father experience a new unity with one another in the Spirit. It is an internal unity that is achieved through external historical involvement. History is swept into the divine life because the Trinity is an open Trinity. The history of Jesus Christ is the promise of the future glorification of God through the eschatological consummation, and this past and this future are both being mediated presently into the life of the church through the Holy Spirit. Moltmann is here extending the line of thought begun in Barth and continued in Jüngel that the historical event of Christ is constitutive of the divine life proper.[48] What this means for Moltmann is that the divine life is not monotheistic.

The God of monotheism cannot suffer with and for us, Moltmann assumes. Yet it is the God who is love and who suffers because of this love who is revealed to us in scripture. So Moltmann's method is to attempt to get behind the metaphysical substantialism of the pre-Nicene and Nicene theologians and return to the original scriptural witness. The problem with the Nicene theologians is that they were beginning with the assumption of a divine unity and then asking about the possibility of a divine plurality. They were beginning with neuter and impersonal terms borrowed from Greek philosophy such as *ousia* and *substantia,* which would tend to lead us toward thinking of God as the absolute individual subject. The Bible, Moltmann says in contrast, begins with the three living persons and then makes unity the problem. This appears to be a clear preference for the Cappadocians over Athanasius, should Moltmann wish to put it in these terms.[49]

The essence of Moltmann's position is that when it comes to divine action we have three subjects, or *loci*, of activity, not one. We have three persons, not one. He complains that when Christians talk in a monotheistic mode they speak of God as *self*-giving. But this is a mistake. The New Testament says that God has given up "his own Son . . . for all of us" (Rom. 8:32) and that the Son "gave himself for me" (Gal. 2:20). This means that there is more than one divine subject. History springs from the Son's coefficacy with the Father and the Spirit. "The history in which Jesus is manifested as 'the Son' is not consummated and fulfilled by a single subject. The history of Christ is already related in trinitarian terms in the New Testament itself."[50]

What, then, is the nature of the divine unity? Moltmann rules out a prior ontological unity in the sense that the three hypostases would share the same substance. It is rather an integrative unity, a unification through dynamic mutuality and relationality. "If we search for a concept of unity corresponding to the biblical testimony of the triune God, the God who unites others with himself, then we must dispense with both the concept of the one substance and the concept of the identical subject. . . . It must be perceived in the perichoresis of the divine Persons."[51] Because he begins with the plurality and only then asks about the unity, Moltmann dubs his a "social doctrine of the Trinity."[52]

On the basis of this conviction, Moltmann lashes out against Barth and Rahner because of their alleged complicity with the tradition of monotheism. He perceives that these two theologians propound the same basic doctrine of the Trinity based upon similar presuppositions.

They both commit the same basic sin, to Moltmann's reading: they both identify the divine subject with the unity and not the plurality. The result is that they end up with a cold, unrelated God who is an absolute individual and who simply expresses the one divine self in the three modes of Father, Son, and Spirit. What Barth and Rahner say they wish to avoid is vulgar tritheism, but Moltmann counters that tritheism has never been a danger to Christian theology. Monotheism is the danger. And monotheism in the form of modalism is the trap into which Barth and Rahner have fallen.

Moltmann's critique of Barth begins by repudiating Barth's starting point—the lordship of God. It is this emphasis upon divine lordship that leads Barth to assert that in God we find only one personal subject with three modes of being. Recall that Barth believed that modern notion of person understood as an independent subject and locus of consciousness was at such great variance with the Nicene notion of person that it no longer communicates accurately the status of Father, Son, and Spirit. To Moltmann, however, Barth's formula of one subject in three modes of being constitutes Sabellian modalism.[53] It seems that Barth starts with God's lordship in order to posit the reverse of Schleiermacher's feeling of absolute dependence. Instead of beginning with the human feeling of dependence, Barth begins with that upon which we are dependent. What this means for Moltmann is that both Schleiermacher and Barth make the same mistake. They presuppose that the fundamental Christian experience with God is monotheistic—that is, there is only one God on whom we are dependent. But on the contrary, Moltmann believes that the primitive Christian experience is already trinitarian.

Moltmann's criticism of Rahner parallels his assessment of Barth. Rahner too fears the application of the modern notion of person to the three hypostases, so he describes God as a single divine subject in three distinct modes of subsistence. What Rahner wants to deny to Father, Son, and Spirit is the idea that there are three different consciousnesses, three different spiritualities, three different centers of activity, three different individualities, and so forth. Moltmann counters that what Rahner describes as the modern notion of person is actually extreme individualism. There is an alternative, says Moltmann, namely, the philosophical personalism of selected German thinkers in which personhood is intricately tied to the I-Thou relationship, in which personality and community are mutual. There must be more than one "Thou" and more than one "I" within the Trinity if there is to be mutual love, because "mutual" presupposes two acts and two actors. Unless we dub the three hypostases as centers of conscious activity, it will be impossible to say that the Holy Spirit proceeds from the love of the Father and the Son and, thereby, constitutes the bond of love between them.[54]

Moltmann condemns Rahner's use of the term *Dreifaltigkeit*, meaning threefold God. In its place he suggests *Dreieinigkeit*, three-in-oneness, which he claims is the better translation of *trinitas*. *Dreifaltigkeit* is modalistic, complains Moltmann. It is too far to go just to avoid tritheism. What Moltmann fails to note here is that Barth too prefers the term *Dreieinigkeit*, yet Moltmann depicts Barth to be just as modalistic as is Rahner.[55]

As we have seen, Moltmann believes the risk of tritheism is a pseudoissue. Tritheism has never existed in Christian theology. Therefore, it is not a problem. Allegedly the real problem is monotheism with its emphasis on divine lordship and divine unity. The challenge, according to Moltmann, is that a monotheistic God makes no room for human liberty. It serves to justify earthly monarchism and political oppression. What we need, he says, is an open divinity within which there already exists a differentiated mutuality and into which the creatures of creation are invited to participate. So, in contrast to Barth and Rahner, Moltmann asserts that the Trinity consists of three distinct subjects who are democratically and cooperatively organized. He unabashedly accepts the modern understanding of personhood as a subject that is the center of action, but he adds to it the idea that personality and mutuality belong together. Who we are and who God is are both constituted by the I-Thou relationship.[56]

Despite his criticisms of Rahner, Moltmann still recites with vigor Rahner's Rule: "I found myself bound to surrender the traditional distinction between the immanent and the economic Trinity, according to which the cross comes to stand only in the economy of salvation, but not within the immanent Trinity. That is why I have affirmed and taken up Rahner's thesis that the economic Trinity is the immanent Trinity and vice versa."[57] Why did the distinction exist in the first place? It existed to protect the freedom and independence and aseity of the divine. It protected the notion that God is perfect, self-sufficient; God is not bound to reveal himself. This is important to Barth, who emphasizes again and again: God is free, therefore, what we know of God is the result of divine grace in the act of self-revelation. Jüngel's *analogia relationis*, similarly, requires the maintenance of the distinction so that he can posit relationality within God apart from God's relationship to the world. All this Moltmann rejects.

Moltmann argues that if God *is* love, then God's freedom cannot consist in the freedom of either loving or not loving. God is bound to love. God is not compelled to love by outward necessity, but God evidently is compelled to express himself as he is and in no other way. Therefore, it follows that the triune God loves the world with the very same love that God in the Godself *is*. This eliminates the need for correspondence between the immanent and economic Trinity. In fact, it comes close to eliminating the need for the immanent Trinity itself. "The notion of an immanent Trinity in which God is simply himself, without the love which communicates salvation, brings an arbitrary element into the concept of God which means a break-up of the Christian concept. . . . It introduces a contradiction into the relationship between the immanent and the economic Trinity: the God who loves the world does not correspond to the God who suffices for himself." Or elsewhere, "The triune God can only appear in history as he is in himself, and in no other way. . . . God can do anything, but he cannot deny himself (2 Tim. 2:13)."[58]

Moltmann does not totally conflate the two. He will permit a distinction between the economic and immanent Trinity on doxological grounds. Assertions about the immanent Trinity issue out of the context of adoration and praise for the God of transcendence. It is important to hear the good news of God's saving work, to be sure; but ultimately our response takes us to the point of worshiping God for Godself, not merely for salvation's sake. The economic Trinity is the object of kerygmatic theology that announces the saving work of God, whereas the immanent Trinity is the content of doxological theology. Having introduced this qualification, Moltmann must add that statements about the immanent Trinity must not contradict statements about the economic Trinity, and statements about the economic Trinity must correspond to doxological statements about the immanent Trinity.[59] Now this might appear to be a return to a position similar to that taken in Jüngel's *The Doctrine of the Trinity,* wherein we almost have two trinities in correspondence with one another. But I think that for Moltmann there finally can be only one Trinity, the economic Trinity. It is the disposition of our piety in a mood of praise that would lead us to conceive of God in Godself, to conceive of the immanent life of the divine apart from the world. In effect, then, the immanent Trinity is the product of pious imagination, an abstraction from the concrete economy of the divine life that is actualized in history.[60]

If we are to assess Moltmann's trinitarianism in the spirit of Claude Welch's work, we need to ask two questions: (1) is it accurate to say that the biblical witness is fundamentally pluralistic and not unitary in its symbols for God? and (2) does a social doctrine of the Trinity succeed in maintaining the unity of God?[61]

With regard to the biblical witness, there is no doubt that the three persons exist at the level of primary utterance. But in no way within the New Testament itself is this construed as a denial of the oneness of God or a denial that one divine subject initiates the saving action. Jesus himself reiterates the *shema,* "Hear, O Israel: the Lord our God, the Lord is one" (Mark 12:29), and the Johannine Jesus says, "The Father and I are one" (John 10:30). There is an unmistakable sense of the singleness of divine intention behind the divine action: God sends the Son; the Word is made flesh; the cross is God's act through which God reconciles the world to himself (2 Cor. 5:18). The coming of God in Christ is not at all thought of as calling into question the oneness of God. The New Testament does not speak of the Son as a divine source of activity alongside and equal to the Father. The Father works in the Son. The Son is the Word of God. Moltmann's reluctance to accept as fundamental the concept of divine lordship or the unity of divine action makes one question just how firmly his antimonotheism can find grounding in the biblical witness.

Welch would argue against Moltmann, contending that "it is not correct . . . to say that the New Testament bears primary witness to the divine plurality. On the contrary, it speaks continually of the one God and Father of us all. In the New Testament there is no interest in Jesus . . . apart from the action of God the Father." Or, "The biblical God is One subject, One Thou, One personal Being."[62] The divinity of Christ is not a separate and distinguishable divinity. It is not even obvious at all that Christ is divine. God is in Christ incognito; that is, God is manifest yet hidden at the same time. When we affirm the divinity of Christ, we do not simply transfer his personality into the Godhead. To do so is to call into question the reality of the incarnation. It is *God* who becomes incarnate. On this point, Welch would have to conclude that Moltmann is not the authentic successor to Barth.

Similarly, with regard to Moltmann's overriding emphasis on the plurality of divine subjects, one cannot help but ask if and how the divine unity is preserved. That the orthodox doctrine of the Trinity proffers an organic or integrative unity should be taken for granted. Athanasius and the Nicene theologians never taught a simple or undifferentiated unity when applied to the Trinity. The Father might have these qualities gleaned from Hellenistic attributes of perfection, but they were not applied to the threefold God, to the Godhead. Greek philosophical categories were employed, to be sure, but they were redefined and transformed to meet the needs of the biblically based revelation of the one God as Father, Son, and Spirit. The God of Nicea simply is not intended to be identical to that of Aristotle or Islam. One wonders if Moltmann's attack against Trinity-denying-monotheism just might have an element of the straw theologian fallacy in it.

If so, then his social doctrine of the Trinity, which he uses to counteract monotheism, may unnecessarily take him too far toward sacrificing divine unity. His emphasis on the three separate subjects or centers of action risks a final plurality. Moltmann does not want to posit the existence of three gods, of course. He is no polytheist. What then can this mean? It may mean that each of the three subjective centers is a part of the one God, that "God" refers to the composite of persons and relationships, just as a society is a composite of its constituents and their relationships. These persons must coexist with one another, define one another in relation to one another. In short, each one must be finite. Should one wish to retain the attribute of infinity when applied to God, then it would have to apply to the divine society and not to the constituent persons. Is Moltmann proferring a view of a single infinite Godhead composed of three finite gods?

Probably not. Moltmann would likely counter any such pluralist interpretation by appealing to the modern concept of the person whose very identity is socially dependent; it would not be right to think of the three persons as parts of the one composite God. Rather, the nature of the relationships that exist between the persons is constitutive of each of their discrete identities, while, conversely, their identities together constitute the Godhead. Nevertheless, his continued emphasis on three discrete subjects or centers of activity makes it difficult to conceive of a principle of unity that is comparable to that of the plurality. It appears that we end up with a divine nominalism.

This has brought Moltmann some criticism. Richard Neuhaus, for example, argues that there is no good reason for making monotheism the enemy of our faith. He says Moltmann "fails seriously to treat the foundational statement of biblical faith, *'shema Israel.'* . . . We are, if you will, trinitarian monotheists and monotheistic trinitarians. Our brief is not against monotheism; our belief is that the One God is Father, Son, and Spirit."[63] Such a criticism, however, seems to be more a matter of words than substance. What Moltmann has done, whether for good or for ill, is draw out vividly some of the implications of the seriousness with which Karl Barth viewed God's interaction with world history.

Of decisive and enduring value in the Moltmann project is the seriousness with which the Tübingen theologian takes the history of God. Echoing Hegel, he says the Trinity achieves its integrative unity principally by uniting itself with the history of the world. God's internal unity incorporates the economy of salvation. God's unity is not simply an original unity. Rather, it is eschatological. As a living and loving God, what we as the human race have experienced is the divine diremption, the separation into otherness that places the creator in the world with the created, the lover in the position of the beloved, the source of healing amidst the misery of suffering. We have experienced Emmanuel, God genuinely with us. What we have experienced within history is brokenness within the divine life proper, a brokenness freely entered into by a God who enters into the stream of our temporal existence. What the Moltmann theology should lead us to repudiate is that there exists some sort of second God, a trinitarian double, a ghostly immanence hovering behind while unaffected by the actual course of divine-historical events. Moltmann reminds us that the relationship between the eternal and the temporal is now broken and, further, God is present on both sides of the brokenness. What we look forward to is the eschatological healing wherein the divine life will integrate its own biography and, in the process, integrate the history of this brokenness into the eternity of its salvation.

Leonardo Boff's Divine Society

Although his antimonotheism and social Trinity mark a detour, Moltmann's emphasis on the self-definition of God through history represents quite an acceleration up the road pointed to by Barth. Robert Jenson and Wolfhart Pannenberg have continued traveling that road, and we will see a little later where this is leading them. Before we do, however, we will pause to look at Leonardo Boff and at process theism. The latter—process theology—represents a detour that leads to a dead end as far as Christian trinitarian thinking goes. The former, Brazilian liberation theologian Boff, seems to start out in the same direction as Moltmann but runs out of gas. He stops short of where Moltmann has taken us. But because he has made an attempt to integrate a social doctrine of the Trinity with the important social concerns of the Latin American liberation project, it will be worth our while to glance at the road's shoulder to see what it is he is saying.

Boff says he wants to make society his starting point for trinitarian reflection. This is supposed to distinguish him from classical trinitarianism, which was founded on the categories of substance and person, making their dominant tone of thought either metaphysical or personalist. In contrast, Boff wants to begin with the idea of women and men living together in community and society. He emphasizes that society is not just the sum total of the individuals who make it up; but it has its own being, a being woven out of the threads of relationships among individuals and institutions that together constitute the political community. Cooperation and collaboration among all members of society produce the common good. These qualities of society, Boff argues, make up the *vestigia trinitatis*. They emulate the Trinity understood as the divine society.[64]

Moltmann is his mentor. He describes God as a community of persons and not simply one. The divine unity exists in the form of communion between the three persons and with history. By adopting Moltmann's notion of the open Trinity, Boff is able to incorporate creation into the divine perichoresis. "The Trinity does not wish to live alone in its splendid trinitarian communion," he writes; "the three divine persons do not love just one another, but seek companions in communion and love. Creation arose from this wish. . . . Creation is external to the Trinity only so as to be brought within it."[65] So far, so good.

In addition to the social starting point, Boff wants to import sexual symbolism into the divine life. While admitting that "on the level of strict theological understanding, God the Father is trans-sexual," he proceeds to argue that divine sexual symbolism is important because it has a social impact. When God is identified with a human father figure, he says, it runs the risk of becoming an idol and legitimizing the domination of fathers as bosses over their children, wives, and anything seen as feminine in nature. Such images play a significant role in molding consciousness and compartmentalizing society. Therefore, Boff contends, we should think of God as bisexual, as both Father and Mother.

The way Boff proceeds to develop his notion of bisexual divinity differs from some feminist proposals, wherein one or another person of the

Trinity is dubbed female in gender. Usually, the hypostasis of Wisdom or the person of the Holy Spirit comes to represent the feminine dimension within God.[66] Boff's proposal, in contrast, combines masculine and feminine traits within each of the three persons. He speaks of "God as maternal Father and paternal Mother."[67] We need both male and female figures to express God's creative work of progeneration. Boff likes to cite a phrase from the Council of Toledo in 675 that speaks of the "womb of the Father." Similarly, the Son would not be understood as strictly masculine, because he shows love and care just as a woman would. And, furthermore, the Holy Spirit can be conceived of in feminine terms (*ruach* in Hebrew is feminine) because of the Spirit's work of consolation and comforting. In short, Boff focuses not on sexual gender per se but rather on masculine and feminine qualities that belong distributively to all three divine persons.

Unfortunately, Boff ties himself up in self-contradictory knots when engaging in such discussions. For example, he writes:

> We need to remind ourselves that God is beyond sex; as St. Gregory Nazianzen said: God is neither masculine nor feminine. Yet masculinity and femininity both find their prototypes in God. . . . [B]y saying that each of the Persons contains masculine and feminine dimensions, we are not conferring sexual characteristics on the mystery of the Trinity, or trying to find them in it. What we are trying to do is discern the ultimate source of the values the Trinity itself has conferred on human beings in their masculine and feminine embodiments.[68]

On the one hand, Boff wants to find prototypes for human masculinity and femininity in God. On the other hand, no such prototypes could possibly be found in God if "God is beyond sex." If it is true that God is beyond sex and that there is no divine prototype, then we ought to conclude, it seems to me, that human sexuality is not a divine but strictly a human phenomenon; that is, sex belongs to the created order of things. Certainly, this is the implication of the passage alluded to but not actually quoted by Boff, where Gregory of Nazianzus repudiates the idea that Christians should believe in a hermaphroditic god.[69]

This is indicative of the wider problem that characterizes Boff's whole approach to the Trinity. On the one hand, he claims to make social community his starting point, which would lead eventually to a social doctrine of the Trinity similar to that of Moltmann.[70] On the other hand, Boff holds so tenaciously to the classical—even monarchian—formula that he risks falling into traditional subordinationism; and he tries to save himself by ascribing all the difficulties to the eternal mystery of the Trinity.

Although Boff stipulates that his method begins with reflection upon society, he in fact begins with a retreat back to the classic doctrine of the immanent Trinity. Accordingly, the Trinity is eternal and beyond time. The Father is the unoriginate source of the divinity for the other two persons. The Word is begotten and the Spirit proceeds. In addition to being the source of divinity, the Father is the source of love. The Son and the Spirit respond by reflecting the Father's love reciprocally, and it is this that establishes communion within the divine life. "There is an order in these relationships," writes Boff; "the Father is always put first, the Son second, as begotten by the Father, and the Holy Spirit third, as the one who proceeds and unites in love."[71]

This position, of course, makes the Father the monarch and risks subordinationism within a divine hierarchy. Boff is aware of this. He believes he can avoid subordinationism by making two moves. First, by stipulating that the relations between the persons are characterized by love and by defining love as being "for, by, with and in one another," he thinks he can avoid ranking one person above the others. Second, Boff insists that these communal relations are eternal. They are without beginning. There is no temporal priority of the Father. Therefore, the three persons enjoy equality. The Son and Spirit are not subordinate to the Father.[72]

Nevertheless, the Boff argument stops short of being convincing. Even though he avoids the temporal priority of the Father, he still makes the divinity of the second and third persons dependent upon the first and the divinity of the first independent of the other two. The same is true of love. It is difficult to avoid a monarchy of the Father under these circumstances. His emphasis on the eternity of the immanent Trinity causes Boff to shrink from the implications of Rahner's Rule. Boff seems to struggle. One would expect him to embrace Rahner's Rule because, like Moltmann, he asserts that creation is drawn up into the trinitarian life. Yet Boff is so committed to the classical position that the idea makes him nervous. So he retreats to an affirmation of the sublime Trinity well beyond creation, unreachable by us because it is shrouded in eternal mystery.

But the Trinity as absolute and sacramental mystery is much more than what is manifested. . . . What the Trinity is in itself is beyond our reach, hidden in unfathomable mystery, mystery that will be partially revealed to us in the bliss of eternal life, but will always escape us in full, since the Trinity is a mystery in itself and not only for human beings. So we have to say: the economic Trinity is the immanent Trinity, but not the whole of the immanent Trinity.[73]

In effect, Boff is working with the assumption that social hierarchies can exist only in the creation where we have temporal priority and, further, that God as Trinity exists primarily in eternity where a hierarchy cannot be a hierarchy. He is working with the additional assumption that no matter what happens within creation or history, nothing will influence the eternal perichoresis of the divine life. Although he apparently does not recognize it, Boff has actually slipped fully into the position of classical monotheism that repels influence by modern ideas such as personhood and relationality. That Boff is dimly aware of his retreat is indicated in his preference for the traditional concept of person rather than the modern one; and, second, by the near negation of his central thesis: "We must not imagine them [Father, Son, and Spirit] as three individuals who come together in communion and unite; this would not avoid tritheism."[74]

In sum, although Boff starts down the road following Moltmann, he quickly decides he cannot travel that far. Although Boff wants to work with a correlation between a divine society and a human society on a nonhierarchical basis, the divine society of which he speaks is in fact a monarchy; and because this monarchy is shrouded in eternal mystery apart from the time in which we live, no genuine correlation with human society can be made.

Process Theism and Two Makes Three

If, as I suggested earlier, we might think of Boff as having run out of gas, then we might think of Whiteheadian process theism as a detour away from the main direction of trinitarian discussion. This is not immediately obvious, however. One might think at first that the process theologians, who are so vigorous and so creative when it comes to constructing a relational theory of God, would be in a position to make a substantive contribution to trinitarian thought. One would think this especially in light of the vehemence with which process thinkers attack the substantialist ontology of classical theism and support a neoclassical metaphysics that emphasizes dynamic relationality. After all, philosopher Alfred North Whitehead himself was inspired by the Alexandrian theologians. He believed that the Alexandrian speculations on the Trinity and the incarnation marked the only significant metaphysical advance beyond Plato. This is because they offered an understanding of how one person could be truly present in another. Whitehead's own metaphysics expands on this, asking how one actual entity can be present in another. A profound sense of relational unity undergirds process theism.

However, our expectations that today's process theists might lead the way into further trinitarian insight are quickly frustrated. This is because the threefoldness of the divine symbolism found in the New Testament is virtually ignored.[75] When it is addressed, what we usually find are crude attempts at making the biblical symbols fit into already established metaphysical categories. This renders almost laughable the frequent contention that somehow the Nicene theologians were guilty of capitulating to the metaphysics of their milieu, whereas contemporary neoclassical thinkers are innocent of such capitulation.

The essential problem of retrofitting process categories with biblical symbols is that the twoness of Whiteheadian metaphysics is difficult to reconcile with the threeness of trinitarian discourse. The God of Alfred North Whitehead's *Process and Reality* is binary or bipolar in that it has two natures: a primordial nature and a consequent nature. Similarly, Charles Hartshorne was constantly occupied with reconciling the poles in the bipolar dialectic between God's absoluteness and relativity, between God's necessary existence and contingent actuality, between God's being both creator and recipient. Hartshorne's insights into the double dimensions of the divine mark an achievement in philosophical theology. Yet he stops here, virtually ignoring the trinitarian symbols of the absolute God of Israel who became relative in history. The Trinity is clearly not intrinsic to process metaphysics, so the value of the threefold revelation becomes doubtful. John Cobb and David Griffin simply throw in the towel by admitting that "process theology is not interested in formulating distinctions within God for the sake of conforming with traditional Trinitarian notions."[76]

Lewis Ford is, however. He wants to tackle the classical conundrum of how three can be one and one can be three. This was difficult for medievalists who operated with Aristotle's dictum that one substance—that is, one actuality—cannot be in another. Whitehead's philosophy, in contrast, is designed to show that this may be so when one concrete actuality is objectively present in the concrescence of another. With this in mind, Ford draws up a set of correspondences in which he pairs the Logos with God's primordial nature and the Spirit with God's consequent nature. The Father is simply God, not another member of the Godhead. The Father is the ultimate transcendent source of the manifest structure of primordial and consequent natures. To illustrate his point, he refers us to occasional depictions of the Trinity in medieval art where we find one man, the Father, with two outstretched hands, one for the Son and the other for the Spirit.

What warrants trinitarianism, in Ford's mind, is the recasting of the problematic. He says that the fundamental problematic for classical theism was to understand how God could be both transcendent to the world yet immanent within it. What Whitehead adds to this is something the classical theologians never entertained, namely, the problem of understanding how the world can transcend God and yet be immanent in God. By adding this second concern, Ford argues that a threefold distinction becomes necessary.[77] God is the source of all creativity, making God transcendent; yet actual events at concrescence are creative on their own. They are independent of God, and in this sense they transcend God. What we need is an organizing principle so that creative activity does not become mere amorphous chaos. This we get with the primordial nature. In addition, we need a principle of reintegration whereby all events are brought once again into the divine harmony. This we get with the consequent nature.

The Logos corresponds to the primordial nature because, as Whitehead conceives it, the primordial nature embraces all eternal objects as the source from whence all initial aims for finite occasions derive. It is the totality of all divine aims, both large and small, both relevant and irrelevant. It is God's "creative word." It issues nontemporally from the source of all creativity. Because the primordial nature is the outcome of a single nontemporal concresence, it corresponds to the eternal Son who is "begotten of the Father before all worlds."

The Spirit corresponds to the consequent nature, God's receptive activity by which God experiences the temporal occasions of the world and in response to which God reinjects successive novel aims into our experience. Ford has to wrestle here a bit. The problem is that the concept of the consequent nature in Whiteheadian thought explains how the world can be immanent in God, not how God can be immanent in the world. Thus, Ford cannot make a one-to-one correspondence between Spirit and consequent nature. Nevertheless, Ford presses on with the point that we experience God through the ordinary aims within day-to-day living, and this gives us evidence that God has experienced us. The Spirit guides us or lures us. The Spirit is the Lord and Giver of life in providing novel aims by which organisms can actualize a living response to a dynamic environment. This applies to all of creation, of course, but we humans become especially aware of the Spirit's lure through ethical injunctions. It is through awareness of divinely proffered values that we are inspired to seek out the divine source and are eventually led to reconciliation with God.

Ford's proposal differs from traditional trinitarian formulations in that here it is not the Spirit but rather the Father who unites the other two. If we were to contrast Eastern Orthodox trinitarianism, with tendencies toward subordinationism in behalf of the Father, with Latin trinitarianism, with Augustinian tendencies toward seeing three equal persons sharing a single divine nature, then Ford would come closer to the Eastern camp here. What this inclusivity of the Father reinforces for Ford is that there cannot be in the Trinity three separate subjectivities, just as in Whiteheadianism there cannot be more than one subjectivity in God. Whatever has actual unity enjoys its own subjectivity, and God is an individual actuality in this sense. Consequently, Ford need not depict the Father as one person in addition to the other two. He chooses rather to see the Father as the one subjectivity inclusive of primordial and consequent natures.[78]

Joseph A. Bracken, S.J., ventures as does Ford to advance trinitarian thinking by using Whitehead's metaphysical categories. In comparison, however, Bracken takes a shorter lead off the classical base. He wants to run toward a revised doctrine of the Trinity that employs process rather than substance as its basic metaphysical category, yet he wishes to stay close to the safety of his own dogmatic commitment to Christian orthodoxy. So, to do so, he extends Whitehead's social understanding of the human person and applies it to the divine life. The result is a social doctrine of the Trinity as a society of societies.

Bracken believes that each of the three divine persons is a separate "I" who can address the other two as a "Thou." Each serves as the bond of union between the remaining two. What makes them together one divinity rather than three gods is the ongoing process of self-giving love that is their common nature. Complementing Whitehead's notion of society with the metaphysics of community developed by philosopher Josiah Royce, Bracken contends that the divine community that is the Trinity represents a higher level of being and activity than would be proper to the persons on the level of individual existence.

The community cannot exist without its individual members, but the members cannot become fully themselves except through participation in the community. The community in this view becomes almost a supraindividual person while not denying individuality and mutuality to the discrete persons.[79]

To be more specific regarding Bracken's use of Whiteheadian metaphysics, he says God as Trinity can be conceived of as three personally ordered societies whose unity as one God is itself the unity of a democratically organized structured society.[80] God is a society of societies. The unity of God is a corporate unity of unities.

Bracken objects to Charles Hartshorne's view that God and the world constitute a compound individual, with God acting as the mind or soul of the world, and the world as the body of God. This organismic mind-body model for the God-world relationship makes God look unipersonal, and Bracken feels this cannot be reconciled with the tripersonal understanding of traditional Christian belief. In addition, Bracken objects because Hartshorne's model perpetuates an inadequate conception of societies coming from Whitehead. To remedy this situation, Bracken suggests we think of Whiteheadian societies as structured environments or unified fields of activity for the emergence of successive generations of actual entities. The field understanding renders Whitehead's metaphysics internally more consistent, he argues, because only societies as fields survive the becoming and perishing of actual occasions. Then, Bracken applies this revised notion of society to God.

> A trinitarian understanding of the God-world relationship in terms of hierarchically ordered fields of activity seems quite possible. If the three divine persons, for example, are interpreted as three personally ordered societies of actual occasions which by their dynamic interrelation from moment to moment sustain a democratically organized structured society, then, their joint field of activity could be said to envelop and support the field of activity brought into existence at every moment by the interrelated activity of all finite actual entities.[81]

Bracken seems to be asserting here that the three fields of activity merge to form a fourth comprehensive field, which is God. The result is a single unified field of activity with three foci or interrelated centers of activity. This will work, Bracken thinks, because the one God is itself a democratically ordered society, mutually dependent upon the three sub-societies. This means the divine persons are incapable of existence apart from their life together as a community. Therefore, they constitute one God, not three gods in close collaboration.

With regard to inner-trinitarian dynamics, Bracken says that through knowledge and love each of the three persons transcends itself within the immanent Trinity. Each person has self-knowledge and unlimited understanding of the other two. Love between the persons is mutual, to be sure, but it is more. It is shared love. A shared love requires a lover, a beloved, and a third person to share what is mutual.[82] Where this leads Bracken is to affirm a higher unity and greater actuality than would be possible for each of the three as individual persons, even if each person is understood as a separate democratically ordered society. What Trinity means here is that, only by virtue of their relationship to one another within the structured society that is the divine community, the three become truly God. God as the divine community is the Supreme Being: that than which nothing greater can be thought.[83]

Each of the three persons has a distinguishable role in this divine community, especially in reference to the economic Trinity. The Father is the transcendent deity, creator of the world process. He is the primal cause and, hence, associated with the primordial nature of God in Whitehead's system. He is the aboriginal condition for all creativity in the universe. He is the primal cause in every event, though he is not the sole cause. He constantly shares his creativity, first with the other two divine persons, and then with all finite actual occasions. He is not the creator in that he first exists and then brings other things into existence. Rather, he is the creator in the sense that he himself is the aboriginal condition that qualifies the existence of all other existing things. The Father prehends himself and is prehended by the Son and the Spirit as the one who continually—moment by moment—proposes for them and for the world a new possibility for shared existence.

The Son, identified with Jesus, is the founder of the church as the beloved community that over the centuries has been intended to be a model for all other communities. The Son is the primal effect of the Father's creativity; so Bracken associates the Son with the consequent nature. Both within the divine life proper as well as in the work of creation, the Son responds affirmatively to the Father's aim by converting pure possibility into actuality for all three divine persons. The Son prehends himself and is prehended by the Father and the Spirit as the one who always says yes to the Father's proposals. It is the Son who provides the concrete unity of the divine life from moment to moment by integrating the particular decisions of the myriad actual occasions of the world into the ongoing concrescence of the consequent nature of God.

What about the Spirit? The Spirit is the chief interpreter of God's community within history who keeps history moving along under its supervision. For this reason, Bracken identifies the Spirit with the superject. Within the divine life, the Spirit prompts the Father to offer new possibilities of divine existence and also prompts the Son to say yes to the Father's offer. The Spirit is the hypostatized condition for this exchange between Father and Son.[84] With regard to the divine economy in creation, the Spirit prompts the Father to offer initial aims to all actual occasions and prompts each of the occasions to say yes to the Father's aim. Now Whitehead only made one mention of the superjective nature of God, but this is important for Bracken because it refers to God's causal influence on the created order.[85] More than the Father and the Son, argues Bracken, the Spirit is responsible for the integrity of the God-world relationship from moment to moment.

In sum, for Bracken there is a Cause, Effect, and Condition of the divine being. The Cause is the primordial nature identified with the Father. The Effect is the consequent nature identified with the Son. And the Condition is the superjective nature identified with the Spirit.

Marjorie Hewitt Suchocki objects to such one-to-one correlations between the Christian symbols of Father, Son, and Spirit and the categories of process metaphysics. It certainly is necessary, of course, for process theists to speak of God in the threefold way: primordial nature, consequent nature, and superjective nature. But "the reason against utilizing these terms as an interpretation of trinity is simply that the terms are abstractions for our understanding, ways of describing the reality that is God."[86] Her criticism is that abstract metaphysical vocabulary is not sufficiently rich in nuance to catch the richness of subjectivity in the divine life. She wants to keep the symbols as they are and let them simply refer to the complexity that is God.

David Mason is a bit more forceful than Suchocki in registering his objection to the method employed and conclusions derived by Ford and Bracken. In a paper that he read at the annual meeting of the American Academy of Religion in Anaheim, California, in 1985, he objected to the idea that Christian symbols should be made to match metaphysical configurations. He has two reasons. First, the religious symbols were never intended for this. Second, metaphysics should be free to speculate on its own terms and not be encumbered by symbolic constraints.[87]

The obvious differences between Ford and Bracken should tell us something. They both start with the same biblical symbols and the same metaphysical structure, yet they arrive at quite different pictures of the inner life of God. Ford identifies the Son with the primordial nature, the Spirit with the consequent nature, and the Father with the primordial envisagement which comprehends both. Bracken, in contrast, identifies the Father with the primordial nature, the Son with the consequent nature, and the Spirit with the superjective nature, each as a separate person united socially. Ford comes across as a modalist, whereas Bracken's social Trinity risks tritheism.[88]

Mason, who is also of the Whiteheadian orientation, believes that the trinitarian symbols function mythically and should be left to do so. The symbols should be interpreted existentially as indicating the meaning God has for our lives. They should not be taken literally as referring to metaphysical concepts. As such, they may be demythologized. Whiteheadian metaphysics, in contrast, should be free to illumine our understanding of the existence and nature of God, of the essential being of creatures, and of the general features of the God-world relation. For Mason, it seems that the trinitarian symbols have existential reference, whereas metaphysics has objective reference. This is what permits him to eschew the desire to turn our symbols into specific metaphysical concepts.

In sum, the conversation within the circles of process theism marks an eddy leading away from the mainstream of current trinitarian discussion. It leads us away insofar as it attempts to replace—replace, not interpret or supplement—the classical metaphysical system with a neoclassical system. The problem here is that it gives too little attention to the religious fact that the originary symbols of Father, Son, and Spirit indicate differentiated experiences with the divine. These must be attended to directly, prior to metaphysical construction.

On the other hand, the process thinkers have one foot in the mainstream as well. Despite their reluctance to identify with the classic trinitarian symbols, Whiteheadians have much to teach regarding temporality in the divine life. David Griffin, for example, argues that God experiences the world, and this requires that God be temporal. Experience requires time. To experience a temporal world, God in the Godself must be temporal as well. Griffin adds that we should consider temporality in God a blessing, not a defect. It is God's temporality that makes intimate relation to the world possible.

Griffin goes on to distinguish temporality in the divine experience from ours. God is not subject to many of the limitations we are. Our memory is selective and subject to fading. God, in contrast, remembers all that has occurred. The remote past is as vivid to God as is the most recent moment. In this sense, Griffin suggests, we might think of God as timeless. What he means here, I think, is that God's memory is not subject to the deterioration that accompanies passage. He does not mean that God is not subject to passage.

God differs from us also in that, though temporal, God is not subject to anxiety. Uncertainty and sometimes fear of the unknown future is a source of distracting anxiety for us humans. Worry about our survival may even lead us to preemptive strikes against others in a fruitless attempt to protect ourselves from the ravages of time; that is, anxiety may prompt us to sin against others. Not so with God, says Griffin; God is free from anxiety. God is able to love us even in the face of uncertainties regarding the future. This leads Griffin to think of God's temporality as free from the imperfections of our temporality; yet it is this temporal dimension of the divine life that makes God's experiential relationship to the world possible.[89]

In sum, what process theists such as Griffin have in common with the Barthian legacy is exploration of the temporal character and process character and relational character of the divine reality. The understanding of God emerging from the work of Whitehead and Hartshorne is one in which the divine is deeply involved in the world processes. God's relation to the world is internal as well as external. The process school has no patent on such ideas, however. They are now the common property of nearly all participants to the current trinitarian discussion.

The relational character of the divine life is the most salient concern of the work of Catherine Mowry LaCugna, for example, whose work places her much more squarely in the Barth and especially the Rahner tradition.

Catherine Mowry Lacugna's "God for Us"

A real jewel among the works of current Trinity talk is Catherine Mowry LaCugna's book *God for Us: The Trinity and Christian Life*. With lapidary precision, this University of Notre Dame theologian cuts through the roughly hewn doctrinal conversations through the centuries to polish the primary facets. "The doctrine of the Trinity is ultimately a practical doctrine with radical consequences for Christian life," she says.

The aim of the Christian life is "to participate in the life of God through Jesus Christ in the Spirit." This means that trinitarian theology is best described "as par excellence a theology of relationship, which explores the mysteries of love, relationship, personhood and communion within the framework of God's self-revelation in the person of Christ and the activity of the Spirit."[90]

LaCugna starts with the question, Why has the doctrine of the Trinity been marginalized? This is a variant on the question I asked earlier: Why have our theologians given us a brain-knocking problem and then frustrated us by consigning the answer to the impenetrable mystery of God? The contribution offered by LaCugna's work is that it presents a historical analysis of the rise of these problems plus a constructive proposal that extends the Barthian insight into practical spirituality. She does not footnote Karl Barth per se; but she does capitalize on Rahner's Rule and develops her constructive proposal for understanding the eternal life of God on the basis of the historical economy of salvation.

The root cause of the marginalization of the doctrine of the Trinity is the split that occurred at Nicea between *theologia* and *oikonomia,* she argues. The term *oikonomia,* which we identify with the economic Trinity, refers to the self-communication of God in the person of Jesus Christ and the activity of the Holy Spirit in the history of salvation. Everything we know about God is a result of this economic activity. *Theologia,* or our knowledge of the eternal being of God, should, in principle, be coextensive with what we have learned from revelation in the divine economy. We have no access to the immanent life of God that goes beyond what has been revealed. So if we consign the trinitarian life to a realm beyond what has been revealed, we can only consign it to incomprehensible mystery.

This is a mistake, contends LaCugna. *Theologia* and *oikonomia* should be one. And they were until the fourth century. What happened in the process of writing the Nicene Creed was the separation of soteriology from the doctrine of God, so that *theologia* came to refer to the inner workings of the divine life apart from the work of salvation. The intradivine relations of the three persons lost their link to God's activity in the world.

Of particular importance in the Nicean century was the unresolved problem of God's suffering. On both the Arian and Athanasian side of the debate, patripassianism was rejected, and this seemed to leave the sufferings of the redeemer out in the cold, external to the divine life proper. The Trinity and even the Logos were thought to be isolated and immune. This history leads LaCugna to conclude that "Christian theology was held back in both its Christology and trinitarian theology by its inability to attribute suffering to the Logos as divine (also Arius' idea), because without examining and revising the axiom of divine impassibility, Christian theology could not find a coherent way around Arius' suffering Logos who was, though a lesser God, still divine."[91]

The repercussions of this failure have lasted down to the present day, when the doctrine of the Trinity is presumed to deal with God's inner life apart from any relation to creation, redemption, or consummation.

> Given the trajectory set by Nicaea, in combination with the long-lasting controversies over Arianism and neo-Arianism, Christian theologians focussed their attention more and more on the nature of *theologia per se,* that is, the interrelationship of the divine persons. While the motive was no doubt consistently soteriological, in time the economy became less and less decisive in shaping conclusions about the intratrinitarian relations. . . . The result of this was a one-sided theology of God had little to do with the economy of Christ and the Spirit, with the themes of Incarnation and grace, and therefore little to do with the Christian life.[92]

In short, the tie between the immanent Trinity and its accompanying *theologia* became severed from the economic Trinity and the *oikonomia* of salvation.

In response, LaCugna recommends that we reconceive the doctrine of the Trinity and retrieve the primal connection between the intratrinitarian relations and the economy of salvation. She says the direction toward reconceiving the Trinity has been pointed out by Karl Rahner, especially by his idea that God is by nature self-communicating. The mysterious and incomprehensible God is God in the act of expressing and sharing the Godself. God's actions reveal who God is. We can be confident that the God revealed in salvation history is in fact the real God, even if God's mystery remains absolute. This banishes once and for all the possibility of a hidden God *(Deus absconditus)* who lurks behind the revealed God *(Deus revelatus).*

Rahner's Rule is key here: the economic Trinity is the immanent Trinity, and vice versa. The LaCugna corrolary is this: "Theology is inseparable from soteriology, and vice versa."[93]

The LaCugna corollary carries her beyond the problem as formulated by Rahner—or by Jüngel and others, for that matter. The formulation of

Rahner's Rule seems to presuppose that what theologians need to do is get the two trinitarian concepts, the immanent and economic, back together again. By revising the vocabulary slightly so that what we are identifying is *theologia* with *oikonomia,* the LaCugna reconceptualization— "more accurately, the return to the biblical and pre-Nicene pattern of thought"—dispenses with the distinction between God's life *ad intra* and *ad extra.* There is but one trinitarian life of God, and it spans and incorporates the entire scope of temporal history.

She envisions a chiastic model of emanation and return. There is neither an economic nor an immanent Trinity; rather, there is only the mystery of the *theologia* manifest in the concrete events of time, space, history, and personality. God as Father begets Jesus Christ the Son. From this proceeds the Holy Spirit. Then the world. The Holy Spirit consummates the world into the eschatological unity of Jesus Christ, who remits all to God the Father. It is a movement from God into creation, redemption, consummation, and back to God. It is a movement *a Patre ad Patrem.* There is no reason to stop at any point along the path, she says. There is no reason to draw a sharp line between Christology or pneumatology. There is no reason to separate God's immanent from God's economic relations.

> *Oikonomia* is not the Trinity *ad extra* but the comprehensive plan of God reaching from creation to consummation, in which God and all creatures are destined to exist together in the mystery of love and communion. Similarly, *theologia* is not the Trinity *in se,* but, much more modestly and simply, the mystery of God. As we know from the experience of being redeemed by God through Jesus Christ, the mystery of God is the mystery of God with us. [94]

This position has drastic implications for our understanding of spirituality. By collapsing the distinction between the immanent Trinity and the economic Trinity, the inner life of God no longer belongs to God alone. No longer can we speak of God in isolation. The divine life is also our life. As soon as we free ourselves from thinking of two levels of Trinity, one *ad intra* and the other *ad extra,* then we can see again that there is but one life of the triune God; and that life includes God's relation to us. LaCugna is quick to incorporate the vocabulary of Eastern Orthodoxy to affirm that God's motive in self-communication is union with the creation—union with us—through *theosis.* The divine economy of salvation is the economy of divinization and glorification. For us human beings, this means entering fully into a life of love and communion with God and with one another. "The life of God is not something that belongs to God alone. *Trinitarian life is also our life.*"[95]

The concept of person employed in this position is one of the most developed of the contemporary options. LaCugna holds that persons, whether human or divine, are constituted by their relationships. To be personal is to be interpersonal, intersubjective. Yet a person is something ineffable. It is impossible to communicate completely who or what one is. The mystery of each person is inexhaustible. In addition, LaCugna, like Zizioulas, says persons are "catholic." This means two things: namely, that we have been created to be open to all that exists, and that each person, though unique, also exemplifies just what it means to be human. Similarly, each person of the Trinity is unique yet also exemplifies what it means to be divine. Finally, personhood defines fulfillment. Living in right relationship—that is, living in communion—is the meaning of salvation and the ideal of the Christian faith. Our personhood attains its fulfillment in *theosis,* in full communion with God.

When LaCugna affirms that the economic Trinity is the immanent Trinity and vice versa, or that God's energies express the divine essence, she is saying that God's way of being in relationship with us is God's personhood. She is saying furthermore that this is the perfect expression of God's being as God. Furthermore, in God alone do we find the full correspondence between personhood and being, between *hypostasis* and *ousia.* "God for us is who God is as God."[96]

Now, we might ask, To what should we apply the term "person," the one nature or the three identities? LaCugna's answer might be surprising. She does not take sides in the skirmishes between Barth and Moltmann or others. "It does not so much matter whether we say God is one person in three modalities, or one nature in three persons, since these two assertions can be understood in approximately the same way. What matters is that we hold on to the assertion that God is personal, and that therefore the proper subject matter of the doctrine of the Trinity is the encounter between divine and human persons in the economy of redemption."[97]

The LaCugna position also puts the divine mystery closer to where it belongs. As we noted in the first chapter of this volume, mystery does not belong to the doctrine of the Trinity as a doctrine. We ought not use mystery as an excuse for our inability to explain contradictory theological propositions. Nor does mystery refer to the inner trinitarian life of God apart from the creation, apart from what has been revealed in the economy of salvation. To apply the term "mystery" to an alleged transcendent reality that has not been revealed is to make theology indistinguishable from fantasy. Rather, LaCugna applies the term "mystery" to our inability to comprehend what we have experienced. What we have experienced is the saving activity of God in the missions of Jesus Christ and in the Holy Spirit. Despite our participation in it, we cannot fully understand it. It remains ineffable. This is the paradox that pervades theological knowledge in general. God freely and completely bestows the Godself in the encounter with human persons, yet God remains ineffable because we creatures are incapable of fully receiving or understanding the one who is imparted.

Finally, LaCugna's reconception of the Trinity has political implications of the type previously drawn out by Moltmann and Boff. She will not let the monarchy of the Father become translated into justification for social patriarchy or any other form of human inequality. She grants that support for patriarchy might come from unitarianism or from a doctrine of the immanent Trinity wherein the image of the divine Father is one of self-definition, self-sufficiency, and isolation. However, drawing upon the Cappadocians and her own exposition of person-in-relationship, LaCugna argues that a trinitarian view of God supports the shared rule of equal persons in communion. Trinitarianism disavows domination by some persons over other persons. It disavows hierarchy. It promotes mutuality.[98]

The insightful scholarship of LaCugna marks a further step up the path first blazed by Barth and widened by Rahner. She knowingly or unknowingly follows the Barthian trail of analysis by arguing that the pre-Nicene biblical apprehension of God's revelation comes already in the form of Father, Son, and Holy Spirit. With full awareness, she follows and then passes Rahner when he stops with his rule: the economic Trinity is the immanent Trinity and vice versa. Her own corollary—*theologia* is *oikonomia* and vice versa—leads her to the grand vision of the divine life spanning and incorporating the whole of creation within itself. What we thought was external to God is now internal. The God we thought was *in se,* for the Godself alone, is now God in relation to us. Without a doubt, the dominant and pervasive theme of her work is the relationality of God.

What is missing, however, is the temporality of God. One would have expected that in formulating the problem as she did, the question of the relationship between eternity and temporality would have appeared on her agenda. The concept of person in relationship implies dynamism, change, and growth. The concept of *theosis,* or divinization, sets our sights on eschatological fulfillment of our personhood. The chiastic route taken from the Father to the Son to the Spirit to the creation and redemption of the world and back again requires that we look forward to the return to the Father. The movement *a Patre ad Patrem* is just that, a movement through time toward a still outstanding future. If the internal relationality of the divine life is as tied to the course of world history as LaCugna seems to believe it is, then one would expect some investigation into the possible temporal dimensions of God's life.

There are other theologians for whom the relationality of God is decisive and for whom Rahner's Rule is taken seriously, yet who also recognize the importance of exploring the connection between the eternal and the temporal in the divine life. To the work of two such theologians we now turn.

Robert Jenson's Triune Identity

"There is one event, God, with three identities," writes Robert W. Jenson.[99] Jenson continues to navigate in the direction set out by Barth, according to whom the threeness in God must be understood not as three instances of one deity but as three events of one deity: God is God, and then God is God again and again, each time in a different way.[100] With this as his point of embarkment, Jenson attempts to go further than Barth in emancipating the Christian Trinity from captivity to Hellenic thinking.[101] Having escaped from the substantialist ontology into the realm of event and becoming, Jenson now turns to cutting our bonds to the classical concept of an atemporal eternity. God is eternal, to be sure, but Jenson wishes to draw out the point that God's eternity embraces time and takes temporal events up into the divine life. Jenson offers two noteworthy contributions to the current trinitarian discussion: (1) he extends Barth's understanding of the relationship between time and eternity so that the immanent Trinity becomes understood as eschatological, and (2) he makes an interesting case for rendering *hypostasis* and *persona* into English as "identity."

The first item on Jenson's agenda is to rescue Christian trinitarian thought from the idea of eternity as timelessness, according to which God is eternal and hence unrelated to the world. He, like Barth and so many other theologians in our century, believes that scripture-based thinking is antagonistic to Hellenic metaphysics. The chief reason is that the Greeks thought of temporal movement as a loss of perfection. Time destroys. Chronos devours his children. So Greek religion became a quest for the rock of ages, for an eternity that was immune to temporal change and deterioration. The defining character of the gods was immortality, immunity to destruction. We are in time, but the gods are not. This makes our mortal situation desperate. Therefore, the religion of late antiquity became a frenzied search for mediators, for beings of a third ontological kind between time and timelessness.

Not so in ancient Israel. Here Yahweh was experienced as eternal, but this eternity was understood as a faithfulness through time. The prophets spoke of God making and fulfilling promises. Yahweh constantly challenged the past from a future that is Yahweh's own freedom. Time destroys, but Yahweh is faithful. In Yahweh we find freedom and a future. Unlike the other gods of ancient Asian polytheism or the one inclusive being of mystical monism, Yahweh does not transcend time by being immune to it. There is a continuity over time that strains forward toward the future when Yahweh's identity will become fully revealed. This continuity is not a constancy of being, an ontological immutability. Rather, it is a continuity that Jenson describes as "personal." It is established through Yahweh's words and commitments, by faithfulness of his later acts to the promises made in his earlier acts. So Jenson can say that whereas the Hebrew Yahweh was faithful *through* time, the Greek gods' eternity was due to their abstraction *from* time. Yahweh's eternity is intrinsically a matter of relation to his creatures, whereas the Greek gods' eternity is the negation of such relation. This contrast did not go unnoticed. The Cappadocian fathers in particular resisted the Hellenization of the Bible's God. Whereas divinity for the Greeks at the time of Nicea consisted of a motionless center with time circling round about it, the God of Gregory of Nyssa, in contrast, is eternal in that God envelops time, is ahead and so before it. The Hellenic God stands still, so that we may ground things in it. Gregory's God keeps things moving. [102]

In appropriating the work of Gregory and the other Cappadocian fathers, whom Jenson favors somewhat over Athanasius, he develops a future-based concept of time that he dubs "temporal infinity." The essential mode of divine temporality is unbounded futurity, he says. This means time is neither linear nor cyclical and, therefore, we ought not understand reality in terms of enduring substances. It is the on-coming of the future that creates time for us, because it forces the present reality to go beyond itself. It is the reality of the future that temporalizes us. It is the structure of the still outstanding eschatological future that determines the character of time and becoming in our present experience. What we experience as endurance is given not by persisting substances but rather by the reinterpretation that the future gives to all past occurrences. What is significant here is that what we experience as the temporal movement of events is taken up into the divine relationality proper. This is the ongoing transformative work of the Spirit.

The transformative work of the Spirit, especially the promised eschatological transformation yet to come, has ontological priority. Because of the event character of the divine being, the future affects the past as much as the past affects the future. Both the generation of the Son and the proceeding of the Spirit free the Father from a role of mere persistence. The Father is free toward the future. Jenson frequently speaks of the Father as the given, the Son as present possibility, and the Spirit as the eschatological outcome.[103]

This temporalization of the divine life is the means whereby Jenson overcomes the substantialist notion of God and affirms a relational understanding. This should make him kin with Moltmann. However, when it comes to the issue of the divine subject and the referent for the term "person," Jenson seems to side with Barth and Rahner over against Moltmann. "God is indeed describable as personal in the modern sense," he writes, "but it is the triune event of which this is true, not the Father merely as Father. The person that is conscious is the Trinity." This focus on the Trinity as God rather than the Father as God, derives from his antimonarchian and antimodalist emphasis that "only the Trinity as such is God by himself."[104] With the term "God" we are not referring simply to the Father for whom the Logos and Spirit are modes of expression. It is the Trinity that is the divine subject.

So Jenson is appreciative of Tertullian's introduction of *una substantia et tres personae,* because Tertullian's use of *persona* here constitutes a defense against modalism. It adequately explicates the sense of address and response found in scripture between the Father and Jesus and the Spirit. This establishes in God the reality of relationship just as do relations between human individuals. They are three in that they speak to and about one another in such scriptural accounts as Jesus' baptism.

They are three also because they have mutually recognized proper names—that is, Father, Son, and Spirit. The unity of the three persons is conceived on the model of the Christian community, in which mutual identification makes one reality, "one body."[105]

What about the one being *(ousia)* these three hold in common? Jenson notes that *ousia* and *hypostasis* both came into theology from the Greek philosophical tradition, where prior to Nicea they were used almost interchangeably to refer to what-is. But Jenson contends—as do Barth, Rahner, and Lonergan too—that the Christian theologians did not simply take over an already existing ontology. The force of biblical explication so dominated the patristics that even though Greek philosophical categories were employed, they were transformed as Christian doctrine took shape. Specifically, the requirements of trinitarian explication led to a division between the terms, wherein *hypostasis* came to mean that which can be identified as an individual, and *ousia* came to mean what such an identifiable individual is. This dropped *hypostasis* to the level of individuals and located *ousia* as the word for the kind of being any one group of individuals have in common. What the Cappadocians did was to affirm that God only *has* an *ousia;* God *is* not one. This move eliminates the necessity of linking attributes to the *ousia,* attributes that the *ousia* must continue to exemplify if it wishes to qualify as divine. This opens the door for the divine being to take up into itself the attributes of particular historical events such as the life of Jesus. The biblical God cannot be bounded by some timeless and unrelational essence or being that we think of as eternally and immutably divine.

When the Cappadocians apply the concept of infinity to God's *ousia,* they defy us to put limits on it, to define it, to specify what it is. God is not infinite because God timelessly extends to all reality, but because time cannot exhaust or keep up with God's activity. In the Hellenic tradition, that something was infinite meant that it lacks definition. The God of Gregory of Nyssa, on the contrary, is infinite in that his God overcomes all definitions. The one divine *ousia* is temporal unhinderedness.

What about the term *hypostasis?* Should we use it today? Should we render it in English as "person"? Jenson is willing to employ the term "person" and mean it in the modern sense of a self-reflexive agent. He will then apply it to each: Father, Son, and Spirit. In addition, he will apply it to God, speaking of God as a "person." He stops short of admitting that he holds to a social doctrine of the Trinity or that he in fact is working with a quaternity that posits God as a fourth item.

A major contribution he offers is the use of the term "identity." Jenson writes: "As a piece of trinitarian language, *hypostasis* is merely an item of linguistic debris knocked from Hellenic philosophy by collision with Yahweh. Present understanding would be advanced if we replaced it with a word not philosophically active; readers will not be surprised that I propose 'identity.' "[106] The upshot is that Jenson can say the Trinity is one, but it has three identities, three names. There is no name for the being of God as one, no name for the divine *ousia*. But each *hypostasis* can be identified: Father, Son, or Spirit. There is no single identity, but three. Yet the three are one reality. The reality of the one God is repeatedly identified and so has identity without being defined by any one timelessly exemplified set of characteristics.

Thus, Jenson is sympathetic to Rahner's criticism of the position that the saving works of God *ad extra* are indivisibly the work of the whole Trinity. Jenson says that the Augustinian tradition on this point represents the bankruptcy of trinitarianism. Whereas in the New Testament titles such as "the Son" or "logos" were given to Jesus with respect to his saving work within history, we have allowed them to lose their relationship to Jesus and become a pure metaphysical entity. If the eternal Logos loses its tie with the historical Jesus, then in principle any of the three divine persons becomes available for whatever duty comes along. The saving works become indifferently the work of each person and of all. "Put the disaster thus: as the rule was applied, 'The Trinity's works toward what is outside are indivisible,' Jesus and the church were taken to be part of 'what is outside.' " But, Jenson insists, "it is Jesus, not a supernatural entity, an unincarnate Logos, that is this second and objective identity of God."[107]

This permits Jenson to hold that there is a single divine subject, yet still deny patripassianism. One of the Trinity suffered and died on the cross. When the patripassianists have extended the suffering of Jesus' death to the Father, this has rightly been promptly rejected. This critical assessment seems to apply to Moltmann as well, for whom the passion of Jesus spills beyond to the passion of the Father. Jenson, no more than Moltmann, of course, is advocating a return to the immutable God above passion. But it is Jenson's contention that we must understand that the suffering is borne by the second person of the Trinity in particular if we are properly to understand God as Trinity. Jenson insists that the one

God has three identities that should not be confused. Jesus' death is constitutive for his relationship to the Father and so for both his deity and the deity of the Father. Jesus is not God despite his death; he is God in that he died. The understanding of God's mortality must remain trinitarian.[108] According to Jenson's analysis, curiously enough, Moltmann's apparent embrace of patripassianism would seem to throw him back into the camp of substantialist monotheism.

Jenson pits the Cappadocians against the more substance-oriented Western tradition of Athanasius and Augustine, which argued in effect that differences of relation in the persons do not necessarily make differences of substance. But the original point of trinitarian dogma and analysis, Jenson argues, was that God's relations to us are internal to him. What should have been emphasized, then, is not the substantial unity of the three persons but rather their relational unity. Had the tradition paid more attention to the Cappadocians, what could and should have been said was that the one Godhead, which each person has, is itself constituted by the relations between the three persons. This means that Father, Son, and Spirit play different roles in their joint realization of divinity, and in so doing each possesses the one and selfsame divinity. Jenson is here giving priority to the relations over their related terms. If one can use the concept of substance at all when speaking of God, Jenson would apply it to the relations that obtain between the three persons rather than the persons themselves.

This would lead one to think that Jenson supports Rahner's Rule. He does. But he perceives a dilemma, a dilemma between two rules. The first is Rahner's: the economic Trinity is the immanent Trinity, and vice versa. Jenson subscribes to Rahner's Rule because it accounts for trinitarian identity and definition determined by the course of events in salvation history. But there is a second rule: the legitimate theological reason for distinguishing the immanent from the economic Trinity is the freedom of God. It must be the case that God in himself could have been the same God he is, and so triune, had there never been a creation or any saving history of God within the creation. So here is the dilemma: Are these two compatible? Yes, says Jenson, they are compatible if we think of the identity of the economic and immanent Trinity as eschatological—that is, if the immanent Trinity is simply the eschatological reality of the economic.[109]

Here Jenson brings his temporalized eternity into play once again. The Hellenized timeless God of impassible substance created a problem when it came to Jesus as the Logos. It placed the nonincarnate Logos into the past as the *asarkos,* the not-yet-incarnate Word, who always was in God and then became the one sent in flesh to us. Because the generation of the Son was timeless and eternal, it could not coincide with the birth of the baby Jesus on the first Christmas day. What we finally get with Jesus in the Bethlehem manger, then, is a human baby plus some sort of preexistent double. This whole pattern must be reversed, says Jenson.

Instead of interpreting Christ's deity as a separate entity that always was, we should interpret it as a final outcome. And as the final outcome, it thereby becomes eternal. "Truly, the Trinity is simply the Father and the man Jesus and their Spirit as the Spirit of the believing community. This economic Trinity is eschatologically God himself, an immanent Trinity. And that assertion is no problem, for God is himself only eschatologically, since he is Spirit."[110] To take seriously the biblical acknowledgment that "God is Spirit" is to recognize that the Spirit is equally principle and source with the Father. The Spirit's witness to the Son and the Son's saving work are equally God-constituting.[111]

It is here that Jenson locates the personhood of God, in the totality of God's self-constituting relations with the history of the world. He recognizes that the modern understanding denies that a person can be a monad devoid of relationships. The internal dynamics of a person are intrinsically communal, inseparable from relations with other selves. What we need to grasp is the communality of God's personhood and our personhood. Here Jenson seems to be siding with Barth, Jüngel, and Rahner over against Moltmann: "Although the triune identities are not as such persons in the modern sense, God is; and if each identity is God, each identity is also personal, and the three a community."[112]

What is of decisive importance for the thesis I am trying to develop in this volume is Jenson's appropriation and extension of Barth's emphasis on the humanity of God and the implications this has for the relationship between eternity and time. This leads Jenson to write: "Time is the form of God's life with and for us. . . . In Christ, God's presence is the temporal present, with a temporal past and future. . . . [W]ithout ceasing to be eternal God took time and made time his own."[113] The eternal beyond has entered the temporally intimate and, because this is a soteriological event, it promises to assume the temporal into the eternal. The absolute has become related, and the promise of this relationship is transformation and consummation.

Wolfhart Pannenberg and Dependent Divinity

Wolfhart Pannenberg is navigating at the point where the flow of trinitarian discussion is currently cresting. His point of embarkment is practically identical to Barth's method of analysis, which he makes clear when saying that trinitarian theology "simply states explicitly what is implicit already in God's revelation in Jesus Christ." He paddles further with "Karl Barth who argued that God in His eternal being must be conceived to be the same as He is in His historical revelation." And it is only a short distance upstream to Rahner's Rule, to the affirmation that what has been revealed incarnately in history applies to God's eternal life. He sails still further in the company of Jüngel, Moltmann, and Jenson.[114] Yet Pannenberg has no intention of throwing anchor. He is steaming forward.

Though an avowed adherent to Rahner's Rule, Pannenberg believes Rahner should have gone yet further and drawn the consequence from which he shrank, namely, that the eternal self-identity of God cannot be conceived independently of the work of the Son and the Spirit within salvation history.[115] Pannenberg believes that the reciprocity in the relationship of the divine persons makes room for the constitutive significance of the central events of salvation history for the Godhead of God and thus for time and change within the divine eternity. And it is not just the sending of the Son with his crucifixion and resurrection that is to be understood as constitutive of the divine life, but also the work of the Spirit who dynamically realizes the kingdom of God in the world. Without this kingdom, God could not be God.[116] The existence of God as Trinity depends upon the future of God's coming kingdom; and the coming of the kingdom depends upon the person of Jesus—in the form of the anticipation of its future and as revealing the love of God—and this provides the occasion for, and the object of, the doctrine of the Trinity.

Pannenberg is critical of Barth for thinking of God as a single divine subject who reveals himself in the three persons as three modes of being.[117] In fact, Pannenberg is critical of the entire western tradition to which Barth is heir—the medieval tradition beginning with Augustine and running through Anselm and Thomas Aquinas down to Hegel—which employs a mental or psychological analogy. According to this analogy, we begin with a single divine mind that contains within itself an object of consciousness, an object from which the divine mind distinguishes itself while remaining united to it. Whether it is the

Augustinian model, which identifies the source of thought with the Father, or the Hegelian version in which the Spirit differentiates itself, the trinitarian relations are collapsed into a single divine subject. Calling this position a "pre-trinitarian, theistic idea of God," Pannenberg objects on the grounds that this is a subtle form of modalism, which assumes an eternal and immutable God insulated from the changes of time and history.[118]

Thus, we can see what direction Pannenberg will take in drawing out the implications of the previous discussion. He is sympathetic to Eberhard Jüngel and Jürgen Moltmann for suggesting that God defines divinity in the Christ event, giving ontological relevance of this historical event to the being of God. Pannenberg concurs with Moltmann and in this case with Jenson when they say that only in the eschaton will the economic Trinity reach completion in the immanent Trinity. Nevertheless, he is critical of both Jenson and Jüngel for repeating Barth's mistake, namely, positing a single divine subject. This Pannenberg believes is incompatible with the constitution of the divine unity through the reciprocal relations of the three divine persons. On this point he is closer to Moltmann. So where Jenson leaves us is where Pannenberg wishes to begin, namely, with the Cappadocian emphasis on the unity of the divine essence as constituted by the trinitarian relations.

Pannenberg's agenda, then, is to try to spell out further the nature of this relational unity. The concept of divine essence *(ousia, esse)* should be relationally structured. The ancients had subordinated the concept of relation to that of substance, so that in Aristotelian language relations belonged among the variable accidents of a substance that is ontologically prior. Modern thought, in contrast, has unloosed the idea of relation from this link to substance. Indeed, it has reversed the situation. Now the concept of substance is subordinated to relation. The substance-accident connection now appears as a subspecies of the category of relation.

This applies to divinity. Pannenberg is not inclined to follow the lead of the ancient Eastern doctrine of generation and procession, according to which the Father is held to be the source of the divinity bestowed upon the Son and the Spirit. He is more inclined to retrieve the mutually determining relational view, which is suggested first by Basil and more fully formulated by Athanasius, then hinted at in Augustine, Hegel, and Barth.[119] The relational view holds that who each person is is determined by its relation to the others. The persons are not temporally or logically prior, so that relationships are simply something extra. Rather, the relations are themselves constitutive. Hence, the Father is the Father only vis-à-vis the Son; the Son is Son only vis-à-vis the Father; the Spirit is Spirit only as the bond of community of Father and Son. The identity of each is dependent upon its relation to the others. What Hegel adds to this view that Pannenberg likes is the sense of self-sublimation—that is, each of the persons surrenders its own independence in behalf of the divine unity. Thus, the Trinity is a unity of reciprocal self-dedication.[120]

Key for understanding not only the relationality but also the temporality of God's trinitarian life is Pannenberg's assertion that the suffering and death of Jesus takes place within the life of God proper. The passion of the historical Jesus is not merely a temporal accident tacked on to an otherwise eternal and immutable Logos. Rather, the divinity of the eternal God is in the process of being determined and defined in the historical events of Jesus' destiny.[121] The eternal nature of God is at least in part dependent upon temporal events.

To be more specific, Jesus defines the first person as Father by differentiating himself as Son and, furthermore, defines the Father as divine by subjecting himself in total obedience. In this fallen and unruly world of ours, Jesus is the first—and until now the only—individual to have obeyed completely the will of the Father. For God to be God, assumes Pannenberg, God must rule. Through his obedience, then, Jesus actually grants God his rule—that is, grants God his divinity. When eschatologically the Son hands all dominion over to the Father (1 Cor. 15:28) and even subjects himself, then God becomes "all in all." By granting dominion to the Father, the Son cedes deity to the Father.

> [The Father's] kingdom and his own deity are now dependent upon the Son. The rule or kingdom of the Father is not so external to his deity that he might be God without his kingdom. The world as the object of his lordship might not be necessary to his deity, since its existence owes its origin to his creative freedom, but the existence of the world is not compatible with his deity apart from his lordship over it. Hence, lordship goes hand in hand with the deity of God.[122]

We must note carefully the steps in this startling argument. The key assumption is that deity is dependent upon lordship, upon kingly rule. The Father may well be an *a se* Lord prior to or apart from creation. Yet once creation enters the picture, the lordship of the Father is called into question. A disobedient or sinful creation denies the existence of a kingdom of God. What the historical Jesus incarnate within creation does is exhaust himself in fidelity to the Father. In his total obedience, he thereby cedes lordship to the Father. Within history, Jesus does this as an individual person, thereby uniting himself with the Father in a unique way. Eschatologically, Christ will finally cede all things to the Father's rule, thereby establishing the kingdom of God. It is in this sense that Pannenberg means that the deity of God the Father is determined by his relationship to the Son. It also shows why the events of salvation within history are constitutive of the divine life; it shows why time must be taken up into eternity.

Where Pannenberg himself goes with this is to affirm that the divinity of each of the three persons is a *dependent* divinity. Divinity comes to each as the result of personhood in relationship. To the Son, divinity manifests itself in the form of the Father, and the Son knows himself only through participation in the Spirit. The Son reveals the Father as divine. To the Father, the Son is the realization of his own divinity through obedience—that is, through the establishment of his kingdom of love. And in the Spirit, the Father finds his unity with the Son and therewith the certainty of his own divinity. Finally, the Spirit serves the Son and serves the Father, thereby finding its own personhood and divinity in the community of Father and Son.[123] Hence, the unity of the Godhead is by no means a simple unity; rather, it is a unity of integrating love.[124]

Tipping closer to Athanasius than to the Cappadocians now, Pannenberg stresses that God is not personal except in one or another of the three persons.[125] When God confronts the world through personal relationship, it will be as Father, as Son, or as Spirit. It will not be in the form of an abstract unity. *God is personal only through one or another of the three hypostases, not as a single ineffable entity.*

Personal identity is also temporal. We human beings form our respective identities gradually through the process of developing self-consciousness. Our biographies with the history of our actual relationships are constitutive of the self and provide the condition for and content of our subjectivity. Our personhood is determined by the whole network of relations that is our life. And, because of Pannenberg's acute sense of holism, he says the meaning of each of our lives is finally determined by our place in the history of the whole of reality. It is similar to divine personhood. If actual historical events and relations are constitutive of the relations between the divine persons, then who the Son truly is and who the

Spirit truly is and even who the Father truly is will be eschatologically determined. The personhoods of Son or Spirit cannot be reduced to their origin in generation or procession from the Father. Personhood is rather a process or a result.

Pannenberg cautions that, even though we use the relational model to enhance our understanding, the divine persons are not simply equatable with human persons. What is the difference? The most important difference, he says, is that human personhood is not so exclusively dependent upon others for its constitution. Each individual has considerable internal capacity for distinguishing his or her own identity. The trinitarian persons, in contrast, are *totally* dependent upon their relation to the others.[126] Perhaps by analogy we might say that although a brick is what it is supposed to be when part of a building's wall, when we find one brick by itself we certainly can identify it. Human personhood must be like this for Pannenberg. But each divine person is more akin to a supporting leg in a tripod. Alter one leg and the whole structure falls asunder, leaving us with mere sticks rather than legs. This makes Pannenberg's perhaps the most radical of the post-Barthian relational proposals.

Human personhood can be distinguished from the divine persons on another count. One of the ways in which Pannenberg analyzes the human experience of estrangement is to point out the split between ego and self. The ego is not mediated through social relations, whereas the self includes the summary of the picture others have of each of us.[127] Much of the pain we feel in life is due to the lack of congruence between these two. The persons of the divine Trinity, in contrast, undergo no such split. The Son is fully himself in relation to the Father; the Father is fully himself in relation to the Son; and the Spirit is fully himself in witness to both.

What Rahner's Rule comes to mean in Pannenberg's theory is that for all practical purposes we need not distinguish between the Godhead *ad intra* and *ad extra*. Identity is dependent and relational on both counts. Pannenberg believes God's relation to the world is necessary for determining God's identity. Pannenberg, no less than Barth and Jüngel, emphasizes that God is free, and this implies that God is eternal and in that sense independent of the world. This is necessary if we are to posit, as the Bible does, that God is the originator of the world. Nevertheless, the identifying essence of God is determined by God's attributes, and these attributes can be discerned only in light of God's existence in relation to what is not-God—that is, only in relation to the world. Specifically, God exists in relation to the world in three modes—through being the world's creator, through reconciliation, and through consummation—each of which constitutes an attribute of the divine essence. The upshot is this: "God, through the creation of the world, made himself dependent on this creation and on its history."[128] For God to be identified with the divine rule, there needs to be a world that is ruled; and in this sense, God has chosen to become dependent upon his creation.

We might break this down sequentially. First, God is present to the world as its creator, as the source of life and goodness. Then, however, when the creatures God has created seek to establish their own independence, disavowing their dependence upon their creator, the existence of God tends to slip into the background. God becomes *Deus otiosus*. The created order becomes the order of death. God's very existence as creator of goodness and life becomes distant if not doubtful.

Second, for this reason God becomes present to the world as its reconciler through the sending of his Son. God must reconcile the fallen creation with himself if the deity of God as the creator is to be retained. The cross throws this into doubt again, however. In the tragedy of the crucifixion, not only is the divinity of the Son brought into doubt, so is that of the Father. Both creation and reconciliation seem to be threatened. In the resurrection of Jesus, however, the sonship of Christ and the divinity of the Father are victoriously affirmed.

Third, at the same time, the resurrection of Jesus Christ is the work of the Holy Spirit. It is the new life shared by believers now and hoped for in the future resurrection—the final reconciliation—of the fallen creation that had been subjected to death. In short, the existence of God as the creating Father, as the reconciling Son, and as the consummating Spirit is determined by the nature of God's relationship to the world.[129]

The Godhood of God as the world's creator is not conceivable without God's ruling in this world, without the existence of God's kingdom, without God's creatures giving praise to God, without our thanking God for our existence, and without our living the same life of love out of which all divine creativity emerges. With this in mind, Pannenberg argues that it will not be until the eschatological consummation of the world—and then with retroactive power—that the existence and hence the identity of God will be conclusively decided.

This does not require Pannenberg to uphold the idea of a divine becoming in history, as though the trinitarian God were the result of a developmental process. Rather, the eschatological event determines what will have been eternally true. On the one hand, historically conceived, the deity of God is dependent on the future coming of his eschatological kingdom. On the other hand, "the eschatological consummation is only the locus of the decision that the trinitarian God is always the true God from eternity to eternity. The dependence of his existence on the eschatological consummation of the kingdom changes nothing in this regard."[130]

The picture one gets here is of a God who jeopardizes his own divinity in order to engage in historical intercourse with created reality. Creation constitutes a divine risk of considerable consequence. Why would a free God choose this destiny? God chooses this path of creative dependence out of love for the world. Pannenberg believes, following Gregory of Nyssa, that infinite love is not just one of God's attributes but is identical with the divine essence itself. Pannenberg goes so far as to say that the divine persons as persons do not have the power to love. Rather, it is love in the I-Thou relationships that lifts them to a level of self-identity. The dialectic of otherness and unity internal to the divine life is virtually the source of the three persons.[131] This has an impact on the world. The love with which the Father loves the Son and that the Son reciprocates is also the love through which God loves the world and the love that, through the Holy Spirit, is poured into the hearts of those who have faith. This love makes us one with another and with God, just as the Father is one with the Son and the Son with the Father. To say "God is love" is to indicate the comprehensive expression of trinitarian fellowship as Father, Son, and Spirit. Hence, the three persons are only one essence, one love.

In sum, there are five post-Barthian commitments that place Pannenberg's proposal in tension with inherited trinitarian thinking. First, the idea of the Trinity cannot be deduced from a general concept of God; it depends upon an analysis of the revelation in Jesus Christ that explicates what is implicit. He rejects access to the Trinity through a metaphysics of monotheism or through Augustine's psychological analogies. Second, in contrast to the classic view that makes the Father the cause of the Son and Spirit, a view that makes causation effective in only one direction, Pannenberg advocates mutual causation. The mutuality of interpersonal relations determines the identity of each, including that of the Father as Father. Third, the self-differentiation through humble obedience on the part of the Son is paradoxically the source of the

Son's divinity. Rather than claim divinity for himself, Jesus subordinated himself totally to God, and in so doing placed himself in total communion with the Father. By submitting himself to the Father, he thereby becomes the eternal Son, the eternal correlate of fatherhood without which the Father could not be Father. This self-distinction constitutes his unity in God. Fourth, in contrast to the tradition, especially in the East, where the monarchy of the Father locates the source of all divinity in the first person, Pannenberg adds the dynamic of redemptive history through which the establishment of the kingdom of God provides acknowledgment and acclamation and, hence, divinity in relationship. Fifth, in Pannenberg's scheme, the Son and the Spirit share in the divine essence of the Father not just by being begotten or by proceeding from a divine origin, but also by contributing to the kingdom of the Father that is entrusted to the Son and returned to the Father through the Spirit.[132]

Because of all this, Pannenberg feels he can contend against Moltmann and in the face of criticisms from Judaism and Islam that only the trinitarian God, who in infinite love is not merely world-transcendent but also immanent in it, can be conceived in a consistently monotheistic fashion. Simply to set God over against the world as a transcendent reality, which is typical of other monotheisms, leaves us at best with a divine correlate to the world. Not a God involved in the world. Not a God who can reconcile the world unto Godself. It is finally only the God conceived in trinitarian terms who, without eliminating the distinction between God and creature, but rather just in the recognition of this distinction on both sides, can truly be "all in all."[133]

Where Have We Been? Where Are We Going?

We began this chapter by acknowledging that Claude Welch pointed the direction for mainstream trinitarian discussion in 1952 when he pointed to Barth.[134] Barth provided the point of embarkment in two ways: first, by giving priority to the threefold revelation of scripture and rendering suspect the inherited Greek understanding of deity as simple, *a se,* and uninvolved with the world; and, second, by suggesting that God's self-expression in the Word is itself an event that constitutes the one Godhead as Father, Son, and Spirit. What has developed since then has been a progression toward greater temporalizing of the self-constituting event of God and the drawing out of further consequences of understanding the divine essence in relational terms.

Eberhard Jüngel posits an *analogia relationis,* according to which we can have confidence that what is revealed in the economy of God's saving work is accurate—that is, it reveals that God is immanently trinitarian. Though he waffles a bit regarding whether to ascribe the modern sense of personhood to the three hypostases, he tends to assert with Barth that there is only one divine subject and center of divine activity. The net effect is that Jüngel, in the name of divine freedom, preserves an *a se* divinity with internal relations that are independent of God's relations to the world.

Karl Rahner formulates his rule—the economic Trinity is the immanent Trinity and vice versa—that at first blush seems to equate the economic and immanent dimensions of Trinity. Should the logical consequence of this be drawn, however, the nature of God-in-himself, *ad intra,* would become dependent upon God's relations *ad extra* with the world. But this is not the route Rahner himself takes. Others will. And, in concert with Barth and Jüngel and the tradition we have loosely identified with Athanasius, in Rahner the Godhead in its unity is designated the divine subject, and the persons are designated three "distinct manners of subsisting" for the one divine substance.

Jürgen Moltmann begins to draw out the full implications of Rahner's Rule. The history of Jesus Christ's passion—that is, the economy of salvation—becomes constitutive of the Trinity itself. In following this track, he tips the scales clearly if not excessively on the side of the Cappadocian theologians. For Moltmann, it is in each of the three hypostases that we find personhood—and in the modern sense of "person"—not in the divine unity or essence. There are three subjects, three centers of consciousness and activity. What we think of as the divine unity or essence is in fact a community. It is the relationships that each of the three persons share that constitute the *ousia* of God. Furthermore, these relationships are the result of historical interaction and mutual definition.

Catherine Mowry LaCugna extends Rahner's Rule, shifts the vocabulary, and collapses *theologia* into *oikonomia,* so that the internal trinitarian life of God becomes "God for us." LaCugna develops the concept of person-in-relationship, applies it both to intratrinitarian relations and to God's relationship with the world. What she leaves underdeveloped, however, is the impact that God's relationship to a world that is temporal might have on God's eternity. This challenge is taken up more directly by Jenson and Pannenberg.

Robert Jenson continues and extends the discussion of the constitutive relationship between God's historical relations with the world through the economy of salvation and God's eternal or immanent being. He further explicates the significance of the Cappadocians, especially Gregory of Nyssa, for apprehending that the divine unity is a relational unity. He offers to the discussion the helpful translation of *hypostasis,* "identity." But, like Barth and Jüngel and Rahner, he continues to maintain that there is a single divine subject, not three.

Wolfhart Pannenberg sides with Moltmann over against Jenson at this point, contending that there is not one divine subject but three. Taking a clear stand with the Cappadocians, Pannenberg elaborates that even the very divinity of the three persons is dependent upon their mutual relations and, furthermore, the identity of God is dependent upon God's relations to the history of the world. Moltmann, Jenson, and Pannenberg all seem to agree that the full application of Rahner's Rule is eschatological—that is, God's self-definition through the economy of salvation will become the immanent Trinity when God's work of creation and reconciliation is finally consummated.

What all—including Boff and the process theologians—seem to agree on is that the God revealed to us through scripture is by no means a simple monad who is satisfied with an existence unrelated to the temporal order of creation. This is a healthy inclination. It reflects well the biblical symbols of a God who loves the world enough to abandon the realms of isolated and protected divinity in order to enter the realm of fallen humanity. By entering into the order of finitude and ephemerality, God has at least in some way taken these dimensions up into the Godself. They are part of God's history. They are part of who God is. God has defined the Godself as one who is in relationship with something other—that is, in relationship with the world.

So when Karl Barth calls us back to the scriptural revelation or Claude Welch calls us back to a Christ-centered revelation, this is not simply the clanging of a conservative bell to return us to the nostalgia of our religious roots. It is a call for theological method to return and attend to the originary experiences with the God of Israel and the symbolism that continues to bear that experience. The doctrine of the Trinity reminds us of this.

It is this insight that impels us to rethink the classical ontology that was earlier invoked to buttress Christian monotheism. For centuries, it seems our church theologians began by thinking there is such a thing as a divine substance or a divine nature that is sharply distinguishable from other natures. Thus God could be God only insofar as God would possess this divine nature. Should God depart from this divine nature—which would be unthinkable—then God would cease to be God. Divinity perdures because it is thought to be a substance that is eternal, timeless, and therefore unchangeable. This also means it is unrelated, of course.

Thus, classical theists who think this way may object to what is being said here. They may worry that God's freedom or God's independence is being compromised when I speak of the divine process of self-constitution through intercourse with the world's history. They may begin to feel pity for a God who is stuck with a world he may not like or want and, hence, be something less than the omnipotent and exalted deity we have always believed in. But such fears are unwarranted. God has not lost any freedom by choosing to enter into a loving relationship with a world that needs him. Incarnation is rather an expression of divine freedom, not a capitulation to a metaphysical principle. In fact, it is the classical theists who would limit God's freedom if they were to insist that God could never abandon the so-called divine nature, that God is somehow stuck in timeless immutability and unable to undergo internal change through his history of external relationships.

In sum, the current impatience with substantialist metaphysics has opened the door to rethinking the way we conceive the doctrine of the Trinity. A reexamination of scripture in light of the contemporary mind is illuminating. We can see that we really have no warrant on the basis of the biblical symbols to posit the existence of such a thing as a divine substance or nature. There is simply God. God is God. It is God who defines what divinity is. We do not need to superimpose upon God an alleged divine nature and then ask God to conform to it. If in the process of historical self-expression God becomes one who is in relationship to the world of temporal transience, then so be it. And this is just the claim made by doctrines such as the incarnation in Jesus, the indwelling of the Holy Spirit, and the resulting Trinity. God is in the process of self-relating through relating to the world he loves and redeems. God is in the process of constituting himself as a God who is in relationship with what is other than God.

4. The Temporal and Eternal Trinity

[God] who lives ever, and for ever reigns,
In mystic union of the Three in One,
Unbounded, bounding all.

—*Dante,* Paradise, *Canto xiv, 28*

U p to this point we have been contending that the doctrine of the Trinity consists of an explication of the biblical symbols that tries to do justice to the paradox of the beyond and intimate dimensions of God's being, to what the philosophers of religion call God's absoluteness and God's relatedness. We have been assuming that the attribute of eternity belongs to the beyond, whereas temporality belongs to the intimate. If God defines the Godself through the event of the incarnation and through the spiritual presence in the world, then this will necessarily include the temporal dimension of the creation. This is how the absolute becomes related. Or, if we take eschatology seriously, we might say this is how the related becomes absolute.

One of the problems bequeathed to us from the classical period in theology is the tendency to disengage these two dimensions of the divine being, usually for the sake of protecting God's absoluteness at the expense of God's relatedness. One way in which this has been done is to attribute eternity to the immanent Trinity, and with this to define eternity so that God as Trinity comes out to be unrelated to the world of creation. Without its being intended, the net product is virtually two trinities, the primary one absolute and the second one related. The inherent fear at work here, it seems, is that temporal relatedness will so contaminate eternal absoluteness that we must render the latter immune. The problem with this is that the paradoxical tension present within the originary biblical symbols is sundered.

146

Although the doctrine of the Trinity borders on arbitrariness of function—associating the Father with the ineffable abyss and source of creative power, the Son with time-space objectivity, the Spirit with inner- and interpersonal subjectivity—the concept of perichoresis holds together the dimensions of absoluteness and relatedness in the single divine life. In its own way, the trinitarian idea maintains conceptually the paradoxical quality of the originary biblical symbols. The supposed split between the immanent and economic life of God, however, inadvertently severs the tie between the beyond and the intimate by cutting at a different angle.

The invocation of Rahner's Rule—that the economic Trinity is the immanent Trinity and vice versa—has the potential for healing. It permits the God of history to be the God of eternity. It also presses us to ask whether it is satisfactory to define eternity as timelessness, that is, to assume that eternity and temporality are mutually exclusive. We must ask if there is any way we can conceive of God's eternity as inclusive of the world's time. Our proposed answer will be positive, suggesting that an eschatological vision of eternity foresees the taking of world history up into the immanent life of the trinitarian God.

In the pages that follow we will explore this proposal.[1] To do so, the context of twentieth-century understandings of the world will need to be examined. This is because in our era the concept of time has undergone the closest scrutiny in the natural sciences, especially physical cosmology. If what we are to say theologically about time and eternity is to make conceptual sense, then we cannot overlook the many new insights regarding the temporal nature of our world. Our immediate task will be to review what we mean by eternity and by time both classically and in light of the theories of relativity, thermodynamics, and quantum physics. We will then move constructively toward the concept of the whole of time as eschatologically determined. This entails at least in part a temporalization of eternity. I will argue that the notion of a temporalized eternity can provide the framework for thinking through a concept of the Trinity in which both divine absoluteness and divine relatedness come to tensive and complementary expression.

What Is Eternity?

Eternity is one of the divine attributes that gives voice to the majestic sense of the divine as beyond, of God as transcendent. With poetic power, the psalmist proclaims that the God of Israel is untrammeled by the passage of time: "Your throne is established from of old; you are from everlasting" (Ps. 93:2). We can expect that "from everlasting to everlasting" steadfast will remain God's love (Ps. 103:17; 106:1), God's righteousness (Ps. 103:17), God's faithfulness (Ps. 117:2; 146:6), and God's glory (Ps. 104:31). The divine eye escapes our human limitations, "for a thousand years in your sight are like yesterday when it is past" (Ps. 90:4). The images employed here are those of strength and endurance and faithfulness through—not outside of—time. In the New Testament, the symbol of the Son raised in glory displays God as the victor over time and savior of time: "I am the Alpha and the Omega, the first and the last, the beginning and the end" (Rev. 22:13).

Although at one point Plato had described time as the image of eternity (*Timaeus* 37d5), the platonic tradition bequeathed to Christianity the tendency to see eternity in opposition to temporality, as timelessness. Time is one thing. Eternity is something different.

Eventually, the eternal became identified with the divine life itself, so that we find Boethius describing eternity as the totally simultaneous and perfect possession of limitless life *(aeternitas igitur est interminabilis vitae tota simul et perfecta possessio)*. Eternity is life in its fullness, without beginning or end, without coming to be or passing away, without the successiveness that cuts the present moment off from past and future. To have life in this way is to be God. To have life in some other way is to be a creature, subject to beginnings and endings and succession within time.[2]

What distinguishes a temporal creature, according to Boethius, is that it has only a present. Its past and future are absent. Even if its life be perpetual or endless, a temporal creature can never be whole.[3] To be whole one must be eternal, and to be eternal is to include the whole of one's temporality—past, present, and future—in a single moment. Thus, God, the only eternal being, is the only whole being.[4] Now a close look at Boethius' emphasis on the whole of time just may reveal that, in contrasting eternity with time, it may not be necessary to describe eternity as timelessness. Perhaps thinking of eternity as the whole of time—which thereby incorporates the reality of temporal passage—may be the better way to conceive this. For the most part, however, Boethius' notion of eternal simultaneity has been taken by the Christian tradition to mean timelessness, the absence of time.

Not so with Barth. As with so much else in our discussion of the Trinity so far, Karl Barth marks an important transition. Barth will not accept a simple opposition between eternity and time. "Eternity itself is not timeless," he writes. "It is the simultaneity and coinherence of past, present and future."[5] The simultaneity of past, present, and future from the point of view of eternity reflects the perdurance of Boethius' influence. Yet Barth goes on to insist that the eternal life of God is dynamized by the temporal actuality of the world. God is not immune to time; rather, God is eminently timely.

> Even the eternal God does not live without time. He is supremely temporal. For His eternity is authentic temporality, and therefore the source of all time. But in His eternity, in the uncreated self-subsistent time which is one of the perfections of His divine nature, present, past and future, yesterday, to-day, and to-morrow, are not successive, but simultaneous.[6]

What I question here is why we need to maintain simultaneity of past, present, and future? What does this add? It is nowhere implied in the doxological descriptions of God's steadfastness found in the Psalms. It contributes nothing to the notion of God's victory over the ravages of time. The idea that God can see all events simultaneously is probably a derivative from a Hellenized image of all-knowingness, of omniscience. The problem with this idea is that it tends to trivialize temporal succession, to render it ontologically exterior to eternal substance. It seems to me that one could construct a model of eternity as embracing temporality that has a yet-open future; that incorporates the redemption and transformation of nature and history, yet does not obviate the course of natural and historical events with the unnecessary positing of simultaneous viewing. One could think of God as having an unlimited future, of the divine being as everlasting, plus a plan for eschatological salvation that catches past and present up into a new chapter in the story of reality.

In sum, as a minimalist concept, eternity could refer to God's transcending the vicissitudes of temporal passage such as deterioration and death. As a maximalist concept, eternity could refer to the consummate unity of all things temporal and spatial that embraces the beginning and the end and everything in between. With this as a proposal, let us now turn to an analysis of the nature of time to see what befits or does not befit the life of the trinitarian God.

What Is Time?

We might define temporality, as Augustine did, as the one-after-the-otherness of events in succession. It is this that makes the distinction between past, present, and future possible. Yet we need to ask whether the successive character of events is cosmic in character or whether it is peculiar to the human perspective. Is the natural world itself temporal, or is temporality merely a structure of human consciousness that we superimpose on an otherwise timeless world? Some philosophers anchor time in human subjectivity. Aristotle began with the human soul as it counts moments of time. Immanuel Kant identified time along with space as categories of the mind. Martin Heidegger focuses on the human sense of the now in the face of anticipated death. On the other hand, there are philosophers who, though recognizing temporality in human consciousness, begin objectively. Plato, for example, held that our idea of time derived from the motion of the heavenly bodies. Here time in nature dictates time in the human psyche.

What we need to do at this point is explore the notion of temporal succession first in the human mind and then in the wider natural world of which this consciousness is a part. What we will find is that the message of twentieth century science is clear: time is as real for the natural world as it is for human consciousness. Reality is temporal. And, if God is engaged in an active relationship with the world, then God must both affect and be affected by the world's temporality.

As we pursue this line of thinking, we need to pause for a moment to observe that the familiar word "time" can actually refer to different things, at least three different things. First, the word "time" refers to passage. Thinking of Augustine, it refers to the quality of one-after-the-otherness that characterizes the successive events that constitute actual existence.

Second, the term "time" frequently refers to the measure of this passage. To answer the question, What time is it?, we normally look at our watch or clock. As we measure the passage of time, we refer to things that repeat themselves, such as the earth's daily rotation, the earth's yearly orbit around the sun, the rotation of neutron stars, the swinging of a pendulum, quartz crystal oscillation, or atomic oscillation. Such repetition provides the parameters that make measure of passage possible. What is amazing is that when these various modes of measure are compared, they seem to repeat in consonance with one another, although in varying degrees of accuracy. An enduring issue is whether time is merely a human psychological phenomenon or belongs to extrasubjective natural processes. To think of time as measure may indicate that it is merely psychological and, hence, possibly illusory. Yet our measuring devices are based upon natural rhythms as Plato long ago suggested, giving credence to the view that both passage and the measure of passage belong to nature proper. We will look at time both in human perspective and in nature in turn, and conclude that temporal passage is a characteristic of the physical world in which we live.

This brings us to the third use of the word "time." It refers to world history, to the realm of creation that is defined in part by passage, decay, and death. Time is shorthand for our reality. Theologically, time refers to God's creation and to the whole reality we hope will be eschatologically redeemed.

Past, Present, and Future: The Human Perspective

Human consciousness of time begins with an awareness of the present marked off by memory of the past and expectations for the future. It is a dynamic present, constantly lopping experiences off into past memories while actualizing what were previously future potentials. This is time's passage. Time here has an arrow, a one-directional movement from what has been to what is now and toward what will be.

Past and future are not actual. What is actual is the present. The present provides the perspective for apprehending past and future realities. What makes the past past and the future future is their respective relations to the present.

Contemporary Christian consciousness combines the sacramental and prophetic understandings of time. Whereas the sacramental understanding of time makes the past Christ and future Christ present to the worshipers, the prophetic vision places the present moment between promise and fulfillment. God's promise lies in the past, the fulfillment in the future. Here, God's presence is not actual. We employ our communal memory to look back toward a past reality, to the event of the crucifixion and resurrection of Jesus Christ. Although what we remember is what happened to Jesus, it has significance for us. That event constitutes for us a promise: as Christ rose from the dead two millennia ago, so also at some point in the future we too will rise into God's new creation. Our present moment is situated between the times, between God's past and God's future.

Whether in the prophetic form of past promise and future fulfillment or in the sacramental form of present presence, Christian consciousness apprehends God in temporal terms. The discrete succession of events, even divine events, never disappears from our awareness of God. Our human encounters with God are timely, as all human encounters must be. Our relationship with God is timely, as all human relationships must be.

The patristic theologians were acutely aware of the inescapable sense of the passing present that constitutes human consciousness, but they sought to drive a wedge between human temporality and divine eternity. God is not subject to time, insisted Augustine. Time is a constituent of creation, and the creator is not subject to what is created. Succession and passage may be all too familiar to us, but they are unknown to God. There is no temporal movement in eternity.

> You precede all past times in the sublimity of an ever present eternity, and you surpass all future times. . . . You have made all times, and you are before all times, and not at any time was there no time. . . . No times are coeternal with you, because you are permanent, whereas if they were permanent, they would not be times.[7]

Augustine had a motive for stressing God's permanence, for describing eternity as supratemporal. Temporality means passage, and passage means decay, and decay means death. If God is to be able to redeem, then God cannot be subject to decay and death. Time and death belong together. Eternity and life belong together. Therefore, it is important to deny passage and affirm permanence. "In the eternal nothing can pass away," he wrote, "but the whole is present."[8]

Yet the enduring problem raised by such a view is this: What is the relation between eternity and time? If eternity is defined as absence of succession, and if cause-effect relations are successive by nature, then it would appear that an eternal God could not cause temporal effects. Conversely, temporal causes could not have eternal effects. The two seem isolated from one another. In his desire to distinguish so sharply the temporal from the eternal, Augustine may have inadvertently isolated God from the affairs of creation. That this is not his intention, of course, is reflected in his notion of the whole. He affirms that "the whole is present" to God.

We find a position similar to Augustine's developed a few decades earlier by the Cappadocian theologian, Gregory of Nyssa. Here time and space belong to the creation. "The world's Creator laid time and space as a background," wrote Gregory, "to receive what was to be; on this foundation He builds the universe."[9] Time and space provide the framework or container, so to speak, within which human activity is carried on. Yet God, the creator, is not limited to temporal and spatial constraints.

But the existence which is all-sufficient, everlasting, world-enveloping, is not in space, nor in time: it is before these, and above these in an ineffable way; self-contained, knowable by faith alone; immeasurable by ages; without the accompaniment of time; seated and resting in itself, with no associations of past and future, there being nothing beside and beyond itself, whose passing can make something past and something future. Such accidents are confined to the creation, whose life is divided with time's divisions into memory and hope. But within that transcendent and blessed Power all things are equally present as in an instant: past and future are within its all-encircling grasp and its comprehensive view.[10]

As with Augustine, divine eternity for Gregory transcends time and escapes the ravages of passage. Yet it would not be quite right to describe eternity as completely divorced from time. One could interpret eternity as enveloping time.[11] If eternity envelopes time, then there must be some intercourse between the two. In at least a minimal fashion, the eternal is affected by the dimensions of the temporal.

What this presupposes regarding the cosmos is noteworthy. It presupposes a created order in which all things are subject to the same temporal sequence. Time and space constitute the cosmic corral within which all natural and historical activities take place. Time and space function like fences, marking the finite limits as well as the arena within which successive events may occur. Temporal and spatial coordinates are objective, at least in the sense that they apply to all things in the world and not merely to one's perspective.

This became the commonsense view of the world in the West. It was refined in the classical physics of Isaac Newton. Here space and time are distinguishable and absolute. Space provides the cosmos with an empty container within which each object finds its definite location. Time passes uniformly and universally, providing a single frame of reference for all observers.[12] Time's uniformity and universality make it possible for all observers to occupy the same present moment. The past and the future are the same for everybody. We all exist in the same shared "now."

According to this container cosmology, one's personal history exists in complete synchronicity with the history of the world. Theologically, this meant that we all share the same objective past with its Christ event. It also meant we all share the same objective future with its promised eschatology. All find themselves located on the same time line that runs from God's past promise through the present challenge of faith toward the future reward for our faith. The salvation of the world and one's own final salvation will be simultaneous.

Consequently, to conceive of the divine eternity as immune to temporal passage consisted in imagining an eternal now that sweeps up a single past and a single future into a single unchanging present. God is not eternity or infinity, wrote Newton, but eternal and infinite. He said that God endures forever and is everywhere present. By existing always and everywhere, God constitutes duration and space. Because every part of space exists *always* and every indivisible moment of duration exists *everywhere,* the Lord and maker of all things cannot be *never* and *nowhere.*

We can here easily distinguish the human from the divine point of view: humans see from a single point in space and time within the container, whereas God sees the entire temporal contents of the container. The human point of view is confined to the present actual moment divorced from its remembered past and from its expected future, a present actual moment that it shares with all of creation. The divine point of view is similarly confined to the present actual moment—for example, the moment of Jesus' crucifixion or our present moment—but in this case, past and future realities are also actual to God. Because past, present, and future are all actual for God, time is not simply a confinement.

In the twentieth century, this Newtonian container cosmology has been severely challenged by new developments in the physical sciences, and now the commonsense understanding of time requires considerable rethinking. Albert Einstein's special theory of relativity challenges the classic assumption that there exists a common frame of reference for all temporal events. The theological temptation since Einstein has been to respond by subjectivizing time, by isolating the human perspective from that of the rest of nature. Many twentieth-century philosophers and theologians have decided to existentialize time, thereby separating human consciousness from the surrounding cosmos. This is a form of ostrichism, however, a burying one's head in the sand. What is happening in the natural sciences is too important to avoid. Developments in thermodynamics, in particular, are of potentially great importance because they may be retrieving a shared arrow of time for both human subjectivity as well as nature on a macroscopic scale. The implications of such developments for conceiving cosmic temporality and divine eternity have yet to be worked out. To this task we now turn.

Time in Special Relativity Theory

With Albert Einstein's special theory of relativity we lose the sense of a universal present, and we end up with multiple frames of reference for the relation between past and future. Here, the only absolute is the speed of light at approximately 186,000 miles per second. Time and space are no longer absolutes. They are relativized.

Einstein's 1905 paper, "On the Electrodynamics of Moving Bodies," argued that just as the forces between electric charges are affected by motion, so also the very measurements of space and time are affected by motion. It has always been common sense that motion changes our location in space. Now Einstein was flouting common sense to say that motion affects the rate of temporal passage. The measurement of ticks of a clock in a fast moving rocket ship is different from that of an identical clock that remains back at the launch site. According to the principle of time dilation, clocks that are moving at a high rate of speed tick more slowly. When we move we change our rate of proceeding toward the future. Furthermore, space and time are so connected as to constitute a single continuum, space-time. Gone is the idea of a fixed spatio-temporal container within which events occur. All motion is relative, not to such a stationary container, but to various inertial frames of reference.

The vital invariant is the velocity of light. The speed at which light travels is constant for all observers. In free space, the velocity of light will have the same value regardless of the motion of the source or the motion of the observer. But each observer observes from a particular inertial frame of reference, within which all the laws of nature apply normally.

The velocity of the frame of reference is itself a factor. The twins paradox illustrates this. Suppose we take twin girls who, naturally, are the same age. We separate them by inviting one to take a seat in a rocket ship and fly off at a very high rate of speed to some destination in space. The other twin we leave here on earth to pursue normal day-to-day activities until her sibling returns some three or so years later. While traveling at a high rate of speed in the rocket ship, time for the astronaut twin would pass relatively slower, even though she would not notice anything out of the ordinary. When they would greet each other upon the space traveler's arrival home, their respective ages would be different. The space-traveling twin would be younger.

The twins paradox is hypothetical. Yet there is more than mere hypothetical speculation. There is empirical evidence. Experimenters have taken very precise atomic clocks and flown them around the earth in jet airplanes. Upon return they have been found to have functioned at slower rates than their control counterparts back on earth's surface. The net impact of this is that inertial frames of reference are contiguous— and hence relative—to one another.

Because, according to relativity, no single frame of reference embraces the whole of space-time, there is no universal present moment, no universal now. This means there is no common slice of space-time at which to divide past and future. The division between past and future will vary according to its inertial frame of reference. Past events for some observers will still be future for others. This does not mean, however, that the directionality of time is altered. For any two events that might be causally connected, the order of before and after will not be disrupted. Relativity does not mean that an effect may precede its cause. One cannot reach from one inertial frame of reference into another to change the causal past. According to the theory of relativity, time still travels in one direction, from the past through the present toward the future. The theory's insight is that it does so at varying rates.

The speed of light constitutes the cosmic absolute because it is universally the same. It is invariant. It also marks the upward limit. It cannot be exceeded by anything physical. It may not even be approached. As an object increases its velocity, its mass increases. At already high rates of speed, it takes a great deal of energy to increase that speed. It would take an infinite amount of energy for an object to attain the speed of light. Due to the equivalence of mass and energy ($E = mc^2$), at that speed its mass would become infinite. Because this is physically impossible, the speed of light commands the position of unattainability for any physical object within the universe.

In 1915 Einstein developed the general theory of relativity, and this added the factor of gravity. Gravity bends space. This means the universe as a whole may be curved. If so, we might leave our present location traveling in a particular direction and eventually find ourselves returning from the opposite direction. Time is also affected. The higher the gravitational pull, the slower the movement of clocks.

Relativity theory has the greatest impact on our concept of reality when we apply it to great distances and high rates of speed, as in astronomy. It pluralizes reality. In our expanding universe, where billions of light-years separate one galaxy from another, even at the speed of light it would take unimaginably long periods of time to communicate.

We are virtually isolated from most inertial frames of reference in the universe.

In our daily activity on earth, however, this seems to have very little consequence. We may operate with our traditional commonsense view that presumes there to be a single frame of reference for all events everywhere. We may delude ourselves into believing that our experience of time within our frame of reference is the absolute standard by which the rest of the universe is to be measured. This is understandable, but it is intellectually confining. We need to imagine how from the point of view of other observers in the universe we might appear to be moving in slow motion or with excessive rapidity. There is no universal standard time, no shared now that marks off a common past and a common future.

So we need to ask, What implications might relativity theory have for our understanding of God? Are we compelled to consign God to one frame of reference among others, preventing God from simultaneously viewing events in all other frames of reference? Does relativity theory in effect eliminate the Boethian idea of eternity?

J. R. Lucas thinks not. The traditional understanding of God's simultaneous apprehension of the course of events is not challenged by Einstein's insights. "The divine canon of simultaneity implicit in the instantaneous acquisition of knowledge by an omniscient being is not incompatible with the Special Theory of Relativity, but it does lead to there being a divinely preferred frame of reference."[13] This preferred frame of reference, of course, would be the eternal frame of reference. Eleonore Stump and Norman Kretzmann take a similar position, arguing that eternity constitutes a separate mode of existence that is not reducible to temporality. God's perspective is not thereby relativized by rendering it one temporal frame of reference among many others. It is a distinctively eternal present in which all events in all temporal frames of reference are perceived simultaneously.[14]

Ian Barbour follows a different but parallel route. He suggests that the limitations set by the speed of light on the speed of physical signals between distant points should not apply to God. This is because God is immanent at all points of the cosmos and in all events. God is neither at rest nor in motion relative to other systems. This means that God must influence each event in terms of the pattern of events relevant to its particular causal past, which, of course, is uniquely defined for each frame of reference.[15]

In similar fashion, Holmes Rolston identifies God with the whole of the cosmos by cultivating a panentheism. He suggests we think of God as "a Great Universal Mind" who stands astride the whole, imparting to it intelligibility. Physicists engaged in research are able to discover this intelligibility and, thereby, actually think God's thoughts after him. Rolston employs a superspatial model for conceiving of what God might be like. He does not identify God directly with ether or with a space-time plasma, but rather places God one or more orders of being beneath it. This permits him to say that space-time is God's creation while also saying that God is the very substrate of the world. Particles, waves, matter in motion, stars, planets, and persons are all warps in space-time. They are also wrinkles in God. As wrinkles in God, they are God's creation. Whether designated *Brahman* or *sunyata* or *Tao*, God is "in, with, and under" the energy pit out of which all comes; God is the prime mover lurking beneath the scenes.

As Rolston develops his idea of God, he moves God further and further away from the course of events and risks confining God to an isolated eternity. "God is not a spatiotemporal entity," he writes. "God is pure spirit. Having no velocity or mass, God has no time."[16] Relativity actually aids Rolston in understanding why for classical Christianity eternity is assigned to God and temporality assigned to the creation. God must be omnipresent, not local. So, he concludes, God has no space and time. But, evidently, Rolston does not want this to mean that God is isolated from the course of events. Quite the contrary. Not having space and time, God can gather past, present, and future into a single whole. Not being physical and not being subject to space-time, God can communicate instantly between various quadrants of the universe at speeds exceeding that of light. Omnipresence means instant communication. The result of Rolston's deliberations is a panentheism with God-in-all and all-in-God, permitting God to materialize and energize at leisure.

In effect, Barbour and especially Rolston have not taken us very far beyond where Gregory, Augustine, and Boethius had left us. God's eternity still transcends the temporal movement of the creation. What is added by reflections on relativity is that the creation now has multiple temporal movements instead of just one. God's interventions into the created order now have to be tailor-made to specific frames of reference, but this marks only minimal change from the previous view. What remains is the larger problem: How can a timeless God experience or act upon a temporal world?[17] For God either to cause a wrinkle in the world or for the world to cause a wrinkle in God, God would in some way have to be temporal. But the difficulty is this: if the first thing we posit of God is that the divine life is eternal and therefore external to the creation, there is no way that temporal action or experience can apply meaningfully to the divine life.

Rolston offers a clue but does not follow up on it. "If God is anywhere known," he writes, "it will be as God 'comes through' in our space-time, relative to our local existence, as God is, so to speak, locally incarnate."[18] The key is local incarnation—that is, the entering of God into the created order and taking up residence within a single inertial frame of reference. Through such an incarnation we would then find God on both sides of the ledger, both eternal and temporal, both universal and particular, both acting and acted upon. This, I take it, belongs to the essence of the trinitarian claim. The weakness of the work of Barbour and Rolston is that they try to solve the problem by developing the idea of God apart from the trinitarian claim.

Time's Arrow in Thermodynamics

As we suggested during the discussion of relativity theory, the overall movement of time is in one direction, toward the future. If there were any doubts, the second law of thermodynamics would seem to eliminate them. Following on the heels of the first law regarding the conservation of energy, the second law sets a boundary condition so that energy may never flow spontaneously from a cold body to a hot one. The natural movement is always from hot to cold, never the reverse. Alternatively put, the movement is from order to disorder. Entropy is the measure of disorder. In closed systems that have no input of energy from outside and the law of conservation applies, entropy increases uniformly until a state of equilibrium has been reached. At equilibrium no more energy can be spent. If certain conditions prevent a system from going to complete equilibrium, then it does the next best thing: it goes to a state of minimum entropy production—that is, to a state as close to equilibrium as possible. The upshot of the second law is that time is asymmetrical: entropy increases in the direction of the future, never the past. The temporal movement of the physical world is irreversible. Time has an arrow.[19] Time is unidirectional.

The second law applies inexorably to closed systems. In open and far-from-equilibrium systems that interact with their wider environment and receive energy input, however, creative fluctuations take place. High energy input at first increases randomness and chance, that is, chaos. Chaos may lead to previously undetermined possibilities. Sometimes a bifurcation point is reached. At this point the system may disintegrate into further chaos. Or it may leap to a new, more differentiated and higher level of order. The fluctuating chaos becomes the source out of which new order emerges. Ilya Prigogine calls this "order through fluctuation."[20] In short, chaos in an open system can be creative.

Chaos and creativity lead to what some physicists call "depth." Depth is organized complexity. In a manner recalling the earlier work of Teilhard de Chardin, physical cosmologists at the end of the twentieth century are tracking the process of complexification in the cosmos. This is the evolution from rather simple beginnings to star and planet formation, the origin of life, the rise of consciousness, and other uncountable creations of higher levels of complexity. With this as nature's past, we can only predict future creations of unpredictable depth. This means time's arrow has two subarrows. The subarrow of entropy presses us toward a future of overall dissipation and degeneration. The subarrow of depth presses us toward localized depth and higher levels of organized complexity. Entropy is the price paid for depth.

Although some scientists hold out hope that depth will win out over entropy, the standard view is that localized depth may peak our optimism for a period; but in the long run, entropy will eventually bring the entire universe to a cold equilibrium—that is, to a heat death. This is because we cannot work with the notion that the universe as a whole is an open system receiving energy input from outside. If there were such an energy source, our notion of the universe would expand to include it, and then we would be right back where we started. The result is that the second law of thermodynamics applies to the cosmos as a whole. The entire universe finds itself in a monodirectional movement from hot to cold, from order to disorder. It is headed for a future equilibrium in which all its energy will be forever dissipated. Although chaos will be creative of new order in local subsystems, cosmic time is irreversible, and all things will eventually wind down to a state of maximum entropy.

When combined with the big bang cosmology, the second law suggests a finite history for the cosmos. We can press our thoughts backwards to a point perhaps 15 to 20 billion years ago, to $t = 0$ (time = 0), when everything began. It began with a singularity of maximum density and heat. After the bang, matter shot out in all directions. The universe is now expanding and cooling. Oh, yes, certain far-from-equilibrium systems such as galaxies are temporarily creating order out of chaos, but the overall movement is toward greater entropy. If the universe is open—that is, if there is insufficient gravity to cause it to recollapse—then it will expand and cool for another 65 billion years or so. Then the energy of the cosmos will be so dissipated that no new order will be able to arise. The end will be death by dissipation.

It is important to note that the concept of temporal irreversibility is not merely the product of human subjectivity. It is more than just a projection of the human consciousness of past and future. We do not superimpose a mental idea of time on an otherwise timeless natural world. Rather, nature itself is speaking and telling us that it is temporal and monodirectional. "We are becoming more and more conscious of the fact that on all levels, from elementary particles to cosmology, randomness and irreversibility play an ever-increasing role," writes Prigogine. *"Science is rediscovering time."*[21]

What is said here about the scientific understanding of nature should, in my judgment, elicit theological reflection in a number of ways. Of most importance, it permits us to look at nature historically. Nature can be thought of as historical. For nearly two centuries now, theologians have been saying that "God works in history." God's actions are events. Contingent historical events in which divine action is identified become the basis for Christian claims regarding ultimate reality. Thus, Wolfhart Pannenberg can assert that "history is the most comprehensive horizon of Christian theology."[22] Pannenberg is inspired in part by physicist C. F. von Weizsäcker, who believes nature has a history. "Man is indeed a historic being," says von Weizsäcker, "but this is possible because man comes out of nature and because nature is historic herself."[23]

Just how God acts in the history of natural events deserves some attention. We might ask, Does God necessarily act in every natural event? Or, are natural events normally *sui generis* so that we can say that God acts in some events but not others? Arthur Peacocke opts for the former. He contends that God's activity is a constituent component of all natural activity within the universe. He holds that "we must conceive of God as creating within the whole process from beginning to end, through and through, or he cannot be involved at all."[24] God is continually creative; and God prompts creativity within nature. The dialectic of chance and law are the means whereby creativity is elicited and depth achieved. Taking what we have said about Prigogine's notion of creative fluctuation whereby order emerges from chaos, Peacocke applies it to evolutionary appearance of biological systems. Peacocke then asserts that the interplay of chance and law makes possible the emergence of living structures and propels them through evolution. He emphasizes that the history of nature is open. It is a fabric of turning points, open at every step to new choices and new direction. Randomness and chance are responsible for this openness, and God is responsible for randomness and chance. "It is as if chance is the search radar of God," he writes, "sweeping through all the possible targets available to its probing."[25]

What about time? Peacocke acknowledges that time in relativistic physics is an integral and basic aspect of nature. Matter, energy, and space-time constitute together the created order. "Hence, on any theistic view," he says, "time itself has to be regarded as owing its existence to God, something Augustine long ago perceived." This "owing its existence to God" is the central core of our understanding of the *cosmos as creation.* "Thus," he continues, "the fundamental otherness of God must include the divine transcendence of time."[26] Note how Peacocke places together transcendence of time with God's otherness. Yet this otherness and transcendence is not all there is to God. God is also immanent to the natural processes. Peacocke strongly advocates a doctrine of *creatio continua,* continuous creation. God is continually producing new forms of emergent matter within the flow of nature's history. God creates continuously, and this creative activity takes place within time.

This is all well and good. But let us carry the discussion a bit further by asking, Might we conceive of the eternal God as enveloping time? After all, time seems to have edges, fences beyond which we might peer into eternity. A thermodynamic big bang cosmology has a beginning and an end. It originates with a very dense, very hot singularity, and at the moment it begins to expand, time begins. Did God act at the beginning? Did God exist prior to the beginning? Was it God who created the original singularity? Did God create that singularity out of nothing, *creatio ex nihilo?* Was it God who lit the fuse on the original dynamite that exploded with the big bang? Did the first moment of cosmic history drop from divine eternity to follow its independent path of successive events?

Then, what about the future end? Will God be there to sweep up the dissipated debris after it is all over? Will God then take the history of the cosmos up into the eternal, or will its dispersed remnants forever lie there in memoryless equilibrium? Does God have sufficient patience to wait until the end, or might God intervene earlier to stop the inevitable? In either case, does the eternal reality have what it takes to redeem what becomes lost in the epic of temporal passage? Whether looking backward or forward, should we look beyond the edges of time for God's eternity?

Time's Edge in Quantum Creation

Stephen Hawking is a physical cosmologist who would say no to such questions. Hawking is fully aware that if time has edges then God-talk could begin to make scientific sense. He fully recognizes that the concept of the absolute beginning implied in the standard big bang model implies the existence of God. The notion of a beginning means that there is a front edge to the cosmos, and the acknowledgment of an edge requires us to ask what lies beyond the edge. "If there is an edge," he once told Renée Weber in an interview, "you would really have to invoke God."[27] Yet Hawking wants to avoid God. So he goes hunting for a theory that will eliminate the edge. He does this by challenging the hypothesis that there once was a singularity prior to the cosmic expansion we know as the big bang.

Hawking's argument begins with the assertion that relativity theory is not enough to solve the problem of the nature of the originating singularity. Why? Because relativity theory applies only to the macrouniverse, to the cosmos in expansion. And, because the alleged original singularity was in fact very small and very dense, we need to include another theory that applies more appropriately. That theory is quantum mechanics. The central thesis of Hawking's work is this: the theories of relativity and quantum mechanics combine into a single uniting *quantum theory of gravity*. This means ultimately that we might be able to describe the universe by a single mathematical model that would be determined by the laws of physics alone. Incorporated into the uniting theory is Heisenberg's uncertainty principle. This implies, among other things, that the subsequent course which the developing universe would follow was not fixed by original boundary conditions. In fact, there are no boundary conditions for either time or space. There is only a curved space-time dimension, which is finite; but it does not take us back to a point of absolute zero, before which were was no time. Time has no edge, he says.

What Hawking has produced is a mathematical model of a block universe of space-time in which no present moment can be isolated from its past and future. The mathematics of his model leads him to distinguish between real time and imaginary time. Real time is time's arrow that we experience as sequence. Imaginary time cannot distinguish directions in space nor the difference between forward and backward in time. This imaginary time Hawking introduces as necessary to implement his proposed unification of gravity with quantum mechanics.

> In real time, the universe has a beginning and an end at singularities that form a boundary to space-time and at which the laws of science break down. But in imaginary time, there are no singularities or boundaries. So maybe what we call imaginary time is really more basic, and what we call real is just an idea that we invent to help us describe what we think the universe is like.[28]

Might there be any theological implications to this loss of time's edge? Most definitely, says Hawking himself. To Hawking's reading, there are antitheological implications. He believes the universe needs no transcendent creator to bring it into existence at $t = 0$, nor does it need God to tune the laws of nature to carry out a divinely appointed evolutionary purpose. If no edge, then no God.

> The quantum theory of gravity has opened up a new possibility, in which there would be no boundary to space-time and so there would be no need to specify the behavior at the boundary. There would be no singularity at which the laws of science broke down and no edge of space-time at which one would have to appeal to God or some new law to set the boundary conditions for space-time. One could say: "The boundary condition of the universe is that it has no boundary." The universe would be completely self-contained and not affected by anything outside itself. It would neither be created nor destroyed. It would just BE.[29]

One major effect of this quantum gravitational vision is to untie the relation between time's arrow and the essential nature of the universe. By no means does this reduce time's arrow to a mere psychological phenomenon experienced in human consciousness. Temporal passage remains physical and suprasubjective. Yet unidirectional temporal passage now applies to regions of physical activity within the universe. The cosmos at a quantum level, however, is judged to be atemporal.

Now, if we wished to press the point, Hawking's atemporal mathematical model of the universe would begin to look somewhat like the timeless eternity with which we began this discussion. It transcends while enveloping regions of temporal passage. And it does so without God.

What motivates Hawking to follow this path? Is it the desire to clean up the mathematics describing the transition from the quantum to the temporal world? Perhaps. Yet one cannot avoid asking about the possible role played by religious skepticism, a skepticism that comes from beyond the realm of strictly scientific warrants. Hawking admits that his denial of an original singularity is based only on a proposal for a future theory. He grants that no strong case can be made. The result seems to be a thin smoke screen blurring an apparently antireligious agenda. He belongs to that subculture of natural scientists who, on the one hand, drive as big a wedge as possible between rational science and allegedly irrational religion, while, on the other hand, invoking scientific discoveries to buttress their belief that belief in God is out of date. Carl Sagan, writing in the introduction to Hawking's book *A Brief History of Time,* somewhat smugly advertises Hawking's argument for "the absence of God" on the grounds that there is "nothing for a Creator to do."

Let us treat this theologically. Let us ask, Just what kind of God are Hawking and Sagan rejecting? What they are rejecting, it seems to me, is the "God-of-the-gaps." What they object to is the God affirmed by the kind of physico-theology that once sought to find a divine explanation wherever scientists failed to give us a natural explanation. In the case of the big bang in particular, many of us are tempted to think of God as the one who set the original boundary conditions, who brought time and space out of a prior nothingness. The point of the Hawking proposal is to shut this door to divinity.

To be more precise, the God that is being rejected here is the God of deism. According to deism, God brought the world into existence at the beginning and then departed to timeless eternity, leaving the universe to run according to its built-in natural laws. God has only one job to do for the deists, namely, create at the beginning. Thus, if the Hawking proposal holds, God is not needed for this.

In light of this challenge, we need to observe that Christians, along with their monotheistic comrades, Jews and Muslims, are not deists. They are theists. The theistic belief is that, in addition to God's creative work at the beginning, God is still active in world events today. The temporal trinitarian understanding of God I am trying to develop here is theistic in that it affirms an ongoing personal concern for the world on the part of an active divine life.

British theoretical physicist C. J. Isham has taken the Hawking pro-posal into account and argues that the Christian doctrine of divine cre-ation could still make good sense, even in the form of *creatio ex nihilo*. Rather than view it simply as crossing time's front edge from pretempo-ral existence into temporal existence at t = 0, God's divine work of cre-ation should be seen as ongoing. The reasonableness of divine creativity does not depend on positing time's edge. What we ordinarily think of as the initial event undergoes a change of status in Isham's theory. The positing of an initial event that originates the macrouniverse arises from within a more comprehensive quantum model in which space-time is a single mathematical entity. Time is finite even without a beginning edge. If we are to draw theological implications, says Isham, we should think that all "times" are copresent to God, and the ongoing indeterminacy of quantum processes represents the continuing activity of God's bringing something out of nothing. What is at stake for the theist is to understand God as a contemporary factor—not merely a past factor—in world events. This means that God's creative work is not limited to a one-time event in the ancient past, but it continues now, and we can expect more things yet in the future. Today's research in physics challenges us to think through what this means.[30]

What is significant about pondering time's finitude is that it leads to questions regarding a possible eternal reality beyond it. Does time have an edge, or does the quantum realm replace eternity as the time-less realm beyond time's edge? Even Hawking and Sagan in their skep-ticism cannot avoid entering into theological discussion. Finite time cannot readily account for itself. It takes eternity or quantum origina-tion or both to understand it.

Eternity as the Whole of Time

If time has no edges, can we think of the quantum realm as the whole of time? Or better, if time has edges, can we think of a whole of time between the edges? And if we can conceive of a whole to time, could we then put it together somehow with the idea of eternity? Wolfhart Pannenberg is perhaps the most helpful contemporary scholar here.[31] He is seeking to retrieve the insights of Plotinus for the purpose of understanding the relation between eternity and time. What he finds in Plotinus is the notion of eternity as the whole of time.

Plotinus followed Plato by defining time as the image of eternity. But he could not reason as Plato did: the circular motion of the heavenly bodies provides the basis for temporal consciousness and calculation. Plotinus could not make time dependent upon motion, because he thought motion was dependent upon time. Time is prior. So, rather than appeal to the sun and the stars in motion, Plotinus appealed to the human soul (and to the world soul) for mediation between eternity and time. What the soul can apprehend is that the eternal is the whole of life, namely, "life that is fixed within Sameness, because the whole is always present in it—not now this, then another, but all simultaneously" in the sense of "completion without parts."[32]

The human soul for Plotinus, of course, has fallen from eternity into time and now experiences temporal reality in terms of parts and intervals that are alien to eternal reality. Instead of a single undivided moment, the human soul undergoes the passage of moment after moment. What was a whole is now fragmented into parts. Yet, despite this association of time with the fall, what attracts Pannenberg to Plotinus is the notion that there is a future return to wholeness. He interprets Plotinus to be saying that the eternal whole is present in the sense that it hovers over the parts as a future whole or totality. The whole becomes the future goal of all striving within the realm of the temporally finite. The path to this goal is time. "In short," writes Pannenberg, "when the theory of time is oriented toward the eternal totality, the consequence is a primacy of the future for the understanding of time."[33]

Although definitely sympathetic to the notion of eschatological wholeness, I am less certain than is Pannenberg that Plotinus can be garnered for support. Plotinus' idea of eternity is immune to temporal succession and also to the part-whole dialectic. He states that eternal life is "instantaneously entire, complete, at no point broken into period or part." Eternity as "Ever-Being" can have "no this and that; it cannot be treated in terms of intervals, unfoldings, progression, extension; there is no grasping any first or last in it."[34] If eternity cannot grasp any first or last, we must ask Pannenberg, how can it envelope and enfold the temporal history of the world without annihilating it?

To make matters more difficult, it appears that Plotinus repudiates the dynamic of the future that Pannenberg seems to find so fruitful. On the one hand, Plotinus admits that for engendered temporal beings to have life they must have a future. On the basis of this observation, Plotinus speculates regarding an engendered All or totality, "in so far as it is a thing of process and change."[35] Such a totality would keep hastening toward its future, dreading to rest, seeking to draw all things into itself. Such a whole understood as totality would seek perpetuity by way of futurity. It appears that this is what Pannenberg has latched on to when pressing Plotinus into the service of eschatological wholeness.

Yet, on the other hand, this generated All is not what Plotinus identifies with eternity. Rather, eternity has to do with what he calls "the primals." The primals exist in an unbroken state of blessedness with no aspiration for things to come in the future. They are whole now. "They, therefore, seek nothing, since there is nothing future to them, nothing external to them in which any futurity could find lodgement." The primal existents that are incapable of increment or change make up the resident plurality within the eternal. And the eternal is the divine.

> Eternity, thus, is of the order of the supremely great; it proves on investigation to be identical with God: it may fitly be described as God made manifest, as God declaring what He is, as existence without jolt or change; and therefore as also the firmly living. . . . Thus, a close enough definition of Eternity would be that it is a life limitless in the full sense of being all the life there is and a life which, knowing nothing of past or future to shatter its completeness, possesses itself intact for ever.[36]

This is not a doctrine of eternity understood as everlastingness, as reality with an unlimited future. It is, rather, eternity understood as timelessness, as an unqualified now with everything in full manifestation.

It seems to me that it would be better to say Plotinus is at least partially mistaken and proceed to develop a concept of eschatological wholeness in which unlimited futurity plays a decisive role. Eternity must include everlastingness if it is to be understood as living and creative. The eternity in which we place our hope consists in the integration of parts and whole and the consummation of temporal history, not in their virtual annihilation into an everpresent now.

This is what Pannenberg is rightly pursuing. Though wrongly attributing it to Plotinus, Pannenberg's eternal whole consists in the integrated unity of finite being. He wants to see the "participation in the interrelatedness of everything divided by time at the moment of eternity."[37]

Temporal Holism

Pannenberg's argument demonstrates that there is a theological warrant for a holistic principle. There is also a scientific warrant. Holism—sometimes spelled wholism—is now playing a significant role in current physical and biological theory. Negatively, it is known as antireduction-ism. Positively, it is known as top-down causation.

In its positive form as downward causation, holism functions as an explanation for the behavior of complex organized systems and the emergence of living organisms. The principle that the whole is greater than the sum of its parts makes it antireductionistic. The behavior of a living organism, though dependent upon its physical and chemical components and their respective laws, cannot be adequately explained on the basis of those physical and chemical or even biological laws. A qualitatively new factor has entered the picture, depth in the form of a higher principle of ordering that derives from the organism as a whole. Although in complete harmony with the underlying physical and chemical and biological processes, the holistic principle frees the ordered system or organism for independent behavior that cannot be reduced to those underlying processes.[38]

There is more than antireductionism going on here. Holism recognizes that the higher levels of systems organization and even the level of individuality in living selves act downward on the lower physical processes, thus pressing these physical processes into the service of the higher level ends. Water molecules remain what they are even when whirled about by a vortex. Metabolism remains what it is, even though a person's decision either to play tennis or to go to sleep will have an impact on its rate. "The component description does not contradict the holistic description," writes Paul Davies; "the two points of view are complementary, each valid at their own level."[39]

Can we extrapolate the holistic principle to cover the cosmos as a whole? We cannot apply top-down causation to the universe in the literal sense because, as we saw in our discussion of special relativity, the universe is not united in a single causal nexus. Yet we must ask: can we conceive of a temporal holism? On analogy with top-down causation, can we conceive of a temporal whole to the cosmos precipitated by an eschatological event that brings fulfillment to all inertial frames of reference?

In making this conceptual move, we need to make three qualifications. First, we need to avoid the temptation to vitalize the world. Because the most complex system we empirically know is that of the living organism, especially the human organism, we will be tempted to extrapolate and describe the cosmos as an even greater living organism. We might then want to ascribe to God the distinct principle of life.

The problem with such a vitalization is that it adds an unnecessary component, a life-force or soul or something that goes beyond what the notion of holism warrants. In addition, if we were to divinize the living whole, we would risk falling into pantheism. The problem with pantheism is that it threatens the idea of God's transcendence. God is more than the animating principle of the world. God is more than the world. God would have to be more than the world if redemption is possible.

The second qualification has to do with time. The whole of which we speak theologically is the whole of history. It is more than simply a higher principle of systems organization that explains what is happening at any given moment. Eschatological wholeness has to do with fulfillment, with the consummation of the entire history of creation that preceded it. Wholeness requires an eternal reality that sweeps up all that has been into a divine presence that affirms its original spatio-temporal actuality while redeeming it for the good of the grand whole. It requires a completeness of time.

The third qualification is a suggestion of prolepsis. This would help constitute the trinitarian dimension. The scientific model of holism makes sense regarding the dialectic of whole and parts. The whole is dependent upon the parts, yet the parts function according to the bidding of the whole. Causation is both upward and downward. So far, so good. Yet, whereas in the scientific model the parts are present within the whole and exhaust the physical being of the whole, in trinitarian theology we want to add that the whole is also present among the parts. In the incarnation of Jesus Christ, the whole is present as one part among others. The eternal has become temporal. The infinite has become finite. And the work of the Holy Spirit anticipatorily binds the part to the whole, the present to the future, the expectation to its fulfillment.

Tracing Our Trajectory

Where have we been to this point? We began by asking how God can be both absolute and related, posing the question in terms of the tie between eternity and time. We began by asking, How can an eternal God act in, and be affected by, a temporal world? The question arises as a problem when eternity is assumed to be a state of timelessness that contrasts sharply with the temporal world in which humanity and the rest of nature are condemned to exist. What this calls for, I have suggested, is that we modify our concept of eternity so that it is not thought to stand in exclusion of what is temporal. Eternity needs to transcend time, to be sure; but it need not cancel or annihilate time. If God's creating and redeeming action is to be effective in this world, then there must be some fashion in which God can be affected by the temporal process. If eternity is to be identified as the locus of our salvation, it must be an eternity "for us."

The path to the answer I have been suggesting is found in the concept of God as Trinity. As Trinity, God is both eternal and temporal. God is the transcendent and hence eternal source of the created world. God is also immanent to the world as one finite being among other beings, as incarnate in Jesus of Nazareth, as a single objectifiable person in a single temporal-spatial frame of reference. God is also paradoxically immanent and transcendent as the Spirit, which ties times together and which promises the consummate unity of the whole of time in the eschatological kingdom of God.

In attending to our contemporary context, we have made a brief inquiry into the concepts of time on the frontier of twentieth-century physics. Because the subject matter of physics is nature, this discussion has taken us quickly beyond the mere subjectivity of temporal passage we experience as human beings into the encompassing realm of cosmology. The subject matter is nature itself, not merely human nature. The subject matter is the whole of creation's history, not merely human subjectivity within it. It readies us to think of God's saving work in light of the biblical symbol of the "new creation."

What we found in contemporary physics is that thermodynamics and the big bang cosmology seem to support the notion that nature as a whole is characterized by a monodirectional arrow of time. Although the special theory of relativity indicates that there exist differing inertial frames of reference that prevent the whole of the cosmos from experiencing a simultaneous present, this does not obviate the overall direction of the cosmos as moving from the past toward the future. This is challenged in part by Stephen Hawking's quantum gravitational pretheory of creation, in which the arrow of time is limited to regions of the universe such as ours; it allegedly does not apply globally to the universe itself. According to Hawking's view, nature itself takes on qualities of a timeless eternity enveloping time, but it does so without the benevolent activity of a creating and redeeming God. What this leaves open as a scientific issue is whether or not time has edges. What this leaves open as a theological issue is whether we can speak of God's eternity as transcending time's edges that may or may not exist.

The Hawking challenge is significant. Given the path we have been blazing, following the theological compass in seeming consonance with theories about the big bang and entropy, Hawking's quantum demur appears on the horizon as a roadblock. What should we do? We have three options. The first option is to assume that the Hawking roadblock makes the path impassible. We might thereby conclude that his theory of quantum creation disconfirms what we have thought to be the relationship between Trinity and temporality. The second option also assumes that the Hawking roadblock is impassible. But, rather than accept disconfirmation, we might want to return to our point of departure and set out in a way that would bypass it. The most common method would be to invoke the two-language theory—that is, to adopt the assumption that theology and science each play separate language games and do not converse with one another. We could assume that we could engage in *strictly theological Trinity talk* and simply ignore what is said in physical cosmology. A third option is to assume that the Hawking roadblock is passible by driving around it, by continuing down the theological road looking for scientific theories that seem to provide greater consonance with theologically guided perspectives. A close look will show that the Hawking roadblock is by no means anchored solidly in concrete. It is speculation not even yet at the status of a theory. It is a mental extrapolation of the assumption that mathematical singularities cannot exist. It is an interesting idea, but it is far from empirically confirmed. Therefore, it is by no means irrational to drive around it and follow the notion of the monodirectionality of a time span with edges, with a beginning and an ending. A fourth option is to assume that the Hawking roadblock is passible and argue from within the Hawking position that time in the macrouniverse—the actual universe in which we live—does in fact have edges. This is consistent despite Hawking's mathematical model of the quantum world with its imaginary time without edges. The quantum realm is the edgeless envelope, so to speak, within which beginning and end occur. Hence, we may still assert with scientific confidence that the universe has a front edge, a beginning, within the quantum realm. We may further assert with confidence that monodirectional time characterizes the overall direction. On the basis of what we know, I am recommending that we continue forward with the trinitarian inquiry with the third and fourth options in mind. Let us see what conceptual fruit it might bear. If at some future date we find that this path of inquiry is fruitless or that Hawking's speculation becomes fact, then we may want to stop and either give up or change direction. In the meantime, we have set a course based on the reasonableness of thinking of the cosmos in terms of a temporal movement from beginning to end.

This has led us to raise the question of the whole of time. This question prescinds from the theological agenda, because the unity of temporal history is implied by the notions of a single God in creative and redemptive relation to a single world. The Christian notion of eschatology points to a future event initiated by God that will not simply put an end to temporal history; it will unify it and fulfill it. The theological vision seems to warrant a principle of cosmic holism. To think of the cosmos as a temporal whole is conceivable in the context of thermodynamics and big bang cosmology, but how this might be done in the context of Hawking's proposal has yet to be worked out.

We have noted further that the scientific idea of downward causation appears to have sufficient consonance with the holistic principle that we might try to press it into theological service. Top-down causation will have limited application, however, because, although we can stretch it to bind creation's history into a unity, it does not say enough about God's action in history. We will need to rely on the originary biblical symbols as our source for this.

To move the discussion forward, I would like to propose some theses. I offer these theses in the spirit of *theologia viatorum,* of theology on-the-way toward more adequate conceptualization. My proposals are not offered with the intent of seeking canonization on the order of Nicene orthodoxy. They reflect rather the combination of explication and construction with the heuristic motive of promoting further theological reflection.

Trinitarian Theses

1. To understand God as Trinity in the economy of salvation requires that God be both temporal and eternal. What we refer to as the incarnation in the second person of the Trinity places the divine presence in a temporal frame of reference as one objectifiable being among others. Jesus of Nazareth is other to us. He is similarly other from the perspective of the first person of the Trinity, the Father. This otherness permits us to think of him as God's Son while, at the same time, due to the unifying work of the Holy Spirit, he constitutes the presence of God in the finite world.

This interpretation of the incarnation presses for a divine involvement in the temporal world that may go further than the ontology of the Chalcedonian period. According to the classic Christology of one person (one: *hypostasis*) with two natures (two: *physis*), the divine nature communicates its attributes to the human nature, but not the reverse. The incarnate Christ, therefore, is a divine *hypostasis* without a human *hypostasis* (*anhypostasis*), a divine person with both a divine and a human nature. This permitted theologians of the Chalcedonian period to combat patripassianism—that is, the belief that the Father suffered on the cross. Jesus Christ in his human nature suffered, to be sure; but his divine nature was said to be exempt. What motivated this scheme was categorical opposition to subjecting the immutable God to passage and decay. Hidden and disguised within the intricacies of the Chalcedonian ontology is the living legacy of docetism. In contrast, my first thesis is more forcefully antidocetic than Chalcedonianism because it posits with utter seriousness the experience of God as human within finite time, an experience that includes passage, decay, and even death. The saving power of God comes not from deafness to the communication of human attributes to the divine. Rather, God's saving power comes from the divine future that transforms the dead into the living, the old creation into the new creation.

I press this interpretation as a more adequate explication of the biblical symbols in light of trinitarian thought. The symbol of the Father communicates the sense of the beyond, the eternal and ineffable abyss. The symbol of the Son communicates a sense of the intimate, of Emmanuel, of God subjected to the vicissitudes of ordinary existence just as we are. The Holy Spirit as love binds the two, assuring us that we are speaking here of one divine reality, not two. And, in the process of binding Father and Son, the Spirit incorporates us. We are incorporated presently through faith. The promise in which we live and hope looks forward to the future, wherein the whole history of nature will be transformed and incorporated into the everlasting Father-Son unity of love.

The love of Father and Son into which the Spirit incorporates us is everlasting; that is, it stands despite the passage of time with its accompanying deterioration and death. The first and most dramatic effect of this love was the resurrection of the dead Jesus on Easter. Jesus was raised never to die again. And, as Jesus was raised into God's everlasting kingdom, so also will we (1 Cor. 15:20). Our future resurrection is a defining component in our salvation. We will be raised into the eternity of the new creation.

What we need to see here is that God's eternity cannot be understood as existing outside of time. Rather, it consists in overcoming the destruction that normally accompanies passage, in overcoming the entropy that presently foredooms all physical existence. God's eternity is gained through the victory of resurrection and transformation. And the trinitarian history shows that God first subjects the Godself to the vicissitudes of temporality and then, from within so to speak, brings about the transformation that leads to new creation.

2. The eschatological future is the key that opens the gate to eternity. What we have been exploring is the proposal that the immanent perichoresis of Father, Son, and Holy Spirit is eternal, to be sure; but this eternity is inclusive—not exclusive—of natural and world history. Eternity embraces time. It embraces creation and consummation. Time as we know it comes into existence with the creation at the beginning and ticks its way through cosmic history toward an immense future. Yet we have a divine promise that this will not go on forever. The present creation is slated for transformation. There will be a new creation. Its advent will be the eschatological consummation of all God has promised. Time will be taken up. Eternity embraces the alpha and the omega plus whatever happens in between.

Vital here is the cosmic Christ. In Christ we find the Logos that structures all of creation. In Christ we also find the resurrection, the prolepsis of the new creation. In fact, the best way to understand this, I think, is to envision the prolepsis coming to fulfillment and retroactively defining all reality. The eschatological Christ will turn out to be the Logos by which the creation will have been structured all along. God's ultimate future will determine just what the past has been. For us today to be bound together with Christ is to be bound together with the future event by which the new creation will come into being and bind together the whole of reality.

The biblical symbol of the new creation is being interpreted here to refer to a point in the future where time will be translated into eternity, where the cosmos will undergo transformation and emerge as the everlasting kingdom of God. But this interpretation of the biblical symbol does not go without challenge. There is a challenge from the scientific imagination. Should the final future as forecasted by the combination of big bang cosmology and the second law of thermodynamics come to pass, wherein the law of entropy has the last laugh and the cosmos drifts into a state of irrecoverable equilibrium—and if some consciousness could then say, "that's all there is"—then we would have proof that our faith has been in vain. It would turn out to be that there is no God, at least not the God in whom followers of Jesus have put their faith. Our faith is allied with our hope, and our hope is based upon the promise inherent in the Easter resurrection of Jesus, the promise that a new creation is coming by the grace and power of God. That prophesied event is the focus of eschatological thinking. The upshot of this is that at the present time we will have to base our eschatological hope on specifically theological resources, not scientific ones.

Whether thinking scientifically or theologically, the *when* of the eschatological event is as yet undetermined. The future of present reality is genuinely open. Yet when the new creation does come, its power will be found not in its destruction of the past but rather in its opening up of a still greater future, a future without decay or death. In this respect, the new creation shares something in common with the old creation: both refer to divine action wherein God grants a future to that which he loves. At the beginning of the present creation—if we can speak about an initial edge to time—the first thing God did was to give the universe a future. At the advent of the new creation, God will grant a new future that—to differ from the present future—will not lose the past. The eschatological future will include the whole of the past. The past will find its wholeness and fulfillment in the face of a future in which nothing will be lost. In this sense, the eschatological future can rightly be called "eternity."

This second thesis leads to a set of corollaries. The first is that *the concept of eternity is not conceptually incompatible with that of temporality.* The two can be conjoined if we make eschatology the link.

Perhaps we can find a parallel in the logic of infinity. If we say that God is infinite, it follows that the divine infinity includes the finite world. Otherwise, if we were to say that God's infinity stands over against the world's finitude, then God would be limited to what is not of this world; that is, God would himself be finite. But this cannot be. So we affirm that infinity includes the finite. It does not stand against it.

Infinity and eternity are sister attributes. Although differing from infinity in that it is possible to think of an eternal entity sitting contiguously side by side with a temporal entity, Christian symbolism entails the affirmation that the eternal God is involved in a temporal world. With this in mind, eternity can be thought of like infinity, namely, as inclusive of temporality. Eternity can be thought of as the fulfillment of time as well as the transcendence of time. It is the incarnation and eschatological consummation that makes temporal transcendence and inclusion possible.

This leads to the second corollary: *the coming into existence of eternity—at least salvific eternity—is contingent*. If we refuse to define eternity as some sort of timeless reality that sits contiguous and parallel to temporal history as we know it, then it will be the future that brings eternity to time. To accomplish this there will have to be an advent, a coming, a temporally apprehensible transformation. From the point of view of our inertial frame of reference, we must admit that logically such an advent may or may not come. It is not a necessity built in to present precedents. It is not a scientifically discernible principle of nature. The advent of eternity will have to come as a free act of God, and all free acts are contingent in character.

The third corollary to our eschatological thesis is that *the arrival of consummate eternity creates the wholeness of time*. Time as we currently experience it in human consciousness is disjointed. It separates past and future from the present. The past seems lost, irretrievable. The future seems precarious, for the most part beyond our control. And passage is most threatening, because it marks the inevitability of decay and death. There is no wholeness to time. Yet the advent of the new creation will mark time's second edge, which, in tandem with the first edge at the beginning, will bundle up the history of creation into a single reality, a single story with a divine plot. Further, we understand the new creation to be the fulfillment of the old, not its annihilation. The resurrection combined with judgment will separate the dross from the pure, so that all that has been good and beautiful and loving and harmonious will find its full and final quiddity in the everlasting kingdom of God. Eternal salvation will create a wholeness that does not now exist. It can only be anticipated.

The fourth corollary is that *Rahner's Rule—that the economic Trinity is the immanent Trinity and the immanent Trinity is the economic Trinity—can be affirmed as an eschatological convergence*. In thinking about Rahner's Rule, we must remind ourselves that we ought not be thinking about two separate trinities that somehow need to be reconciled. There is but one Trinity, and in this work I have been arguing that it is the Trinity we have experienced in the economy of salvation. I have been arguing that the trail of salvation traversed by God implies that the divine life *ad intra* has been put at risk by the incarnation of the Son and the indwelling of the Holy Spirit so that it comes to incorporate the divine life *ad extra*. That which needs convergence, then, is temporal history and the otherness of the divine persons with the eschatological advent of the eternal perichoresis.

Within the scope of temporal history, we must acknowledge that the person of Jesus Christ is other: he is other to us just as all other persons are other, and he is other to God the Father just as all persons are other. It is the Son's very indulgence in the creation that makes such otherness within the divine life comprehensible. And the story of this creation is not over. It is still being told. It will not finish until the eschatological consummation writes the final chapter, until we have been conformed by the Holy Spirit to the image of Christ and transformed by that Spirit into his resurrected brothers and sisters. Only then, when death has been put completely under his feet, can he deliver the creation fully to the Father so that God may be "all in all." In short, the economy of salvation cannot constitute the internal perichoresis until the work of salvation has attained its completeness. From our perspective within the finitude of history, this appears to be an event yet to occur in the future. After the advent of the new creation, when eternity will have defined the wholeness of time, then we will be able to say that the economic Trinity is eternally the immanent Trinity and vice versa.

The fifth corollary is that *origination cannot be used as a criterion for subordinating the Son and Spirit to the Father*. It was customary in the ancient discussion to describe the Father as the unoriginate source from which the Son was generated and the Spirit proceeded. Somehow, the unoriginateness of the Father implied an absoluteness higher than that enjoyed by the other two persons. Although it was granted that in eternity there could be no temporal priority, the Father was granted a logical priority or a priority of honor. But, if we are to assert that eschatology is the key that locks the three persons into their eternal and immanent bond, then the logical or honorific priority of the Father vanishes.

I am working here with an ontological vision that reverses our normal perspective. By the normal perspective, I refer to the assumption that "creation" refers to an event in the past, the onset or beginning of nature. I believe there is some warrant to reverse this view, placing the moment of creation in the future, at the end. If we begin with eschatology as that which defines the creation in light of the new creation, then we find that the moment of creation is simultaneous with the moment of consummation. It will be the future that will determine what we have been. In a sense, creation is not done; it is ongoing. We now find ourselves amidst the continuing creative work of God, amidst a *creatio continua* that will climax with the advent of the renewed order of nature. Redemption will determine creation. Similarly, the eschatological Trinity will determine that the hitherto ineffable God and creator of all is in fact the Father of Jesus Christ and our Father as well. Now, having suggested these corollaries, let us move on to the next thesis.

3. There need not be a split between the absoluteness and the relatedness of God if we think of God as the absolutely related one. Perhaps we have been misled by classical ontology into assuming that absoluteness consists of unrelatedness; that is, to be absolute is to be an immutable substance so independent and isolated that its only relations are external. Its relations, being external and accidental, allegedly cannot affect its self-assigned definition. But suppose we turn this around and suggest that absoluteness consists of total inner- and interrelatedness.[40]

The classical philosophical understanding of absoluteness when applied to the God of the Bible will not do for a number of reasons. For one, the very idea of a creation qualifies an isolated absolute because it introduces a creator-creation relationship. The existence of the creation identifies the absolute as a creator so that the absolute is no longer the sole source of its definition. Ancient doctrines such as *creatio ex nihilo* tried to shore up the absoluteness of the creator by suggesting that God could affect the world but the world could not affect God. But even this defensive maneuver was doomed to fail when scripture added the notion that God loves the world, binding the internal life of God to this otherwise external or accidental relationship. When the God of Israel hears the painful cry of his people rising up from their suffering as slaves at the hands of their Egyptian oppressors, the divine heart is affected, and God responds with a mighty hand and an outstretched arm that results in their rescue and deliverance to the promised land. Certainly, the beyondness and holiness of God are not compromised here, but world-relatedness comes indelibly to mark the divine being even before we get to such outrageous New Testament ideas such as incarnation and spiritual indwelling.

In light of this, suppose we shift the weight totally to the other foot and try to conceive of absoluteness as total relatedness. It seems that we would be describing the notion of perichoresis, the total mutuality that characterizes the immanent Trinity as a relationship of Father, Son, and Holy Spirit. Recall now our earlier discussions of the double surrender in the New Testament and the dependent divinity described by Pannenberg. The existence of the Son defines the first person of the Trinity as Father, and the freely given obedience of the Son cedes to the Father the divinity that makes the coming into existence of the kingdom of God possible. To be divine and to be in relationship is to be freely loved and obeyed, and this divinity is what the Son grants the Father through total love and obedience.

This argument may at first appear to be an assault on God the Father who, if absolute, ought to be the original source of his own divinity. But, as already mentioned, the very existence of the creation already compromises any notion of absoluteness understood as unrelatedness. With the advent of a creation, the situation warrants a transition from isolated divinity to divinity-in-relation. Then, if we add to this picture the fact that the creation is fallen and has forgotten its creator, that to which God relates is more than merely other. It is alien. The created order fills its days with violence, suffering, and death, so that a deep sense of estrangement from God comes into view. We cannot avoid saying that our God become creator has placed his own divinity at risk. God has chosen to make his bed with a world that denies him the reverence and holiness and obedience that would otherwise belong to him. Through the mouth of the prophet God can complain, "If then I am a father, where is the honor due me? And if I am a master, where is the respect due me?" (Mal. 1:6). This honor and respect is what Jesus Christ restores through surrender and obedience. As a historical person, the Nazarene represents the creation in proper relationship to its God. As a prolepsis that anticipates a future reality, we look forward to the eschatological event prophesied by Paul: "When all things are subjected to him, then the Son himself will also be subjected to the one who put all things in subjection under him, so that God may be all in all" (1 Cor. 15:28). Whether in history or in consummation, it is the surrender of Jesus Christ that makes God "all in all."

Turning to the Son, the divinity of the Son is gained through his total identification with the Father: Jesus embodies the Father's will; speaks with the authority of God; performs miracles by the same power that created the world in the beginning; and those who put their faith in Jesus find themselves putting their faith in God. This faithful unity of

Father and Son is the accomplishment of the Holy Spirit. It is the Holy Spirit indwelling in Jesus that makes the Father fully present to him. Whether symbolically portrayed as the Spirit via the angel entering the virgin's womb to precipitate the messiah's birth, or the descent of the Spirit at Jesus' baptism, or the mind of God with which Jesus teaches, or the spiritual body with which Jesus is resurrected, it is the Holy Spirit who makes the connection that insures the living Father's presence in Jesus.

In parallel fashion, it is the Holy Spirit that makes the resurrected Christ present to us in faith. To be baptized in Christ is to be filled with the newness of life that sprouts now from Jesus' resurrection and will come to full flower in our own future resurrection. The Spirit makes us brothers and sisters with Jesus. It imbues us with the mind of Christ, the love of God, the will to obey, hope for the future, and the joy of heaven while on earth. It binds us to Christ, to one another, and to God's future transformation of all things in the new creation. The eschatological task will be to actualize the physical unity of the history of Jesus Christ—a history that includes all those bound to him in faith—with the suprahistorical source of creation, the Father. The Spirit, by serving the Father and the Son, finds its own personhood and divinity in the final accomplishment—the loving community of Father and Son with each other and with the world.

What is absolute here is the total dependence of each person on its relationship to the other two. It is this that constitutes the immanent Trinity. Yet the immanent Trinity is consummated eschatologically, meaning that the whole of temporal history is factored into the inner life of God. God becomes fully God-in-relationship when the work of salvation—when the economic Trinity—is complete. The world, similarly, becomes fully itself only by transcending itself, by transcending its current state of otherness over against God.

Pertinent to the issue of the world's relationship to the inner life of God is Pannenberg's contrast between a divine person and a human person. Whereas the trinitarian persons are totally dependent upon their relations to the others to be themselves, human personhood exhibits a greater sense of independence. Recall the distinction between ego and self. The human ego—the sense of being an "I" or a "me"— has the appearance of being self-constituting. This appearance is in part an illusion, of course, because the self as the image we believe others have of us is an inescapable factor in ego development. It makes us more socially interdependent than it first appears. Here we find the roots of estrangement. Not only might there develop an estrangement between ego and self, but also between our own personhood and God's. The human desire to constitute oneself independently of God's view of our self produces the illusory attempt to make ourselves—our egos—the absolute in our lives. Such attempts to absolutize our egos only hasten the destructive powers of passage for ourselves and for those around us. They actually function to destroy relationship, and the result is death. The total relationality within the divine perichoresis, in contrast, is life untrammeled by passage and death. When historicized, it results in victory over death through resurrection. The call to faith in the resurrected Christ is a call for us to find ourselves only in relationship to God. It is a call to enter into the perichoresis that means life and only life. It is the absoluteness of relationship within the divine life that means eternal life.

4. *A concept of the Trinity must be based in part on distribution of functions in order to maintain the beyond-intimate paradox in the one God, but it must be remembered that the beyond-intimate paradox comes to expression in each of the originary symbols individually.* We must recognize that the press for explanatory concepts in theological construction cannot help but distantiate itself from the tensive and multivalent character of the primary biblical symbols. The press for precision cannot help but reduce ambiguity, and ambiguity is the lifeblood of symbolic meaning. It is the ambiguity in the symbol of God as Father, for example, that gives it its evocative power. On the one hand, when identified with the one who must transcend the creation if he is to be known as the creator, and when identified by association with the king who deserves respect and obedience, the symbol of the Father communicates the sense of the beyond. On the other hand, when identified as the loving Father who pursues his wayward Ephriam or who waits patiently for the return home of the prodigal, and when identified as the one who out of grief shakes the foundations of the world causing earthquakes at the death of his beloved Son, the symbol of the Father communicates the sense of intimacy. It is the very ambiguity built into the symbol that permits the paradoxical tension to come to expression.

The same is the case for the symbols of Son and Spirit. On the one hand, the Son is finite and limited and subject to suffering and even to victimization just as the rest of us mortals are; on the other hand, the Son is raised to eternity, exalted above the heavens, depicted as the lamb upon the throne. The Spirit, on the one hand, known as the Comforter, is present to our innermost thoughts and motives, giving comfort to troubled souls by empowering us with new life and inspiring us to love one another; on the other hand, it was this Spirit that hovered over the waters of chaos at creation and will put flesh on the dry bones at the advent of the new creation. The sense that the God of Jesus Christ is both beyond and intimate is present whenever biblical symbols are allowed to resonate with their full power.

As we move toward conceptual clarity in trinitarian thinking, however, the natural tendency is toward univocity. This is inevitable. This is reflected already in the structure of the Niceno-Constantinopolitan Creed, which drifts toward a distribution of functions. In the first article, we find God called "the Father Almighty," followed by his action in creating "heaven and earth." In the second article, we find the redemptive work of the Son, who is *homoousias* with the Father. In the third article, we find the Spirit, "Lord and giver of Life," plus a list of other items that are roughly associated with the Spirit's work, such as the existence of the church and the resurrection of the dead. What this amounts to is a distribution of functions among the three persons. This may lead to a theological problem unless we try to understand sympathetically the move from primary symbols to second order or reflective thought.

Here is the problem. Should one want to press to the limit the implications of Augustine's maxim that the operations of God in the world are undivided *(opera trinitatis ad extra sunt indivisa),* then we would have to say that the Nicene Creed borders on the unorthodox. It divides the work. Whereas the biblical symbols portray both the Spirit and the Logos as necessary agents in the act of creation, the creed assigns it to the Father. Each person of the Trinity, in turn, has a different function. The work of the one God seems divided. Yet, curiously enough, the Nicene Creed is the measure of orthodoxy. How can this be?

No theological crime has been committed. It is all rather innocent. It has to do with the nature of the movement from symbols with multiple levels of meaning to more univocal explanatory concepts. We pay a price as we move toward conceptual clarity. We lose ambiguity. We risk losing the paradox. But the paradox is too valuable to lose. Its sacrifice is too high a price to pay. Hence, the distribution of functions among the trinitarian persons is an attempt to maintain the paradox at the conceptual level. God as Father becomes the primary repository for the appellations indicative of the beyond. The classical attributes of omnipotence and immutability and ineffability fit best the dimension of the divine that exists independent of the creation, that constitutes the transcendent condition that makes the creation possible. God as Son, in complementary contrast, becomes the focus of intimacy as finitude. We can locate the Son in time and place, in an inertial frame of reference he shares with Pontius Pilate and with Calvary. God as Spirit becomes identified with God's presence and glory spread throughout the creation and, of course, most potently experienced within the human soul and within the history of the church. The Spirit binds Father and Son, the ineffable with the revealed, the resurrected Christ with the faith of the believer, the eternal with the temporal. There is but one God, both beyond and intimate; and the idea of distributing functions so that the beyondness of the Father is complemented by the intimacy of the Son and Spirit provides a conceptual way of binding the absolute with the related.

If we combine the insights of the theses advanced thus far, perhaps we could say that, under the conditions of temporal finitude, to conceptualize the three persons requires that we distinguish them largely according to function: creator, redeemer, sanctifier. *Opera trinitatis sunt divisa.* Perhaps we could add that in light of the eschatological advent of the new creation and the eternalization of the temporal, we might look retroactively at the history of salvation and say, *opera trinitatis ad extra sunt indivisa.*

5. *The image of the immanent Trinity ought not be used as a model for human society; rather, we should seek to transform human society on the basis of our vision of the coming kingdom of God in which God alone is the absolute.* Social doctrines of the Trinity, though increasingly popular, are, in my judgment, wrongheaded. What attracts social trinitarians is the category of community rather than personality for understanding God. Sometimes contemporary theologians pit the Cappadocian fathers over against Athanasius or Augustine so as to root the contemporary view in an ancient precedent of plurality in harmony. The point usually advanced is this: if loving relationships of a nonsubordinationist or egalitarian type can be found within the being of God, then this could become a model or paradigm for loving relationships in human society. As a model, the Trinity would serve as an ethical ideal. Our moral task would be one of copying God—that is, of reorganizing society so that nonhierarchical and mutually supportive relationships would provide peace and harmony. The function of the doctrine of the Trinity then, according to social theorists, would not be to construct a conceptual

understanding of the gospel; rather, it would be to serve as a heuristic device for motivating and directing social change.

The problem with this is that the social doctrinalists have chosen the wrong symbol. The doctrine of the Trinity is a second order symbol, a conceptual apparatus constructed for the purpose of clarifying the more primary symbols of Father, Son, and Holy Spirit. The concepts of personhood and community are concepts we import into the process of analysis, synthesis, and construction. They are products of our intellectual context, which we shave and trim so they fit the needs dictated by evangelical explication. This was as true for Arius, Athanasius, and the Cappadocians as it is for us today. Specifically, the ideal of a nonhierarchical community wherein relationships come prior to persons is the product of our modern and emerging postmodern Western mind. The first task of Trinity talk has been to devise a way of speaking so that the doctrinal affirmation of one God in three persons can be understood in a way that retains the beyond-intimate paradox in the message of salvation. For social theorists to then go on to take a further step and say that this revised image of the Trinity provides a divine model for human society is to ask the tail to wag the dog.

There is a better way, namely, to appeal to a primary biblical symbol that is already directed toward human community. I suggest the kingdom or reign of God. The symbol of the kingdom of God thematically ties together nearly the whole of Hebrew and New Testament scriptures. It emits the call for social justice. It calls forth images of a world community at peace. It hearkens forward to the new creation, because we have been promised an eschatological kingdom of God.

In addition, it is by implication egalitarian, although this point is often missed. According to the symbol of the kingdom of God, God alone is king. This means no human being can be king. Any human being who rules over others does so as a steward on behalf of a higher master, not on his or her own behalf. Human authority becomes secularized and equalized. There is here an implicit contrast between human rule and divine rule that makes prophetic criticism of all human institutions possible. None are exempt from prophetic judgment on the alleged grounds that they are sacred, that they are rooted in some alleged eternal form. On the basis of our vision of the coming kingdom of God, we are free to criticize all present social structures. We are free to transform all that is temporal, because only the eschatological kingdom will determine what shall be eternal.

This dynamic escapes the purview of the social doctrinalists. Why? Because they wrongly operate with the model-theory of morality. They treat their idea of God as a model that we humans should copy. Hence, when they think of God as king, they presume this teaches that certain humans should become king over others. As post-Enlightenment egalitarians, however, they are opposed to monarchy and thereby have difficulty with the symbol of God as king. They may even reject the potential moral value in the symbol of God's kingdom.

The root problem here is that social doctrinalists operate conjunctively rather than disjunctively. The primary advantage of the symbol of the kingdom of God is found in its disjunction: where God is king there will be justice, so we are free to criticize and reform all human kingship with its accompanying injustice. Part of the value of the absolute side of the absoluteness-relatedness paradox is to say that God alone is God. We as creatures cannot copy God in all respects, certainly not when it comes to kingship. To let God be king—to worship the lamb upon the throne— liberates us to work freely in a world wherein no individual or class or race or gender can claim transcendent rights for ruling over others.

In sum, the biblical symbol of the kingdom of God is preferable to that of the Trinity when seeking to enlist religious fervor in behalf of social justice and equality. This is the case because the kingdom of God is a primary symbol in which communal justice already inheres. The Trinity, in contrast, is a second order symbol constructed for the purpose of clarifying the relation between three more basic symbols for God at work in salvation. The kingdom of God is a ready-made symbol for exerting social responsibility.

6. *The doctrine of the Trinity provides the framework for understanding the dynamics of divine grace.* It was out of love that God created. It was out of love that the redeemer was sent. It is into an eternal bond of love that we are being drawn by God's Spirit. When God loves us, we experience God's love as grace. We experience this grace as absolute because it comes to us from the beyond. We have no control over it. It comes as a gift we did not ask for. And, of course, we experience grace in terms of relatedness. Through love, God becomes Emmanuel, God with us. Through the Spirit we are drawn up into the love by which God loves, and this imparts to our lives a sense of bond with others that issues in care and service.

God's grace is both cosmic and personal. The birth of the cosmos issues from the same tender heart of God that celebrated the birth of the

Messiah at Bethlehem. The same power by which the galaxies have been hurled through space was at work in the miracles of Jesus, giving sight to a blind man or stopping a woman's hemorrhage. The glory into which all of nature and human history will explode at the advent of the new creation was already there to greet the crucified one as he emerged from his tomb on the first Easter.

God's grace is personal not just for the Jesus of history, but for us today as well. The Holy Spirit brings future eternity into our hearts and minds ahead of time, collapsing the times so that the crucified and risen Christ of yesterday and the glorified Christ of tomorrow become sacramentally present in our faith. The total surrender by which Jesus treated the Father as Lord and King—which in turn made him the Christ and, hence, made him one with the Lord and King—is present to us as gift. His obedience becomes our obedience. His love becomes our love. Despite our human disinclination to bow or surrender to any absolute other than our selves, the Holy Spirit justifies us by placing Christ's obedience at the center of our lives. Our sins are forgiven because the Spirit makes present in our souls the obedient redeemer who gave his life as "a ransom for many" (Matt. 20:28). The Spirit unites us with Christ Jesus in our baptism "so that, just as Christ was raised from the dead by the glory of the Father, so we too might walk in newness of life" (Rom. 6:4b). This newness of life, like a blossoming tree in spring, bursts forth with daily fruits: love, joy, peace, patience, kindness, generosity, faithfulness, gentleness, and self-control (Gal. 5:22).

It is the experience of a gracious God in the lives of faithful believers that eventually led to the construction of the doctrine of the Trinity. The value of engaging in Trinity talk is that it offers an opportunity to remind ourselves that the God of the beyond has become intimate, that the God of creation has entered our world as its redeemer and sanctifier, and that we have good reason to hope for resurrection into the new creation.

Notes

Chapter 1: Introducing the Task of Trinity Talk

1. For example, see Heinrich Schmid, *Doctrinal Theology of the Evangelical Lutheran Church* (Minneapolis: Augsburg Publishing House, 1875, 1961), 129; J. T. Mueller, *Christian Dogmatics* (St. Louis: Concordia Publishing House, 1955), 149f.; Denis Baly and Royal W. Rhodes, *The Faith of Christians: An Introduction to Basic Beliefs* (Philadelphia: Fortress Press, 1984), 123–125; Richard P. McBrien, *Catholicism* (Minneapolis: Winston Press, 1981), 343–344. For a survey of Enlightenment issues regarding the Trinity as mystery, see Jaroslav Pelikan, *Christian Doctrine and Modern Culture in the Christian Tradition* (5 vols.; Chicago: University of Chicago Press, 1971–1989), 5:68–69.

2. Hans Küng, *Does God Exist?* trans. Edward Quinn (Garden City, N.Y.: Doubleday & Co., 1980), 699.

3. "The doctrine of the Trinity is not itself a mystery," writes Catherine Mowry LaCugna, "even though God who 'dwells in light inaccessible' is impenetrable mystery." "Trinity," in *The Encyclopedia of Religion*, ed. Mircea Eliade et al. (New York: Macmillan Co., 1988), 15:55.

4. Gregory of Nazianzus says the Father is the origin and cause of the Son and Spirit "beyond the sphere of time, and above the grasp of reason." *Third Theological Oration: On the Son,* III, in *Nicene and Post-*

Nicene Fathers (Grand Rapids: Wm. B. Eerdmans, 1978), 2d Series, VII:302 (hereinafter abbreviated: NPNF).

5. Basil, *On the Spirit,* XVIII:44–45; *Letters,* XXXVIII:4 (NPNF, 2d Series, VIII:27–28; 138–139); see Pelikan, *The Christian Tradition,* 1:222–223. Earlier, the esoteric character or unknowability of God referred to the essence or *ousia* of the ungenerate Father, the mysterious abyss from which all things flowed. We only know the divine as manifest in the three *hypostases.* As the Cappadocian discussion proceeded, especially in the work of Gregory of Nazianzus and Gregory of Nyssa, however, the Son and Spirit came to share in the Father's mystery beyond human comprehension. The three now reside in a heaven so ineffable that it lies beyond Plato's realm of ideas. The divine Trinity was catapulted up into the realm of unknowable being *(ousia),* leaving us in effect to understand only the extra-trinitarian divine energies *(energia).* Such a reduction to mystery makes further theological discussion of what has been revealed about God's triuneness virtually useless, because it in principle can be quickly obviated by simple appeal to a higher level of mystery. The problem, of course, is that there is no scriptural or even rational warrant for this kind of appeal to mystery.

6. Karl Rahner, *The Trinity* (New York: Herder & Herder, 1970), 46. Walter Kasper writes: "The Trinity is without qualification *the* mystery of faith." *The God of Jesus Christ* (New York: Crossroad, 1986), 273, Kasper's italics; see p. 268. Donald L. Gelpi, S.J., shows he is more aware of the temptation to obfuscation when he writes: "A mystery should not be mistaken for a contradiction or a conundrum. Rather its full intelligibility exceeds and therefore baffles our finite minds. We should not then confuse its theological contemplation with obfuscation or obscurantism." *The Divine Mother: A Trinitarian Theology of the Holy Spirit* (Lanham, Md.: University Press of America, 1984) 127.

7. Leonardo Boff, *Trinity and Society* (Maryknoll, N.Y.: Orbis Books, 1988), 233. William J. Hill similarly assumes that the trinitarian problem is one of arithmetic and proceeds to solve it for us: we should begin with the unity and work toward the plurality "because unity enjoys a logical priority over multiplicity." *The Three-Personed God* (Washington, D.C.: Catholic University of America Press, 1982), 256. In a moment of weakness, even Karl Barth identified the concern of the doctrine of the Trinity as "God's oneness in threeness and threeness in oneness." *Church Dogmatics* (4 vols.; Edinburgh: T. & T. Clark, 1936–1962), I/1:423. So

widely taken for granted is the assumption that the doctrine of the Trinity has to do with arithmetic that Barth himself does not see the significance of his own otherwise profound explication; namely, that the central concern of the Trinity has to do with God's redemptive relation to the creation.

8. Walter Kasper tries to rescue us from some of the confusion by drawing a distinction. Christian theology has never made the absurd claim that $1 = 3$, he says. It has never claimed that 1 person = 3 persons, or that 1 substance = 3 substances. Rather, by distinguishing substance from person, the doctrine of the Trinity asserts that in God there is a unity of substance and a trinity of persons. "The one and the three refer, therefore, to entirely different aspects." *The God of Jesus Christ,* 234; see p. 271.

9. Roger Haight gives us just this confusing historical picture, but then he goes on to make the clarifying point regarding arithmetic by saying, "Even though the history of the doctrine has been obsessed with the problem of mathematical threeness and oneness, and it continues to be a problem today, in reality the doctrine has nothing to do with this issue." "The Point of Trinitarian Theology," *Toronto Journal of Theology* 4, no. 2 (Fall 1988), 195.

10. In those few places where tritheism is mentioned in trinitarian discussion, the assumption comes immediately to the fore that the Christian view has no truck whatsoever with polytheism. For example, see Irenaeus, *Against Praxeas,* III; Augustine, *On the Trinity,* VII:iv:8.

11. *"The point of the doctrine of the Trinity is therefore soteriological,"* writes Roger Haight with his own emphasis. "The doctrine is not intended to be information about the internal life of God, but about how God relates to human beings. It is a formula that guarantees that the salvation experienced in Jesus and the Spirit is really God's salvation." "The Point of Trinitarian Theology," 199.

12. "As always, the central problem for the doctrine of God is how to unite intelligibly the *absoluteness* of God as the unconditioned source of our total being with the dynamic *relatedness* and the *reciprocal activity* of God as the ground, guide, dialogical partner, and redeemer of our freedom." Langdon Gilkey, "God," in *Christian Theology: An Introduction to Its Traditions and Tasks,* ed. Peter C. Hodgson and Robert H. King (2d ed.; Philadelphia: Fortress Press, 1985), 108. Similarly, after denying that

the Trinity has to do with the number three, Paul Tillich writes that "the trinitarian problem is the problem of the unity between ultimacy and concreteness in the living God." *Systematic Theology* (3 vols.; Chicago: University of Chicago Press, 1951–63), 1:228. Catherine Mowry LaCugna says "the claim about God's essential relatedness is crucial to a revised trinitarian theology." "Current Trends in Trinitarian Theology," *Religious Studies Review* 13, no. 2 (April 1987), 145.

13. Jürgen Moltmann, *The Way of Jesus Christ: Christology in Messianic Dimensions* (San Francisco: Harper & Row, 1990), 173.

14. Barth, *Church Dogmatics,* III/2:519.

15. Rahner, *The Trinity,* 21–22.

16. It is common fare among today's theologians to fear that a collapse of the immanent into the economic Trinity would imply the loss of God's freedom. I wonder if this is completely correct. The understanding of freedom is key here. If freedom means God needs to act in eternity unaffected by the world of time, then this only begs the question in behalf of the classical position. If, however, freedom for God means anything close to what it means for us, namely, the capacity to make decisions and take actions that will be effective in an otherwise open future, then the economy of God's saving work becomes understood as the very expression of God's freedom. With this understanding of freedom, Rahner's Rule could be pressed to its extreme consequence.

17. Robert W. Jenson, "The Triune God," in *Christian Dogmatics,* ed. Carl E. Braaten and Robert W. Jenson (2 vols.; Philadelphia: Fortress Press, 1984), 1:155–156, Jenson's italics; see Robert W. Jenson, *The Triune Identity: God According to the Gospel* (Philadelphia: Fortress Press, 1982), 141. Carl Braaten similarly lays down the eschatological gauntlet: "The church can no longer hold on to the doctrine of the Trinity for the sake of tradition or expect assent to it out of deference to ecclesiastical authority. The church is badly in need of a key by which to unlock the treasury of meaning that once was cached in its doctrine of the Trinity. Here we suggest that the right key is the presence of God's ultimate future in the man Jesus of Nazareth. The doctrine of the Trinity describes the identity of God's future under the different modes of his appearance to the world." *The Future of God* (New York: Harper & Row, 1969), 107–108.

18. Jürgen Moltmann, *The Trinity and the Kingdom* (San Francisco: Harper & Row, 1981) 161.

19. Arthur Peacocke, *Theology for a Scientific Age* (Oxford: Basil Blackwell, 1990), 132, Peacocke's italics.

20. "Message of His Holiness John Paul II," in *John Paul II On Science and Religion: Reflections on the New View from Rome,* ed. Robert John Russell, William R. Stoeger, S.J., and George V. Coyne, S.J. (Vatican City State: Vatican Observatory Publications, Notre Dame, Ind.: University of Notre Dame Press, 1990), M10. Avery Dulles, S.J., adds a cautious commentary: "Theologians should, however, be on guard against a facile concordism that would link the doctrines of faith too closely with fragile scientific hypotheses. Conversely, scientists, while they should refrain from proposing their theories as deductions from doctrines of Christian faith, may allow their religious faith to suggest lines of scientific investigation that would not otherwise have occurred to them." "Science and Theology," ibid., 12.

21. "Hypostatizing" for Eric Voegelin has a meaning similar to that of "reifying" for Marxists. It refers to literalizing inappropriately otherwise tensive symbols; it refers to denying the transcendent reality of the beyond by reducing it to propositional statements as if it were one object among others. Voegelin's choice of the word *hypostasis* here signals a haunting warning to Christian theologians. This is the term used to describe Jesus Christ as a divine person. The trinitarian dogma is guilty, he thinks, of presuming that we know more than we do about God in order to foreclose reverence for the mystery that lies beyond. To see how Voegelin uses this as a critical principle, see his *The Ecumenic Age,* vol. 4: *Order and History* (Baton Rouge: Louisiana State University Press, 1974), 37, 113, 237–238.

22. Robert L. Wilken, "The Resurrection of Jesus and the Doctrine of the Trinity," *Word and World,* 2, no.1 (Winter 1982), 28.

Chapter 2: A Map of Contemporary Issues

1. John Hick, *God Has Many Names* (Philadelphia: Westminster Press, 1982), 124.

2. Cyril Richardson, *The Doctrine of the Trinity* (New York: Abingdon Press, [1958]), 148–149.

3. Dorothy Sayers, *Creed or Chaos* (New York: Harcourt, Brace & Co., 1949), 22.

4. Timothy F. Lull, "The Trinity in Recent Literature," *Word and World* 2, no. 1 (Winter 1982), 61.

5. James A. Pike, *A Time for Christian Candor* (New York: Harper & Row, 1964), 124.

6. Ibid., 126.

7. Ibid., 128.

8. Claude Welch, *In This Name: The Doctrine of the Trinity in Contemporary Theology* (New York: Charles Scribner's Sons, 1952), 218; Welch's italics.

9. Robert W. Jenson, *God After God* (Indianapolis: Bobbs-Merrill, 1969), 96.

10. Catherine Mowry LaCugna, "The Trinitarian Mystery of God," in *Systematic Theology: Roman Catholic Perspectives,* ed. Francis Schüssler Fiorenza and John P. Galvin (2 vols.; Minneapolis: Fortress Press, 1991), 1:153.

11. Tertullian, *Against Praxeas,* II (ANF, III:598).

12. In his "Preface to the Second Edition," Immanuel Kant writes: "I must, therefore, abolish knowledge, to make room for belief." *Critique of Pure Reason,* trans. J. M. D. Meiklejohn (New York and London: Dutton, Everyman's Library, 1934), 18.

13. See John O'Donnell, *The Mystery of the Triune God* (New York: Sheed & Ward, 1988; New York: Paulist Press, 1989), 3.

14. See, for example, Schubert M. Ogden, *The Reality of God* (New York: Harper & Row, 1966), and John B. Cobb, Jr., *God and the World* (Philadelphia: Westminster Press, 1969).

15. Joseph A. Bracken, S.J., "Process Philosophy and Trinitarian Theology II," *Process Studies* 11, no. 2 (Summer 1981), 84.

16. Joseph A. Bracken, S.J., "Process Philosophy and Trinitarian Theology," *Process Studies* 8, no. 4 (Winter 1978), 223.

17. Protestant process theologians such as John Cobb and Schubert

Ogden are likely to emphasize common human experience. Roman Catholic Donald Gelpi, who borrows the emphasis on experience from James and Whitehead, however, will focus on the experience of God. In doing so, he shifts the locus of reality from being in substance to experience in process. This leads him to argue that "if God is an experience rather than a substance, the need to conceive of Him as an absolute simply vanishes." *The Divine Mother,* 130.

18. Wolfhart Pannenberg, "Person und Subjekt," in *Grundfragen Systematischer Theologie: Gesammelte Aufsätze, Band II* (Göttingen: Vandenhoeck & Ruprecht, 1980), 82–83.

19. Until the attempt at refinement in the fourth century, *hypostasis* and *ousia* had overlapping meanings, both referring to that which exists as a substance or essence. The Latin *substantia* is the equivalent of *hypostasis* in the intransitive sense, meaning to exist under. The Greeks used *hypostasis* in the transitive sense, meaning the concrete character of a substance in relation to others. It was possible to use the word *hypostasis* as Arius did to refer to three substantially different beings; and it was equally possible to say *"one hypostasis"* as the Greeks did to refer to the unity of being. The Cappadocians paved the way to compromise with their formula, *mia ousia, treis hypostases,* with *ousia* referring to what the three share in common and *hypostasis* to that which makes them distinct. See Basil, *Letters,* XXXVIII:1–3; CCXXXVI:6 (NPNF, 2d Series, VIII:137–138; 278); and Catherine Mowry LaCugna, *God for Us: The Trinity and Christian Life* (San Francisco: Harper & Row, 1991), 66.

20. Between the councils, the term *ousia* seemed to grow in meaning, coming finally to signify the fundamental being of something as distinguishable from its qualitative attributes. To say the Son is *homoousias* with the Father is to say the two share an identical internal being even if, from an external or objective viewpoint, each *hypostasis* is distinguishable from the other.

21. The equivocation is recognized by Augustine, who throws up his hands, saying, "They intend to put a difference, I know not what, between *ousia* and *hypostasis*." Ordinarily, he says, we should render *mia ousia, treis hypostases* into Latin as "one essence, three substances," but after a debate with himself, Augustine concedes to "one essence or substance and three persons." Augustine, *On the Trinity,* V:10.

22. Boethius, *Against Eutyches and Nestorius,* III.

23. Barth, *Church Dogmatics,* I/1:411–413.

24. Jenson, *The Triune Identity.*

25. Rahner, *The Trinity,* 110.

26. Boff, *Trinity and Society,* 63.

27. To paint Barth the color of modalism will not stick, however. The classical modalist position as we find it in Sabellius describes God as appearing to be three in relation to us while asserting that the divine life itself is that of a bare monad. Barth, in contrast, affirms that what we experience in the economy of salvation is in fact the same as the inner or immanent trinitarian life of God.

28. This postmodern relational understanding of person may claim roots in the Cappadocian notion of Trinity. These fourth-century trinitarians understood each *hypostasis* relationally. The Father as ungenerate and unknowable was, of course, an essence *(ousia)* independent of any relations. Yet God as Father was also understood a second way, namely, in relation to the Son. The *hypostasis* of the Father is what it is only by virtue of its relationship to the *hypostasis* of the Son. See Gregory of Nyssa, *Against Eunomius,* II:2 (NFPF, 2d Series, V:102).

29. J. D. Zizioulas, "Human Capacity and Human Incapacity: A Theological Exploration of Personhood," *Scottish Journal of Theology* 28, no. 5 (October 1975), 408.

30. Boff, *Trinity and Society,* 149. Another even more radical interactive model is that of Donald Gelpi. Gelpi begins by defining "person" as "a dynamic relational reality, not only subsistent in its own right (that is to say, as an autonomous center of responsive evaluation and decision), but also imbued with vital continuity and with the capacity for responsible self-understanding, for decisions that flow from that same self-understanding, and for entering into responsible social relationships with entities like itself." Here both relationality and autonomy are emphasized. When applied to each of the divine three, would this definition of person lead to tritheism? No, says Gelpi, because the persons are not self-existent. They are mutually "inexistent." Their existence depends upon the perichoresis, their total interpenetration within the Godhead. *The Divine Mother,* 115–116; 131–132.

31. Joseph Bracken, S.J., "The Holy Trinity as a Community of Divine

Persons," *Heythrop Journal* 15 (1974), 180. See John O'Donnell who, when trying to exclude a "monadic consciousness," proceeds to posit "the one divine consciousness as a shared consciousness, shared by the three persons." *The Mystery of the Triune God,* 110. O'Donnell seems to accept the interpersonal emphasis of Bracken, but he lacks Bracken's holism as the glue that binds the three together. Perhaps this misleads O'Donnell into criticizing Bracken for "tritheism . . . an accidental unity, the moral unity of a social aggregate rather than the ontological unity of substance affirmed by Nicea and the subsequent magisterium of the church." "The Trinity as Divine Community," *Gregorianum* 69, no. 1 (1988), 29. The weakness with O'Donnell is twofold. First, he begs the question by simply appealing to substantialist metaphysics, which is just what is at stake here. Second, his appeal to the authority of Nicea and the magisterium seems to be a veiled attempt to cut off further free thought, as if orthodoxy has the right to put an end to metaphysical explorations.

32. John O'Donnell, for example, assumes the importance of person-in-relationship while affirming substantialism and avoiding holism. He argues by analogy of human experience that "we may speak of three centres of consciousness in God, in the sense that the Father knows himself to be Father, to be the begetter of the Word; the Son knows himself to be Son, to be the one uttered; the Spirit knows himself to be Spirit, to be the bond of communion between the Father and the Son. Thus each of the divine persons is aware of being himself, distinct from the other persons and in relation to the other persons. At the same time, each person is conscious of being the one God. Relation, then, provides the key to the divine community." "Trinity as Divine Community," 33.

33. LaCugna, "The Trinitarian Mystery of God," 1:180.

34. Norman Pittenger, *The Word Incarnate* (New York: Harper & Brothers, 1959), 216.

35. Gregory of Nazianzus writes: "When I say God, I mean Father, Son, and Holy Ghost. For Godhead is neither diffused beyond these, so as to bring in a mob of gods; nor yet is it bounded by a smaller compass than these, so as to condemn us for a poverty stricken conception of deity; either Judaizing to save the monarchia, or falling into heathenism by the multitude of our gods." *Orations,* XXXVIII:8 (NPNF, 2d Series, VII:347).

36. The Trinity, thinks William Ellery Channing, is a holdover from polytheistic idolatry because it apotheosizes a human, Jesus Christ. "Men want an object of worship like themselves, and the great secret of idolatry lies in this propensity." "Unitarian Christianity," in *The Works of William E. Channing* (Boston: American Unitarian Association, 1875), 373.

37. Channing belongs in the camp of the unitarians of the Father or of the Creator, says H. Richard Niebuhr. Niebuhr sees three tendencies toward unitarianism within Christian faith and practice, one for each trinitarian person. Along with Channing and the Unitarians, Niebuhr puts into the camp of unitarians of the first person monarchianism, Arianism, deism, Socinianism, and so forth. They emphasize natural knowledge of God and seek to preserve the unity of the divine in the first person. In practice, there exists as well a "unitarianism of Jesus Christ," better called a "henotheism of the Son," that comes to expression in Marcion, in the Jesus-cult of pietism with hymns such as "Fairest Lord Jesus," and in Ritschl's liberal ethics, where Jesus is the ideal human being. Finally, there is a unitarianism of the Spirit that includes Christian spiritualism, mild mysticism, Joachim de Fiore, the Spiritual Franciscans, certain Protestant sects, the Society of Friends, and Roger Williams. These tendencies within Christendom, argues Niebuhr, should make us seek an ecumenical formulation of the trinitarian faith so as to provide unity for the church. "The Doctrine of the Trinity and the Unity of the Church," *Theology Today* 3, no. 3 (October 1946), 371–385.

38. Friedrich Schleiermacher, *The Christian Faith* (Edinburgh: T. & T. Clark, 1928, 1960), par. 8, p. 35.

39. Ibid., par. 170, p. 738.

40. Ibid., par. 56, p. 230.

41. Ibid., par. 8, p. 37.

42. Not everyone interprets Schleiermacher thusly. Carol Jean Voisin, for example, takes exception to the prevailing interpretation that Schleiermacher viewed the Trinity as a mere appendix to Christian theology. She argues that the doctrine of the Trinity is central to Schleiermacher and that it provides the key for unlocking his entire system. "A Reconsideration of Friedrich Schleiermacher's Treatment of the Doctrine of the Trinity" (Th.D. diss., Graduate Theological Union, 1980). In contrast to Voisin, I here follow Welch's interpretation in *In This Name*.

There Schleiermacher is depicted as synthesizing primal utterances of the one God into a constructed Trinity, and this synthetic method appears in sharp contrast to the analytic method of Karl Barth.

43. Barth, *Church Dogmatics,* I/1:406.

44. Ibid., 403.

45. Moltmann, *The Trinity and the Kingdom,* 139.

46. Ibid., 191.

47. Ibid., 130.

48. Ibid., 131. The problem of ambiguity in Moltmann's argument can be seen right here in this citation. If monotheism and monarchism belong together, and if Christianity is trinitarian and not monotheistic, then why does he have to caution Christianity against the notion of divine lordship?

49. Jürgen Moltmann, *Jewish Monotheism and Christian Trinitarian Doctrine: A Dialogue by Pinchas Lapide and Jürgen Moltmann* (Philadelphia: Fortress Press, 1981), 46.

50. Ibid., 32, 49, 55.

51. Wolfhart Pannenberg, "Problems of a Trinitarian Doctrine of God," *Dialog* 26, no. 4 (Fall 1987), 256.

52. An introduction to the biblical and patristic discussion is offered by G. W. H. Lampe, *God as Spirit* (Oxford: Clarendon Press, 1977), 162–166, and Kasper, *The God of Jesus Christ,* 144–147.

53. John Hick, "Jesus and the World Religions," in *The Myth of God Incarnate* (Philadelphia: Westminster Press, 1977), 178.

54. Maurice Wiles, *Faith and the Mystery of God* (Philadelphia: Fortress Press, 1982), 96.

55. Geoffrey Wainwright, *Doxology: The Praise of God in Worship, Doctrine, and Life* (New York: Oxford University Press, 1980), 57.

56. Ibid., 59.

57. Ibid., 60.

58. Calvin, *Institutes,* I:xiii.

59. Rosemary Radford Ruether, *Sexism and God-Talk* (Boston: Beacon Press, 1983), 68–69; Sallie McFague, *Metaphorical Theology* (Philadelphia: Fortress Press, 1982), ch. 1. "For my money," writes Daniel A. Helminiak, "the combination of 'Mother-Father' is a real winner. It retains the concreteness of the original image that Jesus gave us. It includes the feminine and the masculine and so avoids sexist exclusiveness. Best of all, it boggles the imagination. Except perhaps among some parthenogenetic lizards, we know of no such thing that qualifies as a father-mother. All the better! Then this title reminds us that God is not like us." "Doing Right by Women and the Trinity Too," *America* 160 (February 11, 1989),119.

60. Roberta C. Bondi, "Some Issues Relevant to a Modern Interpretation Of the Language of the Nicene Creed, with Special Reference to Sexist Language," *Union Seminary Quarterly Review* 40, no. 3 (1985), 23.

61. Ibid., 28.

62. Gregory of Nyssa, *Answer to Eunomius' Second Book* (NPNF, 2d Series, V:309). While affirming divine ineffability, Gregory grants some specificity to symbols for God because "there is no appellation given to intuition about Him." Ibid.

63. Athanasius cites as decisive Jesus' calling God "Father" in the Lord's Prayer and Jesus' bidding us to baptize in the name of the Father, the Son, and the Holy Spirit. *First Discourse Against the Arians,* IX:35 (NPNF, 2d Series, IV:326). For similar reasons, Pheme Perkins writes: "Thus St. Augustine would have theological difficulties with some feminists' proposal to replace traditional trinitarian language with the functional categories of creator, redeemer and sanctifier. The Trinity is not an organizational chart for getting the divine jobs done." "Beside the Lord," *The Christian Century* 106 (May 17, 1989), 521.

64. Gregory of Nyssa, *Against Eunomius,* I:23 (NPNF, 2d Series, V:63).

65. Deborah Malacky Belonick, "Revelation and Metaphors: The Significance of the Trinitarian Names, Father, Son and Holy Spirit," *Union Seminary Quarterly Review* 40, no. 3 (1985), 36.

66. Catherine Mowry LaCugna, "The Baptismal Formula, Feminist Objections, and Trinitarian Theology," *Journal of Ecumenical Studies* 26, no. 2 (Spring 1989), 238.

67. Patricia Wilson-Kastner, *Faith, Feminism, and the Christ* (Philadelphia: Fortress Press, 1983), 122.

68. Jenson, *The Triune Identity,* 16. There is some precedent for treating the terms "Father" and "Son" as unexchangeable names in the work of Karl Barth, even though Barth recognizes that they are "figurative" and not literally applied. *Church Dogmatics,* I/1:441–458, 495.

69. Alvin F. Kimel, Jr., agrees, perhaps going beyond the name toward a substantialist understanding of divine maleness, on the grounds that masculinity is necessary for transcendence. "Divine paternity is not an arbitrary metaphor chosen by humanity and then projected onto the deity: God is self-revealed as Father in and by his Son Jesus Christ." "The Holy Trinity Meets Ashtoreth: A Critique of the Episcopal 'Inclusive' Liturgies," *Anglican Theological Review* 71, no. 1 (Winter 1989), 26, cf. p. 41.

70. *Guidelines for Inclusive Use of the English Language,* Office of the Secretary and the Commission for Communication, Evangelical Lutheran Church in America, 8765 W. Higgins Road, Chicago, IL 60631. In an editorial response to the *Guidelines,* Leonard Klein says: "The issue at hand is what language shall be used to describe God. . . . [T]he issue is not the metaphorical and analogical character of language. The issue is whether the language of Holy Scripture shall govern and shape our talk of God. . . . Scripture is not our Word but God's." "ELCA's Confessional Crisis Bottoms Out," *Lutheran Forum* 24, no. 1 (Lent 1990), 4.

71. Perhaps surprisingly, there are very few who approve of substituting "Creator, Redeemer, Sanctifier" for "Father, Son, Spirit." The Anglican Blue Book rejects the substitution because it confuses operations of the Godhead with the persons of the Trinity. *Supplemental Liturgical Texts* (New York: Church Hymnal Corporation, 1988), 106. Catherine Mowry LaCugna says that Creator-Redeemer-Sanctifier language does not adequately reflect the language and view of scripture that God creates *through* the Son (Col. 1:16) and by the Spirit (Gen. 1:1–2) or that God redeems through Christ (2 Cor. 5:19). "The Baptismal Formula," 243. Patricia Wilson-Kastner writes that "'creator, redeemer, and sanctifier' can be helpful, but indicate only the relationship of God to us, rather than the inner life of the trinitarian God, in which we are to participate." *Faith, Feminism, and the Christ,* 133.

72. Carl Braaten, "Trinity as Dogma," *Dialog* 29, no. 1 (Winter 1990), 3. Braaten's position on the divine name emerges from his commitment

to a "new trinitarian paradigm" based on Karl Barth's approach to the Trinity through Christology and on Rahner's Rule: "The economic and the immanent Trinity are one and the same." This means that our God-language will reflect the very structure of revelation, and what has been revealed is the three persons of the Trinity. He goes on to speak of "Father, Son, and Spirit" as proper names, citing the dictionary definition of a proper name as "designating a specific person." "The Problem of God-Language Today," in *Our Naming of God,* ed. Carl Braaten (Minneapolis: Fortress Press, 1989), 29, 32.

73. There is another nuance here that needs sorting out. It has to do with whether one is working within theology proper or invoking cultural analysis. Susan Brooks Thistlethwaite, for example, is convinced that trinitarian language is both sexist and patriarchal. "Terms such as Father or Son are heard as referring to males." "On the Trinity," *Interpretation* 45, no. 2 (April 1991), 159. Catherine Mowry LaCugna says just the opposite: "Trinitarian theology need not be looked upon as inherently sexist and patriarchal." "The Trinitarian Mystery of God," 1:183. The discrepancy is due in part to the employment of different audiences. Thistlewaite employs popular culture, whereas LaCugna employs Christian theology. Thistlewaite relies upon media interviews of pedestrians on New York streets to argue that popular culture imagines God to be a male. "On the Trinity," 160. LaCugna, in contrast, relies upon the actual claims made by the history of trinitarian teaching.

74. Barth, *Church Dogmatics,* I/1:360, 400, 444–456.

75. This applies to a closely related issue, namely, that of hypostatizing Wisdom *(Sophia, Hokmah)* into a near goddess figure and, in some instances, then identifying Wisdom with a female Holy Spirit in the Trinity. For example, see Elisabeth Schüssler-Fiorenza, *In Memory of Her* (New York: Crossroad, 1984), 132–135; and Gelpi, *The Divine Mother,* 9–11. Roland Mushat Frye argues against this practice on a number of counts, including its drift toward both Gnosticism and Arianism. "Fiorenza and other feminist theologians are in line with Gnostic heresy, as when Ptolomaeus declared that the 'celestial mother Sophia' bestowed the Logos upon Jesus at his baptism. Furthermore, it is interesting that those who argue that *Sophia-Hokmah* is in some way a divine being are repeating a favorite Arian argument for the subordination of Son to Father by interpreting Jesus Christ as the incarnation not of God but of God's wisdom." "Language for God and Feminist Language: A

Literary and Rhetorical Analysis," *Interpretation* 43, no. 1 (January 1989), 50. The trend toward Arianism is present, I think, but inadvertent. When applied to trinitarian thought, the feminized Holy Spirit is an attempt to put female representation into an already masculine triumvirate. This has its weaknesses, even from a feminist perspective, because the female Holy Spirit still gets outvoted by males two to one. See Ruether, *Sexism and God-Talk,* 60, and the discussion of Leonardo Boff in Chapter 3.

76. See Welch, *In This Name,* 56–57, 220–225.

77. McFague, *Metaphorical Theology.*

78. David Tracy defines Christian theology as "an interpretation of the central symbols of the Christian tradition for some construal of our present situation." "Theological Method," in *Christian Theology,* ed. Hodgson and King, 35. Then, with more precision, he adds: "Theology is the attempt to establish mutually critical correlations between an interpretation of the Christian tradition and an interpretation of the contemporary situation." Ibid., 36. This involves retrieval, critique, suspicion, explanation, and understanding. Ibid., 57.

79. Richard Rhodes, *The Making of the Atomic Bomb* (New York: Touchstone, 1988), 572.

80. Mary Daly, *Beyond God the Father* (Boston: Beacon Press, 1973), 122.

81. Mary Grey, "The Core of Our Desire: Re-Imaging the Trinity," *Theology* 93, no. 755 (1990), 363–365 passim.

82. Jerome, *The Dialogue Against the Luciferians,* XIX. The standard version leaves some questions unanswered, such as, if Nicea condemned the Arian view in 325, then why did so many Eastern bishops embrace it? The newer studies emphasize a few relevant things. First, in the decades immediately following 325, Nicea was not taken to have the orthodox authority it later garnered. Second, the Eastern bishops did not realize Athanasius and others were calling them "Arian" until 341, at which time they repudiated the label. Third, Athanasius used the label "Arian" rather loosely to describe all of his opponents.

83. Cf. Joseph T. Lienhard, S.J., "The Arian Controversy: Some Categories Reconsidered," *Theological Studies* 48 (1987), 415.

84. Athanasius overtly draws the analogue between the Arians of his own day and the Jews of New Testament times. "Both the Jews of that day and the new Jews of the present day inherited their mad enmity against Christ from their father, the devil." *On the Opinion of Dionysius,* 3. This kind of rhetoric has in later times come to be associated with anti-Semitism, as Robert C. Gregg and Dennis E. Groh point out, *Early Arianism: A View of Salvation* (Philadelphia: Fortress Press, 1981), 46. His point here actually has nothing directly to do with the Jews. It is that Athanasius sees Arius as a Christ-hater, which Gregg and Groh try to prove was not in fact the case.

85. Gregg and Groh, *Early Arianism,* x.

86. "We have no substantial evidence of Arian reticence to revere and honor the Son." Ibid., 49.

87. Arianism is not crude adoptionism, because Christ's future title of "Son" was given him proleptically out of the Father's foreknowledge. Although in principle the historical Jesus could have willed to disobey the Father, the Father knew in advance that he would not. Ibid., 22.

88. Ibid., 50.

89. Ibid., 193.

90. Lienhard tells the story a different way. Prior to Nicea, he says, two broad schools of thinking could be discerned: the dyohypostatic (two hypostases) school, which includes Arius' emphasis on will, and the miahypostatic (one hypostasis) school, which includes Athanasius' emphasis on being. Their collision surrounding Nicea forced new thinking and creative solutions such as one *ousia* and three *hypostases*. Although Lienhard emphasizes the existence of the two lines of thinking prior to Nicea, he tacitly agrees with Gregg and Groh when he says of the Arian controversy that "the very collision prepared the way for a resolution." "The Arian Controversy," 437. So does Rowan D. Williams who, though critical of Gregg and Groh for depending too much on Athanasius as a source for Arius' teachings, agrees that the Arian controversy stimulated a more complex yet more profound way to state Christian commitments. He says that "theology continues to need its Ariuses." "The Logic of Arianism," *Journal of Theological Studies* 34 (1983), 81.

91. Mary Ann Donovan, S.C., adds that, even though Gregg and Groh may not see it, there are two differing concepts of God at work

here too. Arius' position is monarchic, and the Alexandrian position allows for a pluralistic understanding. "Seminar on the Trinity," *CTSA Proceedings* 36 (1981), 182.

92. Augustine, *On the Trinity,* VI:x:11; V:xiv:15; XV:xxvi:45–48; cf. Hilary of Poitiers, *On the Trinity,* II:29.

93. Photios, *On the Mystogogy of the Holy Spirit* (Astoria, N.Y.: Studien Publications, 1983), 71–72, 51–52. When Augustine comes to this text, John 15:26, he pauses; but then he goes on to John 20:23: "He [Jesus] breathed on them and said, 'Receive the Holy Spirit.' " Augustine remarks that this was done "so as to show that he [the Spirit] proceeded also from himself." *On the Trinity,* XV:xxvi:45. Barth attacks the Eastern exegesis because it isolates John 15:26 from the wider context of texts. *Church Dogmatics,* I/1:549.

94. The humorous absurdity of thinking the Holy Spirit to be the Father's grandson goes back at least as far as Gregory of Nazianzus, *Fifth Theological Oration: On the Holy Spirit,* VII (NPNF, 2d Series, VII:319).

95. Timothy Ware, *The Orthodox Church* (New York: Penguin Books, 1963), 221.

96. Some Western Christians have taken this to heart. The 1985 General Convention of the Episcopal Church adopted Resolution A-50 to restore to liturgical usage the original form of the Nicene Creed without the *filioque,* provided that this restoration be endorsed by the Anglican Consultative Counsel and the Lambeth Conference. The rationale behind the resolution supported a historical return to the original liturgical text but suspended any judgment regarding the doctrinal or theological issue. Can we separate the liturgical from the doctrinal so cleanly? Some Eastern Orthodox ecumenists are demanding from the West more than a mere liturgical change; they want the West to disavow the doctrine of *filioque* as well. John C. Bauerschmidt argues that the Anglican divines of the sixteenth and seventeenth centuries were fully committed to *filioque* as they identified completely with the Western trinitarian tradition and, further, that if Anglicans affirm *lex orandi, lex credendi,* they cannot easily separate the liturgical from the doctrinal. The appeal to historical argument alone while disregarding the theological argument will fail to make friends with the Orthodox and at the same time will alienate Anglicans from their Western friends

in the faith. "'Filioque' and the Episcopal Church," *Anglican Theological Review* 73, no. 1 (Winter 1991), 7–25.

97. Vladimir Lossky would disagree with the argument I advance here, because he, along with other Orthodox, wants to find the unity of the Godhead in the Father, not the Spirit. "This is why the East has always opposed the formula of filioque which seems to impair the monarchy of the Father." *The Mystical Theology of the Eastern Church* (London: James Clarke, 1957), 58.

98. Augustine, *On the Trinity*, V:11 (NPNF, 1st series, III:93). In commenting on Augustine here, David Coffey says that "the Holy Spirit cannot be the common gift of the Father and the Son in the immanent Trinity . . . because it is of the essence of a gift that it be bestowed gratuitously, whereas all that happens in the immanent Trinity does so with a necessity of nature." "The Holy Spirit as the Mutual Love of the Father and the Son," *Theological Studies* 51, no. 2 (1990), 197. The problem with Coffey's assessment is that he presupposes such a split between the immanent Trinity and the economic Trinity that the historical Jesus is excluded from the immanent life of God. As Coffey's own exegesis will show, Jesus gives the Spirit to the Father. Hence, if we affirm there is one Trinity and not two, then the life of Jesus itself constitutes the free act of gift giving that meets Coffey's criterion.

99. Augustine, *On the Trinity*, VI:5 (NPNF, 1st series, III:100). See Augustine, *Faith and Creed*, XIX. The Latin tradition has pretty much followed Augustine to the dismay of the Greeks who complain that here the "Holy Spirit is no more than a reciprocal bond between the Father and the Son." Lossky, *The Mystical Theology of the Eastern Church*, 62.

100. Karl Barth puts it this way: "As God is in Himself Father from all eternity, He begets Himself as the Son from all eternity. As He is the Son from all eternity, He is begotten of Himself as the Father from all eternity. In this eternal begetting of Himself and begotten of Himself, He posits Himself a third time as the Holy Spirit, i.e., as the love which unites Him in Himself." *Church Dogmatics*, I/1:483. "The problem with this statement," says Michael von Brück, "is in the way it determines the Holy Spirit, who . . . is seen as the unifying bond between the Father and the Son, and thus in effect is not really a hypostasis." *The Unity of Reality* (New York: Paulist Press, 1991), 130–131.

101. Augustine wants to avoid a quaternity. "And, therefore, they are not more than three: One who loves Him who is from Himself, and One who loves him from whom He is, and Love itself." *On the Trinity,* VI:5.

102. Coffey, "The Holy Spirit as the Mutual Love of the Father and the Son," 218.

103. Ibid., 219.

104. Wolfhart Pannenberg, *Systematic Theology* (3 vols.; Grand Rapids: Wm. B. Eerdmans, 1991), 1:383, 430. Not all recent theologians embrace Augustine's mutual-love theory. Yves Congar, for example, argues mildly against it because it cannot be supported by Thomas Aquinas and because it depends upon an analogy drawn from human relationships. For Congar, metaphysical truths about God's relationships are evidently independent of the human pattern. *I Believe in the Holy Spirit* (3 vols.; London: Geoffrey Chapman; New York: Seabury Press, 1983), 1:88–90.

105. Augustine, *Faith and the Creed,* XIX. Old concerns reappear. One of Augustine's models for the three persons is lover (Father), beloved (Son), and the love (Spirit) passing between and uniting them. *On the Trinity,* VIII:10. Kalistos of Diokleia objects because this "tends to depersonalize the Spirit. He [Augustine] himself believed the Spirit to be a person, but the analogy that he has here adopted does not in itself imply this. For, while the lover and the beloved are both in the full sense persons, the mutual love passing between them is not a third person alongside the other two. His model has the disadvantage of being bipersonal rather than tripersonal." "The Human Person as an Icon of the Trinity," *Sobernost* 8, no. 2 (1986), 9.

106. Rahner, *The Trinity,* 12 n. 6.

107. Zizioulas, "Human Capacity and Human Incapacity," 409. Zizioulas distinguishes human personhood, a creaturely openness that is subject to decay and death, from divine personhood, which is equally open yet not subject to decay and death—that is, God's *ekstasis* is impassible or apathetic. Ibid., 419.

108. Paul S. Fiddes, principal of Regent's Park College at Oxford, formulated the issue in these terms in a paper, "Persons in Relationship: Perspectives on the Trinity from East and West," delivered at the Eastern

Orthodox Studies Consultation of the American Academy of Religion, New Orleans, November 1990.

109. Lossky, *The Mystical Theology of the Eastern Church,* 58. J. D. Zizioulas says that God exists on account of a person, the person of the Father, and not on account of a substance. *Being as Communion* (Crestwood, N.Y.: St. Vladimir's Seminary Press, 1985), 42.

110. Karl Rahner, *Theological Investigations* (21 vols.; Baltimore and London: Helicon and Darton, Longman & Todd, 1961–1976; New York: Seabury, 1974–1976; New York: Crossroads, 1976–1988), 1:46. Gregory Havrilak sees rapprochement between Rahner and Orthodoxy. "Rahner is faithful to classical formulations of the Greek fathers from the fourth century. His trinitarian theology uses as its springboard the eastern approach whereby a definite priority of 'persons' is expressed over the common essence. The personalistic emphasis of each hypostasis in the Trinity is maintained." "Karl Rahner and the Greek Trinity," *St. Vladimir's Theological Quarterly* 34, no. 1 (1990), 76–77.

111. See Catherine Mowry LaCugna, *God for Us: The Trinity and Christian Life* (San Francisco: Harper & Row, 1991), 192–193.

112. Ibid., 223; and *idem,* "The Trinitarian Mystery of God," 1:177.

113. In Book IX of *On the Trinity,* Augustine identifies vestiges of the Trinity (such as the tripartate structure of lover, beloved, and love itself) in human experience, and these vestiges are universal to the human condition. Yet Augustine is by no means satisfied that this universal human experience of threeness is in itself sufficient to establish an apprehension of the true God. Special revelation is required. The *vestigia* cause us to seek, revelation to find. "We certainly seek a trinity,—not any trinity, but that Trinity which is God, and the true and supreme and only God." *On the Trinity,* IX:i:1.

114. Nicholas Berdyaev, *Christian Existentialism,* trans. W. Lowrie (New York: Harper & Row, 1965), 53.

115. Tillich, *Systematic Theology,* 3:283, 293.

116. David L. Miller, *Three Faces of God: Traces of the Trinity in Literature and Life* (Philadelphia: Fortress Press, 1986), 13–14. Miller takes "a poetic and dramatic perspective on the Trinity," and with some eloquence declares that "the Trinity may itself be a perspective

on the theater of everyday life-experience." Ibid., 129.

117. Ibid., 17.

118. Raymond Panikkar, *The Trinity and World Religions* (Madras: The Christian Literature Society, 1970), 42.

119. Ibid., 5–6.

120. Ibid., 46. Ordinarily the Christian tradition applies kenosis or self-emptying to the Son, not to the Father.

121. Ibid., 51.

122. Ibid., 61.

123. Ibid., 54.

124. Ninian Smart and Steven Konstantine, *Christian Systematic Theology in a World Context* (Minneapolis: Fortress Press, 1991), 21.

125. At this point, Smart and Konstantine side with the Greek Orthodox over against the Latin tradition by denying that the Spirit can be simply identified with the risen Lord. They attack in particular Karl Barth for his confused identification of the Holy Spirit with the spirit of Christ. Ibid., 157–158, 187–189. Smart and Konstantine claim to be followers of L. S. Thornton's version of a social doctrine of the Trinity, which requires the Spirit to be a more distinct person. Ibid.,157, 173.

126. Smart and Konstantine work with a version of *lex orandi, lex credendi,* according to which the rule of worship leads to and governs the rule of belief. Ibid., 193–194.

127. Ibid., 163.

128. Ibid., 176.

129. Von Brück, *The Unity of Reality,* 10; cf. 87, 143. Von Brück recognizes the prevalence of triadic thinking in various religious traditions, but this recognition does not play a decisive role in his own method. This is because what is decisive for Christian faith is not triadic thinking but rather the event of Jesus Christ. Ibid., 78–79.

130. Ibid., 129. His conclusion is that "God is the source, the realization, and the fulfillment of the unity of reality." Ibid., 163.

131. Ibid., 91.

132. Ibid., 127–128; see 138, 155.

133. Ibid., 152.

134. Ibid., 158.

135. Ibid., 156.

Chapter 3: Trinity Talk in the Last Half of the Twentieth Century

1. Welch, *In This Name,* 217.

2. In addition to the Enlightenment challenge, Welch identifies two factors within theology proper that led to the virtual disappearance of trinitarian discussion in the modern period: (1) Schleiermacher's demotion of the doctrine and (2) because of historical criticism, the loss of faith in the Bible, especially the Gospel of John, to serve as a primitive historical source. Ibid., 4–5.

3. Ibid., 219; 218.

4. Ibid., 243.

5. Ibid., 119.

6. Ibid., 126; 119.

7. Schleiermacher, *The Christian Faith,* sec. 170:1, p. 738; cited by Welch, *In This Name,* 5.

8. Welch, *In This Name* 159–160 (see pp. 227–229); 229–230.

9. Ibid., 161.

10. For Barth, the doctrine of the Trinity is a construction of the church based upon its "root" in scripture; cf. Barth, *Church Dogmatics,* I/1:353–354, 383–304.

11. Ibid., 349.

12. Ibid., 344. This formal argument based on the concept of the Word has variants. Dorothy Sayers identifies human creativity with the *imago dei* and likens the threefold activity of God with that of a story writer: the Father corresponds to the idea of the writer; the Son to the expression of the idea in the story; and the Spirit to the completed story as it fulfills or fails to fulfill the intention of the writer plus the reader's

response. *The Mind of the Maker* (London: Religious Book Club, 1942). Robert Jenson suggests a trinitarian view of God in which language is the first hypostasis, utterance is the second hypostasis, and new understanding the third. "The Futurist Option in Speaking of God," in *New Theology* No. 7, ed. Martin Marty and Dean Peerman (New York: Macmillan Co., 1970), 219. William H. K. Narum sees Sayers and Jenson as proposing ways in which "triune structures in human expression may be used to understand the Christian experience of God." "The Trinity, the Gospel, and Human Experience," *Word and World* 2, no.1 (Winter 1982), 50. This is not quite what Barth is doing. Barth's method of analysis seeks a guarantee that in the very structure of divine revelation itself the threefoldness of the divine reality is uncovered.

13. Ibid., 343. Barth's argument, based as it is on the subjectivity of God, has precedents in the psychological analogy of Augustine as well as the differentiation of consciousness in Hegel's view. Wolfhart Pannenberg is critical of Barth here, arguing that trinitarian thinking ought to begin with reflection on the symbol of the Son and asking about the Son's relationship to the Father. See Pannenberg, *Systematic Theology*, 1:304. But to reiterate: Barth's formal analysis of revelatory discourse functions only as a preliminary preparation for the Trinity. For the substance of trinitarian thought, Barth turns as well to the person of Jesus Christ and his relation to the Father and Spirit.

14. Welch, *In This Name,* 234. Cyril Richardson is not happy with Welch's method. He grants that the Father, Son, and Spirit symbolism is already present in the New Testament; but he also says that as symbols, they are too ambiguous in meaning to make the method of analysis yield a neat three-personed Trinity. He also accuses Welch of engaging in a "sleight of hand" to construct a Trinity that accepts both a single trinitarian self-consciousness and a social Trinity without acknowledging his indebtedness to the paradox involved. *The Doctrine of the Trinity* 127–132. What Richardson fails to appreciate in Welch, and Barth as well, is the distinction between the "root" of the Trinity found in the biblical symbols and the admittedly constructive growth necessary before one smells the fragrance of full trinitarian flower.

15. Welch, *In This Name,* 235–237, 250.

16. Ibid., 206; see p. 218.

17. Ibid., 238.

18. Ibid., 240.

19. Barth, *Church Dogmatics,* III/2:457. In his insightful analysis of Barth, Colin Gunton writes: "There is a kind of temporality in God, which preserves both the ontological distinction of God from the world and the real relation God has with it. God's eternity is not non-temporality, but the eternity of the triune life." "Barth, the Trinity, and Human Freedom," *Theology Today* 18, no. 1 (April 1986), 318.

20. By "aseity"—God's being unto himself—Jüngel intends us to understand the term to mean that we are absolutely dependent upon our relationship with God, but God is not dependent in any way upon us.

21. For many readers, this is the value of Jüngel's work. "His central theological achievement is that of exploring the complementarity of God and the world." J. B. Webster, "Eberhard Jüngel," in *The Modern Theologians,* ed. David F. Ford (2 vols.; Oxford and New York: Basil Blackwell, 1989), 1:105.

22. Eberhard Jüngel, *The Doctrine of the Trinity: God's Being Is in Becoming* (Grand Rapids: Wm. B. Eerdmans, 1976), 16–17. In an excellent doctoral dissertation on the thought of Eberhard Jüngel, Jürgen Moltmann, Robert Jenson, and Wolfhart Pannenberg, Faye E. Schott emphasizes that "the fundamental assertion that binds the four theologians into a specifiable movement is that the revelation of God as Trinity must be established solely through the historical person of Jesus rather than through humanly conceived philosophical structures and categories." "God Is Love: The Contemporary Theological Movement of Interpreting the Trinity as God's Relational Being" (Th.D. diss., Lutheran School of Theology at Chicago, May 1990), 9.

23. Eberhard Jüngel, *God as the Mystery of the World* (Grand Rapids: Wm. B. Eerdmans, 1983), 343.

24. Jüngel, *The Doctrine of the Trinity,* 84–86; *idem, God as the Mystery,* 345–346; see Barth, who argues that God "does not come into conflict with himself." *Church Dogmatics,* IV/1:185; see II/1:287.

25. Jüngel, *The Doctrine of the Trinity,* 32–33 (Jüngel's italics).

26. Ibid., 61.

27. Ibid., 39; 42–44.

28. Ibid., 104; 99 (Jüngel's italics).

29. Cited in ibid., 91. Note how this choice of words automatically applies "personal being" to the *tres personae* and not to the *una substantia* of the Trinity.

30. Barth, *Church Dogmatics,* II/1:297; see I/1:407–415.

31. Cornelius Plantinga, Jr., is critical of Barth's *Seinsweise* in light of the trend toward a social doctrine of the Trinity that will develop through Jüngel, Moltmann, and Boff. "Barth wants in heaven a model of covenant fellowship, the archetype of mutuality that we image as males and females, and a ground for the ethics of agape," writes Plantinga: "But, to tell the truth, his theory cannot consistently yield these fruits. For modes do not love at all. Hence they cannot love each other." "The Threeness/Oneness Problem of the Trinity," *Calvin Theological Journal* 23, no. 1 (April 1988), 49. Plantinga has it backwards. Even if Barth's disciples such as Moltmann and Jüngel are guilty of holding a social doctrine of the Trinity, Barth himself is surely innocent, and his notion of "modes" proves it. Most of Barth's critics claim he is a modalist, not a tritheist. William Hill calls him a "trinitarian modalist," a trinitarian because there is no fourth divine essence that unites the three and a modalist because there is but one seat of divine subjectivity. *The Three-Personed God,* 113–124.

32. Jüngel, *God as the Mystery,* 369–370.

33. Rahner, *The Trinity,* 21–22. Writing a decade or so later on this point, Walter Kasper remarks that "what K. Rahner sets down as a basic principle reflects a broad consensus among the theologians of the various churches." *The God of Jesus Christ,* 274. Faye Schott identifies the major factors "which have intersected to form the basis of the present trinitarian movement [as] Hegel's connection of the Trinity and the world historical process, Barth's connection of the Trinity and revelation as the basis for all theological statements, and Rahner's connection of the economic and immanent Trinity as one identical reality." "God Is Love," 62. Borrowing the term from the work of Roger E. Olson, I first employed the name "Rahner's Rule" to describe this principle in a series of two articles titled "Trinity Talk" for the Theology Update column in *Dialog* 26, no. 1 (Winter 1987), 44–48 and 26, no. 2 (Spring 1987), 133–138.

34. Rahner, *The Trinity,* 34–35.

35. Ibid., 39.

36. Ibid., 55. Does this parallel Barth's distinction and preference for interpretation over illustration? Interpretation consists of analysis, whereas illustration consists of analogy. *Church Dogmatics,* I/1:396–397.

37. Rahner, *The Trinity,* 49.

38. Ibid., 108.

39. Ibid., 11; see p. 86. See also Rahner, "On the Theology of the Incarnation," in *Theological Investigations,* 4:106–107; and *idem, Foundations of Christian Faith* (New York: Seabury, Crossroad, 1978) 214–215.

40. Rahner, *The Trinity,* 23.

41. Ibid., 44; see Barth, *Church Dogmatics,* I/1:412–413; II/1:296–297.

42. Rahner, *The Trinity,* 110; see Welch, *In This Name,* 190–191.

43. Rahner, *The Trinity,* 43, 107; see Rahner, *Foundations of Christian Faith,* 134–135.

44. Rahner, "On the Theology of the Incarnation," 4:113–114 n. 3.

45. Not all would agree that Rahner has advanced the discussion. Paul D. Molnar, for example, argues that Rahner's Rule has contaminated an otherwise pure Barthianism. Hence, when Jüngel, Moltmann, and Pannenberg try to synthesize Barth and Rahner, they tarnish the immanent Trinity with too much economic Trinity. In his litany of complaints, Molnar says that "Moltmann and Rahner accept a form of panentheism which is excluded by the very nature of the Incarnate Logos. Pannenberg accepts a docetic definition of revelation. Jüngel tends to re-define God's love by a phenomenological definition of love. In each instance, the priority of the divine over human is lost." "The Function of the Immanent Trinity in the Theology of Karl Barth: Implications for Today," *Scottish Journal of Theology* 42, no. 2 (1989), 398. What is going on here? Molnar mistakenly thinks the issue has to do with methodology—that is, the priority of revelation. He says that "experience and revelation are in conflict." Ibid. He is wrong here. When the post-Barthian trinitarians speak of experience, they do not refer to common or natural experience but rather specifically to the Christian church's experience of Jesus Christ, which is tantamount to special revelation. The alleged

split between revelation and experience is a nonissue in the current debate. What is potentially an issue (and is obliquely referred to by Molnar) is the possible loss of divine freedom if the immanent Trinity is collapsed into the economic. The theologians in question avoid the problem, I think, in two ways. First, they all affirm both God's freedom and the eternal dimension of the immanent Trinity. Second, God's freedom is expressed in time and, therefore, in the economic Trinity, not just in the immanent. Genuine freedom does not require a timeless eternity. It only requires an open future.

46. Kasper, *The God of Jesus Christ*, 275–276. See O'Donnell, *The Mystery of the Triune God*, 37–38. Yves Congar similarly grants qualified approval of Rahner's Rule while modifying it in favor of an asymmetry, giving priority to the immanent Trinity by denying that the economic Trinity is a full divine self-communication. *I Believe in the Holy Spirit*, 3:13–18.

47. Moltmann, *The Trinity and the Kingdom*, 4. Moltmann seems to embrace patripassianism, but he does not exactly say it. "The Son suffers and dies on the cross. The Father suffers with him, but not in the same way." *The Crucified God* (New York: Harper & Row, 1974), 203. He says this in the context of criticizing the theopaschite position; yet later he himself develops what he calls a "theopathy." *The Trinity and the Kingdom*, 25.

48. Among Moltmann's friendly critics is John Cobb, who does not like Moltmann's identification of Jesus with the Son. Cobb sponsors for trinitarian membership the suprahistorical Logos that he finds in Chalcedon, not the historical Jesus of Nazareth. "Reply to Jürgen Moltmann's 'The Unity of the Triune God,' " *St. Vladimir's Theological Quarterly* 28, no. 3 (1984), 173–177. Yet, Moltmann emphasizes, it is just the prehypostatized historical event of Jesus that gives the divine life its distinctive trinitarian character.

49. Moltmann, *The Trinity and the Kingdom*, 149.

50. Ibid., 64.

51. Ibid., 149–150. Moltmann avoids the term *Einheit*, which describes an original or ontological unity, preferring instead *Einigkeit* or *Vereinigung*, terms that indicate a process of unifying or integration.

52. Ibid., 19.

53. Ibid., 139.

54. Ibid., 147.

55. Barth, *Church Dogmatics,* I/1:423. In commenting on Moltmann, John Wright, S.J., says: "It is not at all clear to me in what sense 'the union of God' is a goal of trinitarian history. If it means that by our entrance into trinitarian fellowship Father, Son and Holy Spirit are now newly related to one another in and through us and the created world, I think I could accept that. If it implies that the divine missions of the Son and the Spirit set up some kind of separation or division within God that is healed through our salvation (as Moltmann does seem to mean), I cannot accept it." "The Holy Trinity: Mystery of Salvation," *CTSA Proceedings* 35 (1980), 199.

56. Moltmann, *The Trinity and the Kingdom,* 126, 145.

57. Ibid., 160.

58. Ibid., p.151; 153.

59. Ibid., 152–154. Not all Moltmann's critics acknowledge this nuance. John O'Donnell insists that Moltmann does away with the economic-immanent distinction; then he accuses Moltmann "of falling into a type of Hegelianism according to which history is a constitutive dimension of God's self-realization." As a prophylactic against such Hegelian contamination, O'Donnell's prescription is that we take a good dose of Rahner's "God is mystery as such." "The Trinity as Divine Community," 20. Hill's criticism is parallel. *The Three-Personed God,* 172–173. I find the response of O'Donnell (and, to a lesser extent, Hill) inadequate on three counts: (1) it fails to give Moltmann proper credit for at least attempting to maintain the economic-immanent distinction; (2) the immediate appeal to God's mystery to solve a doctrinal debate is anti-intellectual; and (3) this response cannot avoid positing two trinities, a ghostly immanent Trinity allegedly hidden behind the one revealed through the historical events recorded in scripture. O'Donnell and Hill continue the classical failure of nerve, the lack of courage called for when looking at Jesus Christ on the cross and saying with the centurion, "Truly, here is the Son of God."

60. What Susan Brooks Thistlewaite appreciates about Moltmann's work is that he avoids the abstractionism of metaphysics and begins with the specific. She also likes the implications for feminism. "God did not create Jesus as the Christ; God bore Christ out of the same substance as

God. . . . Moltmann is quite clear that God's bearing of Jesus is both a motherly and a fatherly activity." "Comments on Jürgen Moltmann's 'The Unity of the Triune God,'" *St. Vladimir's Theological Quarterly,* 28, no. 3 (1984), 182.

61. Welch, *In This Name,* 253.

62. Ibid., 264; 268. Carl Braaten comments that "Moltmann, of course, does not himself hold to his own rule about speaking of God in trinitarian fashion. He reverts time and time again to a simple concept of God, where God as such is the subject of the sentence without any trinitarian differentiation. It proves at last to be as unavoidable to him as it was to Karl Barth." "A Trinitarian Theology of the Cross," *Journal of Religion* 56, no. 1 (Winter 1976), 117.

63. Richard John Neuhaus, "Moltmann vs. Monotheism," *Dialog* 20, no. 3 (Summer 1981), 241.

64. Boff, *Trinity and Society,* 119–120. Max L. Stackhouse similarly embraces the notion of *vestigia trinitatis* and applauds the Boff Trinity because it is "antihierarchical, antipatriarchal, decidedly personalistic and communitarian." This makes Catholic Boff compatible with "many ecumenically minded Protestant churches that have been touched by the arguments of psychology, socialism, and neo-orthodoxy as well as the new awareness of a global vision." "The Trinity as Public Theology: Its Truth and Justice for Free-Church, Noncredal Communities," in *Faith to Creed: Ecumenical Perspectives on the Affirmation of the Apostolic Faith in the Fourth Century,* ed. S. Mark Heim (Grand Rapids: Wm. B. Eerdmans, 1991), 186.

65. Boff, *Trinity and Society,* 222f.

66. Rosemary Radford Ruether considers the option of a female Holy Spirit sharing a Trinity with a male Father and Son. She demurs, suggesting that the Spirit would be outvoted 2 to 1. This would only reinforce the terrestrial patriarchal order of dominance. She goes on to challenge the assumption that the highest symbol of divine sovereignty still remains exclusively male. *Sexism and God-Talk,* 60–61. Boff goes on, I think, in just the direction Ruether might want him to go.

67. Boff, *Trinity and Society,* 121; see p. 170.

68. Ibid., 198.

69. Gregory of Nazianzus, *On the Holy Spirit,* VII.

70. Social doctrines of the Trinity are notorious for their failure to do justice to the divine unity. Cyril Richardson writes: "It is simply impossible to say that God is really one in some ultimate sense, and still retain the idea of discrete centers of consciousness, which stand over against each other. . . . In fact, there is no way to overcome the paradox that we must think of God both as one and as a society. Logically, he cannot be both; yet we must say both." Rather than dissolve the Trinity into tritheism, which no social doctrine can avoid, Richardson throws up his hands and says, "Is it not better to admit the paradox, to confess we have reached the limits of human thought, and to acknowledge that, to guard Christian truths, we must say self-contradictory things?" *The Doctrine of the Trinity,* 94–95. In effect, Boff does something like this when consigning the contradiction to the divine mystery.

71. Boff, *Trinity and Society,* 140.

72. Ibid., 83; 146.

73. Ibid., 215; see p. 114.

74. Ibid., 112, 118; 84.

75. One noteworthy exception is Norman Pittenger, who affirms "the full doctrine of the Trinity, insisting that God reveals himself as he actually is." *The Word Incarnate,* 235. He begins with the threefoldness of the one God already implicit in the Christian experience of revelation, just as Claude Welch would advise. But, then, Pittenger actually uses Welch for his point of departure and acknowledges it. Ibid., 217. Joseph Bracken and Marjorie Suchocki register concern for attending to the trinitarian symbols, but even they have not to date provided what to my mind is a satisfactory fit with Whiteheadian metaphysics. It may yet come.

76. John B. Cobb, Jr., and David Ray Griffin, *Process Theology: An Introductory Exposition* (Louisville: Westminster/John Knox Press, 1976), 110. Elsewhere, John Cobb says that the "church has rightly affirmed a trinity," but we should feel quite free to "reimage" Father, Logos, and Spirit. *Christ in a Pluralistic Age* (Louisville: Westminster/John Knox Press, 1975), 259–264. This permits him to endorse inclusive language such as "Creator, Word, and Holy Spirit." Cobb also distinguishes sharply between Jesus, on the one hand, and Christ or the Word, on the other. "The failure to make that distinction has led Christians at times to

make quite arrogant claims about Christianity and it has led to views of salvation which were quite exclusive and restrictive." "Reply to Jürgen Moltmann's 'The Unity of the Triune God,'" 176. Cobb appreciates the trinitarian relations as coconstitutive. Yet he resists using conventional trinitarian rhetoric. Why? As a form of protest. He complains that the doctrine of the Trinity has been used more as a test of orthodoxy than as a way of clarifying and advancing the good news of Jesus Christ. "Response to Ted Peters," *Dialog* 30, no. 3 (Summer 1991), 243–244.

77. Lewis S. Ford, *The Lure of God* (Philadelphia: Fortress Press, 1978), 99–111.

78. Schubert Ogden's neoclassical position is parallel. For him, the divine essence is properly termed "Father" because he is the fountain of the whole Trinity. God as Father is both loving and loved, both subject and object of the divine love. The Son is the divine objectivity, generated by the Father as an object of love. The Spirit is the divine subjectivity, because it is God loving both himself and all other individuals. "On the Trinity," *Theology* 83 (March 1980). The assumption here that there are modes of being within the single divine essence leads John O'Donnell to suggest that Ogden is a modalist. *Trinity and Temporality* (Oxford: Oxford University Press, 1983), 81. Although Ogden defines the divine essence in terms of "boundless love" and then distinguishes divine objectivity and subjectivity within this love, this structure is at least parallel to that of Ford's, which places the primordial and consequent natures within the inclusive essence of the Father. Perhaps O'Donnell's suggestion of modalism could apply to Ford as well.

79. Joseph A. Bracken, S.J., *What Are They Saying About the Trinity?* (New York: Paulist Press, 1979), 67ff.; see also Bracken, "The Holy Trinity as a Community of Divine Persons," 166–182, 257–270.

80. Bracken, "Process Philosophy and Trinitarian Theology," 224, and "Process Philosophy and Trinitarian Theology II," 83. In identifying each of the three divine persons as a democratically structured society with agency, Bracken describes himself as in continuity with Whitehead though in discontinuity with some Whiteheadian disciples who insist that only actual entities have agency. Bracken wants to emphasize holism, not atomism. The result is a hierarchy of agency: up from actual entities themselves to the structured society of actual entities (which is each divine person) to the divine unity that encompasses

both subordinate levels. What is innovative here is that Bracken, although partially accepting Whitehead's ontological principle that only actual occasions have agency, adds the idea of *collective agency*; that is, an organized society functions as agent in order to maintain its own pattern of organization and identity from moment to moment. God's agency is of this collective type.

81. Joseph A. Bracken, S.J., "The World: Body of God or Field of Cosmic Activity?" in *Charles Hartshorne's Concept of God,* ed. Santiago Sia (Dordrecht: Klower Academic Publishers, 1990), 96.

82. Bracken objects to Jürgen Moltmann, Herbert Mühlen, and Eberhard Jüngel, who equate the Holy Spirit with the love relationship between Father and Son. This, says Bracken, confuses *person* and *nature.* Three separate persons are necessary to constitute the divine nature, that is, the process of self-giving love; but it is the unifying nature, not one of the persons, that binds them together. "Process Philosophy and Trinitarian Theology," 219. What Bracken risks here is positing the divine nature as the functional equivalent of a fourth person, a quaternity rather than a trinity. None of the three persons turns out to be God; only the composite is God. From Bracken's point of view, Moltmann, Mühlen, and Jüngel border on tritheism, because they begin with three separate beings and later unite them with the Spirit as mediator. "Process Philosophy and Trinitarian Theology II," 83.

83. Bracken, "Process Philosophy and Trinitarian Theology," 226.

84. It appears to me that Bracken contradicts himself. On the one hand, he criticizes Moltmann, Mühlen, and Jüngel for depicting the Holy Spirit as the bond of love between Father and Son. Yet, on the other hand, he seems to hold the same essential position, referring to the Spirit as "the common nature itself become a person . . . [T]he bond of love between the Father and the Son is the Primordial Condition for the interaction between the Primal Cause and the Primal Effect within the Godhead itself." "Process Philosophy and Trinitarian Theology II," 84; see 87.

85. "The superjective nature of God is the character of the pragmatic value of his specific satisfaction qualifying the transcendent creativity in the various temporal instances." Alfred North Whitehead, *Process and Reality,* ed. David Ray Griffin and Donald W. Sherburne (Corrected ed.; New York: Macmillan Co., 1929, 1978), 88. Cf. Bracken, "Process Philosophy and Trinitarian Theology II," 91.

86. Marjorie Hewitt Suchocki, *God, Christ, Church* (New York: Crossroad, 1982), 215f.

87. David R. Mason, "Demythologizing the Doctrine of the Trinity" (Paper delievered at the annual meeting of the American Academy of Religion, Anaheim, Calif., 1985).

88. William Hill puts Bracken in "the shadow of tritheism." *The Three-Personed God,* 220. This is overstated. What prevents Bracken from falling into tritheism is his holism: the whole of God is greater than the sum of the parts, and this whole is itself a unity at a higher level.

89. David Ray Griffin and Huston Smith, *Primordial Truth and Postmodern Theology,* vol. 3, *SUNY Studies in Constructive Postmodern Thought* (Albany: SUNY, 1989), 121–125.

90. LaCugna, *God for Us,* 1. "The doctrine of the Trinity is the attempt to understand the eternal mystery of God on the basis of what is revealed about God in the economy of redemption." Ibid., 22.

91. Ibid., 42.

92. Ibid., 209–210.

93. Ibid., 211.

94. Ibid., 223–224.

95. Ibid., 228.

96. Ibid., 305.

97. Ibid.

98. Ibid., 393–400.

99. Jenson, *The Triune Identity,* 114; see also his chapter "The Triune God" in *Christian Dogmatics,* 1:140.

100. Jenson, *The Triune Identity,* 136–138; 179–180. Jenson wants to pursue further than Barth the freeing of the Christian Trinity from Hellenistic timelessness. The problem with Barth is that he identifies the eternity between the Son and the Father as "before all time" and only so "after all time." God predestines Jesus. Thus, Barth's eternal God threatens to undergird the persistence of the past rather than openness to the future. Ibid., 179–180.

101. Jenson seems to use "Greek" and "Hellenic" interchangeably.

102. Jenson, *The Triune Identity,* 57, 165.

103. Faye Schott believes that Jenson is inconsistent when proceeding to say that the being of God can be verified only eschatologically: to predicate God as subject gives logical priority to the conception of an already existent or originating unity for God and therefore undercuts Jenson's own description of the Spirit's priority as the power of the future to surpass all that already exists. "God Is Love," 198.

104. Jenson, *The Triune Identity,* 175; 51, 89.

105. Ibid., 73.

106. Ibid., 108.

107. Ibid., 127; 175.

108. Jenson, *Christian Dogmatics,* 1:189.

109. Jenson, *The Triune Identity,* 140; see *idem, Christian Dogmatics,* 1:154.

110. Jenson, *The Triune Identity,* 141; *idem, Christian Dogmatics,* 1:155.

111. "The Spirit is the power of the eschaton now to be at once goal and negation of what is. In the New Testament, this Spirit is identified as Jesus' spirit, as every human being has spirit." Jenson, *Christian Dogmatics,* 1:101. Colin E. Gunton objects to Jenson's formulation for two reasons. First, it sounds like a natural theological projection from a supposed meaning of *spirit* to a theological conception. Second, by identifying the Spirit with Jesus, he succumbs to Western subordinationism; he reduces the third person to a kind of link between the first two just as Augustine had done. The result is the single-person deity of the Western tradition. *The Promise of Trinitarian Theology* (Edinburgh: T. & T. Clark, 1991), 135–137. What Gunton seems to miss is Jenson's strenuous effort to retrieve the relational insights of the Cappadocians, often at the expense of Augustine.

112. Jenson, *The Triune Identity,* 146.

113. Jenson, *God After God,* 128. Those who want to retain the classical double Trinity and give priority to God's unrelated relatedness are

not happy with Barth and Jenson. William Hill, for example, complains that "what Jenson has done with Barth's thought at this point is to collapse God's eternity into what is rather temporal unsurpassability. What has enabled him to do so is the process of identifying the economic and the immanent Trinity." This is a problem, because Hill wants an *excessus* of divinity, a *Deus in se* about which we cannot speak—that is, an eternal God beyond the one we have experienced in the economy of salvation. *The Three-Personed God*, 126–128. I can only ask Hill, why? There is no warrant for it in revelation or in soteriological reflection. It only hypostatizes a figment of the philosophical imagination that takes our attention away from the God who was present in Jesus and continues to be present in the Spirit.

114. Wolfhart Pannenberg, "The Christian Vision of God: The New Discussion on the Trinitarian Doctrine," *Asbury Theological Journal* 46, no. 2 (Fall 1991), 28–29. See *idem, Systematic Theology*, 1:327–330.

115. "Rahner did not yet draw the consequence that the eternal self-identity of God could not be conceived independently of the salvation-historical workings of the Son and of the Spirit." Pannenberg, "Problems of a Trinitarian Doctrine of God," 251. Faye Schott offers a distinction we have avoided making in this work, a distinction between Pannenberg, whom she says takes a historical approach, from Jüngel, Moltmann, and Jenson, who take a kerygmatic approach. The kerygmatics follow the sequence of language (Word of God as ontological language), then history, and finally personhood, to arrive at the comprehensible account of the Trinity. Historian Pannenberg alters the sequence to history, then language, and then personhood. "God Is Love," 65.

116. Pannenberg had already committed himself to the dependence of God upon his kingdom by saying that "God's being is his rule" in his early book, *Theology and the Kingdom of God* (Louisville: Westminster/John Knox Press, 1969), 55. Roger E. Olson dubs this "Pannenberg's Principle" (as a complement to "Rahner's Rule") in his excellent exposition "Wolfhart Pannenberg's Doctrine of the Trinity," *Scottish Journal of Theology* 43, no. 2 (1990), 175–206.

117. Wolfhart Pannenberg, "Die Subjektivität Gottes und die Trinitätslehre," in *Grundfragen Systematischer Theologie, Band II* (Göttingen: Bandenhoeck & Ruprecht, 1980), 96–111.

118. Pannenberg, "Problems of a Trinitarian Doctrine of God," 251.

Jüngel is critical here, saying that Pannenberg may have underestimated Barth's positive contribution to the idea of a concrete or achieved unity in the divine life, an idea that found its way into the work of Moltmann. Eberhard Jüngel, "Nihil Divinitas, Ubi Non Fides," *Zeitschrift für Theologie und Kirche* 86, no. 2 (April 1989), 221 n. 66. Overall, Jüngel finds himself in extensive agreement with Pannenberg on many trinitarian issues. This is due, most probably, to their common Barthian ancestry.

119. Pannenberg, *Systematic Theology,* 1:272–280, 308–319. Pannenberg is critical of Augustine's psychological analogy because it tended to lead Western theologians toward the concept of a single divine subject that subordinates the three persons. Ibid., 285–286. For Pannenberg, the divine essence is produced by reciprocal relations, not presupposed. There is some precedent for the relational view in Augustine too *(On the Trinity,* V:4, 5), where Augustine affirms that relationality belongs to God's essence and not just the accidents.

120. Pannenberg thanks Hegel for this insight, dubbing it the most profound clarification of the inner trinitarian perichoresis to appear in the history of Christian thought. Wolfhart Pannenberg, *Jesus—God and Man* (2d ed.; Louisville: Westminster/John Knox Press, 1977), 179–183.

121. Pannenberg agrees here with Moltmann's thesis as developed in *The Crucified God* that the passion of Jesus Christ belongs to the inner-trinitarian life of God as well as to history; that is, what is true *ad extra* is also true *ad intra.* But Pannenberg still affirms monotheism. Putting on the best construction, he says Moltmann made a terminological error by repudiating monotheism as such, because Moltmann certainly affirms divine unity. What Moltmann rightly rejects is the abstract monotheism of the nineteenth century, but certainly not trinitarian monotheism. Pannenberg, *Systematic Theology,* 1:335 n.217. Christoph Schwöbel tries to drive a wedge between these two scholars, saying that whereas Moltmann seeks to repudiate monotheism, Pannenberg emphasizes retaining monotheism. See chapter 13 of *The Modern Theologians,* by Ford, 1:283. Actually, Pannenberg argues that trinitarianism is the most consistent form of monotheism. Hence, the pitting of trinitarianism against monotheism by Moltmann and Schwöbel unnecessarily commits the fallacy of false alternatives.

122. Pannenberg, *Systematic Theology,* 1:313; see p. 329.

123. Pannenberg, "Die Subjektivität Gottes und die Trinitätslehre,"

II:110. For the Barthian roots to this, see *Church Dogmatics*, I/1:419. For commentary, see David P. Polk, *On the Way to God: An Exploration into the Theology of Wolfhart Pannenberg* (Boston: University Press of America, 1989), 280–284.

124. Pannenberg seems to think he and Jüngel agree that the biblical statement "God is love" does not refer merely to the activity or attribute of a transcendent subject over against us, but rather it is an idea directly implied by the reciprocal relations within the Trinity. Wolfhart Pannenberg, "Den Glauben an ihm selbs fassen und verstehen," *Zeitschrift für Theologie und Kirche* 86, no. 3 (July 1989), 365–366.

125. Although Jenson agrees with Pannenberg regarding the dependence of deity in the three persons, he will not follow Pannenberg's use of "person" to refer to Father, Son, and Spirit. Jenson is not willing "to give up the tradition from Augustine on" that regards "the one God as personal." Robert W. Jenson, "Jesus in the Trinity: Wolfhart Pannenberg's Christology and Doctrine of the Trinity," in *The Theology of Wolfhart Pannenberg,* ed. Carl E. Braaten and Philip Clayton (Minneapolis: Augsburg Publishing House, 1988) 202.

126. Pannenberg, *Systematic Theology,* 1:431.

127. Wolfhart Pannenberg, *Anthropology in Theological Perspective* (Louisville: Westminster/John Knox Press, 1985), 189, 222; see *idem, Systematic Theology,* 1:331.

128. Pannenberg, "Problems of a Trinitarian Doctrine of God," 255. Pannenberg "is able to develop a trinitarian understanding of the nature of God in which the triune God is truly involved with the historical process—even to the point of suffering with creation—but is not limited by this process." Stanley J. Grenz, *Reason for Hope: The Systematic Theology of Wolfhart Pannenberg* (Oxford: Oxford University Press, 1990), 72.

129. Pannenberg asserts that the Son is not ontologically inferior to the Father. In fact, the Father becomes the Father only in relation to the Son. This would make Father and Son equa-primordial. They share the same origin, or *Ursprung.* We might ask: Can this be reconciled with the creedal commitment to the Father as "begetting" the Son or with the patristic assumption that the Father is the unoriginate source? Yes, of course; but the point is that the trinitarian life cannot be reduced to its

state at origin. For Pannenberg, there is a mutuality in the Father-Son relationship that goes well beyond the begetting. *Systematic Theology,* 1:313. The unity of the divine for Pannenberg is not found in an anterior state, in a primary undifferentiation. Rather, it is found rather in the integration of the plurality of persons who move into unity.

130. Pannenberg, *Systematic Theology,* 1:331.

131. Pannenberg, *Systematic Theology,* 1:427. Because the Holy Spirit is the one responsible for the love that binds otherness, Pannenberg equates the two biblical phrases "God is love" and "God is spirit." In addition, Pannenberg likens Spirit-love to that of a dynamic force field in physics with the Father and Son as singular concretions of the Spirit's reality. Ibid., 383, 430.

132. Pannenberg, "The Christian Vision of God," 31–35.

133. Pannenberg, "Problems of a Trinitarian Doctrine of God," 256–257.

134. Welch was a prophet, and history seems to be confirming his prophecy. Robert Jenson writes: "It can fairly be said that the chief ecumenical enterprise of current theology is rediscovery and development of the doctrine of the Trinity. It can also fairly be said that Barth initiated the enterprise." Chapter 1 in *The Modern Theologians,* ed. Ford, 1:47.

Chapter 4: The Temporal and Eternal Trinity

1. The discussion that follows expands upon research for a paper, "The Trinity In and Beyond Time," prepared for the Vatican Conference on "Quantum Creation of the Universe and the Origin of the Laws of Nature," Castel Gondolfo, Italy, September 21–27, 1991.

2. Boethius, *The Consolation of Philosophy,* V:6. See John Wright, S.J., "Time and Eternity: Some Discussion Questions for Systematic Theology," unpublished paper.

3. Boethius puts together *"semper"* with *"eternity"* to get the word *"sempiternity"* referring to the everlastingness of the flow of successive events. *The Trinity,* IV. Eleonore Stump and Norman Kretzmann object to Boethius' etymology here. If "sempiternity" refers to unending passage, it should be sharply distinguished from "eternity," which is exempt from passage. "Eternity," *Journal of Philosophy* 78, no. 8 (August

1981), reprinted in *The Concept of God,* ed. Thomas V. Morris (Oxford: Oxford University Press, 1987), 221 n. 3.

4. What we are here referring to as the whole of time Stump and Kretzmann dub "fully realized duration." Ibid., 237.

5. Barth, *Church Dogmatics,* III/2:526; see II/1:61–62, 608; III/1:71.

6. Ibid., III/2:437. Eric C. Rust says that "we need to redefine the metaphysical attribute of God's eternity. God is not a timeless being." "The Dynamic Nature of the Triune God," *Perspectives in Religious Studies* 14, no. 4 (Winter 1987), 35. J. R. Lucas argues that God must be temporal because God is personal. "If we are to characterize God at all, we must say that He is personal, and if personal then temporal, and if temporal then in some sense in time, not outside it." *The Future: An Essay on God, Temporality, and Truth* (Oxford: Basil Blackwell, 1989) 213.

7. Augustine, *Confessions,* 11:13, 14.

8. Ibid., 11:11.

9. Gregory of Nyssa, *Against Eunomius,* I:26, NPNF, 2d Series, V:69. That "time was born along with things which exist" was already assumed by Clement of Alexandria, *Stromata,* VI:16, ANF, II:512.

10. Gregory of Nyssa, *Against Eunomius,* I:26, NPNF, 2d Series, V:69.

11. This is certainly the interpretation offered by Robert Jenson in *The Triune Identity.*

12. "Absolute, true and mathematical time, of itself and from its own nature, flows equably without relation to anything external." *Sir Isaac Newton's Principles of Natural Philosophy and His System of the World,* Cajori rev. of 1729, trans. Andrew Motte (Berkeley: University of California Press, 1947), 6.

13. J. R. Lucas, *The Future,* 220. Despite his defense of the traditional position, Lucas can still affirm openness to the future. The course of natural events is contingent; therefore, foreknowledge is precluded "unless quantum mechanics is logically inconsistent, and almighty God could have chosen to make a world that exemplified the laws of quantum mechanics. And if He did, then He would be unable to have detailed knowledge of its future developments." Ibid., 227.

14. Stump and Kretzmann, "Eternity," 228–230.

228   Notes, Chapter 4

15. Ian Barbour, *Religion in an Age of Science* (San Francisco: Harper & Row, 1990), 112.

16. Holmes Rolston, *Science and Religion: A Critical Survey* (Philadelphia: Temple University Press, 1987), 65.

17. John Polkinghorne seems to understand the problem in just this way when he writes: "The God who simply surveys spacetime from an eternal viewpoint is the God of deism, whose unitary act is that frozen pattern of being." *Science and Providence: God's Interaction with the World* (Boston: Shambhala, 1989), 79. Therefore, there must be temporality within the divine life. But how? When confronting the twins paradox in relativity theory, Polkinghorne offers a fascinating theological interpretation. He asks, Which clock does God use, the one on earth or the one on the spaceship? He answers: both. God is the omnipresent observer, experiencing the course of events as they happen within their respective inertial frames of reference. And no frames of reference are deleted. God experiences them all. "That totality of experience is presumably the most important thing to be able to say about God's relation to world history. He would not miss anything and his action would always be causally coherent." Ibid., 82. Polkinghorne helps by offering an understanding of divine temporality that accounts for the effect the world has upon God, but he is less clear on just how God affects the world.

18. Rolston, *Science and Religion,* 62.

19. Noting how the image of the arrow of time is used in physical cosmology, Jenson's use of the term may be unnecessarily confusing. He speaks of three arrows of time, one for each: past, present, and future. Ascribed to the Trinity, the three arrows refer to the Father as given, to the Lord Jesus as the present possibility of God's reality for us, and to the Spirit as the outcome of Jesus' work. *The Triune Identity,* 24. The weakness here is that Jenson too quickly exports the human experience of a present moment detached from past and future into the realm of the divine, bypassing the arrow of time indicative of the creation. See Robert John Russell, "Is the Triune God the Basis for Physical Time?" *CTNS Bulletin* 11, no. 1 (Winter 1991), 7–19.

20. Ilya Prigogine and Isabelle Stengers, *Order Out of Chaos* (New York: Bantam, 1984), 178. James Gleick describes the second law of thermodynamics as a "piece of technical bad news from science that

has established itself firmly in nonscientific culture." It is taking the blame for the disintegration of societies, economic decay, the break-down of manners, and such. Such secondary or metaphorical incarnations of the second law are misguided. If we are looking for scientific models for understanding our culture, Gleick recommends that we pick on the laws of chaos. Here we find the source of creativity. *Chaos* (New York: Penguin Books, 1987), 307–308. Chaos and the second law belong together. We find local eddies of creativity within a larger flow toward dissipation.

21. Prigogine and Stengers, *Order Out of Chaos,* xxviii, author's italics.

22. Wolfhart Pannenberg, *Basic Questions in Theology,* trans. George H. Kehm (2 vols.; Philadelphia: Fortress Press, 1970–71), 1:15.

23. C. F. von Weizsäcker, *The History of Nature* (Chicago: University of Chicago Press, 1949), 7.

24. Arthur R. Peacocke, "Theology and Science Today," *Cosmos as Creation: Theology and Science in Consonance,* ed. Ted Peters (Nashville: Abingdon, 1989), 34.

25. Arthur R. Peacocke, *Creation and the World of Science* (Oxford: Clarendon Press, 1979), 95.

26. Peacocke, "Theology and Science Today," 33, 34.

27. Stephen Hawking, "If There's an Edge to the Universe, There Must Be a God," in *Dialogues with Scientists and Sages: The Search for Unity,* ed. Renée Weber (London and New York: Routledge & Kegan Paul, 1986), 209. When in 1992 his Cosmic Background Explorer (COBE) satellite map showed telltale fluctuations in the temperature of the early cosmos that provided confirming evidence for the big bang theory, George F. Smoot, astrophysicist at the University of California at Berkeley, told an interviewer, "If you're religious, this is like looking at God. . . . Cosmology is where science and religion meet, right?" *Scientific American* 267, no. 1 (July 1992), 34. Physicist John R. Albright responds by saying, "Science cannot prove the reality of God the Creator. It is possible, however, to state with basic consistency one's faith in God who created in exquisite detail the universe. . . . " "God and the Pattern of Nature: A Physicist Considers Cosmology," *The Christian Century* 109, no. 23 (July 29–August 5, 1992), 714.

28. Stephen Hawking, *A Brief History of Time: From the Big Bang to Black Holes* (New York: Bantam, 1988), see p. 143.

29. Ibid., 136. See my previous analysis of this important passage in *Cosmos as Creation,* 54–57.

30. C. J. Isham, "Creation of the Universe as a Quantum Process," in *Physics, Philosophy, and Theology,* ed. Robert John Russell, William R. Stoeger, S.J., and George V. Coyne, S.J. (Vatican City State: Vatican Observatory; Notre Dame, Ind.: University of Notre Dame Press, 1988), 375–408.

31. Pannenberg's help comes in two steps. First, he asserts the necessity for connecting time and eternity. "Now eternity has been interpreted traditionally as timelessness, and in this interpretation its relation to time appears to be purely negative. But this contradicts the Christian hope for resurrection. . . . Salvation cannot mean pure negation and annihilation of this present life, of this creation of God. Therefore in a Christian perspective time and eternity must have some positive relation." "Theological Questions Posed to Scientists," *Zygon* 16, no. 1 (March 1981), 74; reprinted in *idem, Toward a Theology of Nature,* ed. Ted Peters (Louisville: Westminster/John Knox Press, forthcoming). The second step is the move to eternity understood as the whole of time discussed here.

32. Plotinus, *Enneads,* III:vii:11,41. See Wolfhart Pannenberg, *Metaphysics and the Idea of God* (Grand Rapids: Wm. B. Eerdmans, 1990), 76–77, 97.

33. Wolfhart Pannenberg, *Metaphysics and the Idea of God* (Grand Rapids: Wm. B. Eerdmans, 1990), 77.

34. Plotinus, *Enneads,* III:vii:3,6.

35. Ibid., III:vii:4.

36. Ibid, III:vii:4,5.

37. Pannenberg, *Metaphysics and the Idea of God,* 90.

38. Based on the axiom that the whole is greater than the sum of its parts, we can parse the different but overlapping forms of holism. *Ontological holism* affirms that the whole, although not adding any new parts beyond its components, earns its own distinct ontological status.

Causal holism holds that the behavior of higher order entities is not reducible to the laws governing its simplest parts; its behavior demonstrates a distinct level of complexity. *Explanatory holism* asserts that theories of behavior regarding a whole cannot be replaced by logically equivalent explanations referring only to the level of its component parts. *Methodological holism* would be a research strategy that directs inquirers to seek explanations by investigating the behavior of complex wholes in addition to the behavior of their simpler parts. Nancey Murphy parses these four in reverse by identifying their respective forms of reductionism. "Evidence for Creation from the Fine Tuning of the Universe," unpublished 1991 conference paper, "Quantum Creation of the Universe and the Laws of Nature," Vatican Observatory and Center for Theology and the Natural Sciences.

39. Paul Davies, *God and the New Physics* (New York: Simon & Schuster, 1983), 62. Davies adds that with the doctrine of holism we no longer need the idea of a life-force to account for the seemingly miraculous jump from inanimate to living matter. Ibid., 64. Arthur Peacocke would agree. "It is possible to be anti-reductionist without being a vitalist." *God and the New Biology* (San Francisco: Harper & Row, 1986), xv.

40. This is one of the most important insights of Charles Hartshorne, *The Divine Relativity* (New Haven: Yale University Press, 1948). Calling this view "surrelativism" and "panentheism," Hartshorne describes God and the world as internally related to each other on the model of the relation of mind to body. The world is God's body, and God is the world's mind. This is by no means the metaphysics I am developing here. Yet by borrowing the idea of surrelativism, I would like to see if it helps illuminate the immanent life of the Trinity and then, via the economy of salvation, the God-world relationship.

Index